APR 9 3			
MR 1 '94			
OC 17 '94			

HOW TO FIND AND BUY

Your Business In the Country

by Frank Kirkpatrick

STOREY COMMUNICATIONS, INC., POWNAL, VERMONT 05261

Text design by Leslie Fry
All of the illustrations courtesy of Dover Publishing, Inc.
Cover design by Ann Aspell
Cover photo courtesy of the Shelburne Country Store

Copyright © 1985 by Storey Communications, Inc.

The name Garden Way Publishing has been licensed to Storey Communications, Inc. by Garden Way, Inc.

Printed in the United States by The Alpine Press
Third printing, December 1989

Library of Congress Cataloging in Publication Data
Kirkpatrick, Frank, 1924–
How to find and buy your business in the country.
(Storey's country business library)
1. Small business—Purchasing.   2. Country life.
I. Title. II. Series.
HDI393.25.K57   1985   658.1'1   84.51489
ISBN 0-88266-372-0
ISBN 0-88266-373-9 (pbk.)

Contents

Changing Your Life

This is not an ordinary, everyday, run-of-the mill book. Give it a chance and it will change your life. There are a couple of ways you can use the book.

It can provide an *overview*. As you read it you should come away with a real feeling for what country businesses are all about. You'll find out what it's like to be in the country and why a country business is very different from a bookstore in the suburbs of Toledo, Ohio.

For other folks it will be a *step-by-step manual*. After reading the book through, they will go back to each section, each chapter, and pick out the advice they find most helpful in their search for a new way of life.

It is also a *workbook*. There are self-administered tests, checklists to make sure you're not missing things, and a number of important formulas and forms. These, of course, you can fill out right in the book. Most people, however, want to make copies, because the odds are that they'll use these work pages over and over again.

The book is a *resources guide*. All the background, current information, and long-range planning materials you'll need to make intelligent decisions about your business could hardly be put into one book. So, in addition to the reference data in these pages, there are dozens of leads to other sources of up-to-the-minute, highly detailed facts from federal, state, and town governments and national, regional, and local business and industry groups.

How To Find And Buy Your Business In The Country, in itself is a complete *short course* in achieving your goal of peaceful independence (or whatever you want to call what you're looking for). It contains everything you need to know in order to move from where you are now to being right on top of a going business. Maybe running something instead of running *from* something.

How Come We're So Smart?

Well, we've learned a lot over the years, and we learn more every day. We're the publishers; we're Storey Communications, Inc. First of all, we've learned a lot about country living and country life. Since 1973 as Garden Way Publishing we've sent out millions of copies of books about every phase of everything that interests country people, their food and their shelter and what's outside—their trees and plants and animals. Over the years we've made a lot of friends by finding writers and illustrators who wanted to share with others their thoughts and experiences about the big things and the little things of life in the country. And, of course, we hear from the people who read our books. That's what helps us turn out better books for more people whose interests are in the country.

Consulting Firm, Too

We've learned a lot about making a living in the country, too. We're Kirkpatrick Associates, Inc., a consulting firm in Peru, Vermont, specializing in helping people buy country businesses. I'm Frank Kirkpatrick—how do you do?—your writer. For the rest of the book I'll be your consultant, and I'll tell you everything I've learned from a lot of people.

In the fall of 1978 I brought together ten individuals who possessed significant expertise in a particular business category—country kinds of businesses. Each one was either operating successfully in that field at that time or had substantial recent experience.

The idea was simple enough. People looking for a business get advice from brokers who get paid for selling businesses, bankers who are in the business of lending money, accountants who are hired to analyze and certify incomes and expenditures, and, sometimes, real estate appraisers who make money by offering opinions on values.

There are two problems with depending on these people for such advice: one, when you spend money to buy a business, they all get some of it, so their thoughts cannot be totally objective; and two, they simply don't know very much about the business you're going to buy. They know their business; they don't know your business.

Kirkpatrick Associates offers the advice of people who are experts in the business you want to buy—country stores, inns, hardware stores, horse farms, you name it. You can't get better advice than you'll get from someone who either made or didn't make the same mistakes you're about to make. We've shared our experience with quite a few people.

We Made Mistakes

I got started in part-time counsulting work because my wife, Nancy, and I own a country business. It's an attractive, old (1827) general store here in Peru (population 312) in southern Vermont. The business became ours on November 4, 1977, after we made just about every mistake possible in the process of buying it.

For example, we did no research at all on the community in which we were going to make our living. We settled for the services of a lawyer who also represented the broker. We ended up using the seller's accountant, pretty much to check over his own figures. It's hard to believe we made these mistakes, because we're both experienced business people.

We behaved just like most people do when they buy a business in the country. We were guided by our emotions, not our intellects. We just lucked out, that's all. Peru is a wonderful place to live, and the store is doing great. In those days there wasn't much good advice to be had. There's a lot more now. You're fortunate.

Right here in this book—and in the other publications we'll suggest—you'll find out what we've learned over the years about living in the country and making a living there. We'll be sharing the experiences of thousands of people who are happier now than they were in their other lives. They feel they are a lot better off because they were part of the big move to the little town.

CHAPTER ONE

People Are Searching

April Fool's Day fell on a Tuesday in 1980. That was the day when you and almost 90 million people all over the United States sat down to be counted. The white packets from the Census Bureau had arrived in the mail. Or the enumerator from the District Office had crossed your threshold. There were questions to be answered, and your patriotism and your patience were being tested. And for the twentieth time since 1790, you came through with flying colors. You put numbers in all the spaces and told all about the members of your household, and the Department of Commerce thanked you very much.

The computers went to work. In a few months the magnetic tapes and the microfiche and the printouts were starting to accumulate in Washington and in government offices all over the land. The universities were filing the data as fast as they got them. And the private sector was gobbling up the information for which it had been waiting.

Yes, you helped planners all over the country do things for you. You helped them allocate congressmen, reassign teachers, policemen, and nurses, and market toilet paper. One-sixth of you told the statisticians how long it took you to get to work, what you did when you got there, and how worthwhile they made it for you. You told about the elevator in the building where you lived, your crop sales, the cost of your mortgage, and how many vans you owned at the time. Oh, and another thing, you told them where you were living.

That turned out to be the most important thing about the 1980 Census. There was confirmation of what demographers had suspected for quite a while. More and more Americans prefer to live in the country—not in cities.

The Big Move

Rural counties showed a population increase of 15.4 percent, urban counties 9.1 percent. Calvin Beale of the U.S. Department of Agriculture summarized the population shift in a February 1981 report for the press: "For the first time in more than 160 years, the population growth rate in the United States was higher in rural and small town communities than in metropolitan areas. In absolute terms, the numbers of people in non-metropolitan counties increased from 54.4 million at the beginning of the

1970s to 62.8 million by 1980. This includes a net of at least 4 million people who moved in from metropolitan areas and abroad. By contrast, in the 1960s, some 2.8 million more people moved out of the rural and small towns than into them."

Four million new people in the country in ten years!

That's what happened. People moved. And that movement—statistically and philosophically—is continuing. Population experts were impressed by the magnitude of the shift. People with causes dubbed it "the Rural Renaissance." But the move wasn't all that beautiful. Urban sprawl hit Wyoming. Resort communities burst. Agricultural economists were concerned. Howard Conklin of Cornell University wrote as early as November 1979: "We have a new distribution of people upon the land—one that has never existed before in the history of the human race. It is a pattern in which large numbers of nonfarm people live in the country, far outnumbering farmers in most rural communities."

Population growth makes growing things more difficult.

Economic Reasons

Most of the four million people who moved to the country during the seventies did so for reasons that were basically economic. New jobs were opening up in rural areas, such as coal and oil shale mining in the Rocky Mountain states, and more opportunities in recreational occupations. For retirees, small, southern towns offered lower prices and healthier climates than the big cities of the Sun Belt. This is group migration; getting to where the bucks are bigger or the sun is brighter. More money, a longer life. Why not go?

But a significant minority—maybe 20 percent, 800,000 people—of the new country folk quit the metropolitan areas for reasons that were not

States with the Highest Percentage Increase in Nonmetro Population

1970-1980

Florida	53.7%	California	33.4
Nevada	52.3	Alaska	29.1
Arizona	49.8	Oregon	28.7
Hawaii	45.0	Colorado	28.7
Wyoming	41.5	Idaho	28.3
Utah	40.0	Total U.S.	14.4

Source: *U.S. Bureau of the Census, 1980 Census of Population*, volume 1, chapter A. Metro and nonmetro as defined by U.S. Office of Management and Budget, June 30, 1983

primarily concerned with income or occupation. These newcomers chose to live their lives in the country because of its isolation or natural beauty or some other characteristics of the environment or the people. For some, it was urban flight, from crime, filth, carbon-arc street lights, crowds, and dumb bosses. No more room—they were pushed out. For others, it was more a matter of being pulled into the country by the rural attractions. This kind of migration is an individual thing. The reasons are more personal. These people didn't come to the country for their financial or physical health. They came here simply because they wanted to be here. And they keep coming. Nostalgia and fresh air, yearnings for green grass and roots. A quality of life. Whatever.

Why People Are Moving

BY CARRIER-PIGEON—DIRECT.
IMPORTANT
FROM LANDS ALOFT.
Particulars Hereafter.

Nobody really moves their family from one place to another for air and grass (the kind you walk on). The underlying reasons are psychological and physical. A lot of people find, particularly as they grow older, an increasing inability to cope with urban occupations. Jobs, no matter what they are, can be frustrating. And that's not good. Jobs, no matter who holds them, can be taken away. And that's scary. Job security, retiring at sixty-five and the farewell party are—for better or for worse—in the past. By and large, jobs in this country just aren't what they were twenty years ago. Blame managements' love affair with youth, computerization, MBA's, consultants, and themselves. Blame anything you want. The bloom is off the business rose. So folks want to move to the country to get away from the thorns. Others find that they can't cope with urban surroundings. The people, so many, so violent. The noise you hear, the dust you breathe, the things you see. Dependence, defeat, disaster. Depart!

When they get out of their cars with the different-colored license plates, when they unpack their rented moving vans, these new country people don't wear name tags or buttons that say "Failures" or "Succeeders." They're not in groups that identify them as Adventurers, Improvers, Rejecteds, or Gypsies. They look pretty much like people who are already here. Within a few hours, if they get a move on, the van can be dropped off and ready for a trip back to the city. And within a few months there will be home-state license plates on the car. Before too long it will be April 1, 1990, and the Bureau of the Census will be counting us again and telling us that we've moved to the country. As if we didn't know!

What They Do

A lot of them do what they did in the cities. They teach, they doctor. They're lawyers, they're plumbers. They're professionals, they're tradesmen. Others came to jobs they knew existed—in banks, in offices. Some found work when they got here, in stores, at resorts. Clerking, waiting on tables. Country jobs are a lot like city jobs, except there aren't very many of them. In the state of Vermont, for example, the total civilian labor force—all the people who were working on April 1, 1980—is smaller than the population of Virginia Beach. If you're thinking of moving to the country and finding work, change your priorities. Find work, then move.

In the past ten years, many people with hope of a better life have come to the country to work with their brains and ended up working with their hands. Some who came to work with their hands have had to sit on them.

A Business of Your Own

This has been the answer for thousands of businessmen and women, dissatisfied with life in metropolitan areas and anxious to do their own thing. For a long, long time, people thought owning a business in the country was just a good thing to think about. But today those thoughts are becoming reality for an increasing number of families. Suburbia just isn't what it used to be. For a significant percentage of people, the station wagons, cocktail parties, country clubs, and barbecues have become a bore, and they want out. And they're going to get out. Maybe not tomorrow. But next month, next year, ASAP. And they're making plans to make the move.

Just a few years ago, country businesses were pigs in pokes. Hundreds and hundreds of dreamers gambled their life savings on little businesses in beautiful places. And lost. But today, things are a little bit different. Country people know that city people are on their way. Real estate salesmen and business brokers are cleaning up their acts. Chambers of Commerce in country places are out to welcome new business owners and the long-needed sophistication that many of them can bring. There's new blood flowing through the veins of tired, old trade associations. State development agencies are working harder than ever to attract business. And not just the big employers, the big taxpayers who are often the abusers of the environment. The states want other kinds of businesses within their boundaries. Clean ones, modern ones, successful ones, growing ones. Banks are easier to deal with (and that's hard to believe). Even the federal government is doing its part through the Small Business Administration field offices and development centers. The pace of business in the country is still on the slow side, thank God, but there's kind of a new lilt in the step.

There just aren't very many country folk out to take the city slickers anymore. People are ready to cooperate with other people no matter who they are, how they talk, or where they come from. For the most part the natives are friendly. And that's just plain good business.

There Are a Lot of Businesses

There are over a million businesses in what the Census Bureau designates as "rural" areas—places with populations under 2,500. The rest of the United States, 73.7 percent, is "urban." "Metropolitan" areas contain urban centers of 50,000 or more people. The boundaries go to the county lines, and adjacent counties are included if they are of metropolitan "character"—with workers commuting from them. All the other counties are non metropolitan. (Go to the head of the class.)

Most of these businesses are pretty small. They range from small antique shops along back roads, shops that haven't been bothered by a customer for quite a while, to big, busy motels with live entertainment except on Sundays.

You've got your bowling alleys and secondhand stores, fish farms and camera shops, lumber yards, hardware stores, and farms that raise chickens, hogs, and anything else you can think of. There are stores that sell almost anything and plants that manufacture almost everything.

You're into taverns and feed mills, RV parks and greenhouses, general stores and private campgrounds, bait farms, marinas, and laundromats. Gift shops, dance halls, bakeries, and bars. Horse farms, milk routes, and car washes. Gas stations, tack shops, sporting goods, and catering. Name it. You can buy any kind of product or service in the country—including country businesses.

Legend has it that you can walk up to a knowledgeable-looking citizen on any sleepy, small-town street and ask him if he knows of any businesses for sale. Legend has it that he'll tell you he doesn't know of any that aren't!

Logic tells us that of those million-plus businesses in the country at least 20 percent could be yours if the price were right. Figure that there are a quarter of a million country businesses out there that you can choose from. But you'd better be careful. Only a handful are for you. And that's if . . .

If

If you happen to have the personality and skills necessary to be a successful country businessman. You see, most everybody thinks anybody can run a country business pretty well because it doesn't take much know-how or effort. And most everybody is 100 percent wrong! Bear this in mind: of all the businesses started all over the United States, 80 percent have disappeared within five years. If running a country business is so easy, how come eight out of ten people blow it?

And Another If

And there's another if. You can be a truly wonderful person with great ability—and no money. You have no business being in business. Now, you don't need a lot of money. But you do need some and, very

Five Personality Groupings
Test Yourself (Then Ask Three Others to Rate You, too)

	Yours	Spouse	Friend	Neighbor
Drive				
Thinking ability				
Human relations ability				
Communications ability				
Technical knowledge				
Overall rating				

Rate your talent from zero to ten (ten being extraordinary ability) in each area. Average your score. Then average the others' ratings. Pass is sixty, real good is eighty. Where do you think you're better than the others think you are? Watch out if you rate yourself higher than they rate you!

Source: *Starting and Managing a Small Business of Your Own* by Wendell O. Metcalf, 3rd Edition, Small Business Administration, Washington, D.C., 1973.

important, you have to be able to convince the people who are going to lend you more money that you'll be able to pay them back.

No Law Against Dreaming

Not one of the fifty states has a law that says you can't dream. That's one of the eleven great freedoms: you can dream about anything at all, any subject you can imagine, any time of the day or night. As long as you don't appear to be overly zany, no one will haul you off to an institution. The good thing about dreaming of owning a country business is that this particular dream is relatively attainable. You don't have to be rich to buy one. You will have to assure at least a few people, however, that you're not totally destitute and you're not a complete nudnik. Assuming that you have a few bucks in the bank and can add and subtract, let's move on.

BUT FIRST, A CASE HISTORY

The interesting thing about the experience of this couple—we'll call them the Smiths because that's their name—is that it is unfolding as you read these very pages. They bought a country inn right here in Peru, Vermont, just a couple of days ago. As this book is being written, they are going through exactly what you may be going through in a couple of months. It's happening live just down the street. We'll keep you up to the minute on exactly what's going on as they get ready to open their doors

Causes of 16,794 Business Failures in 1981

Incompetence	45.6%
Unbalanced experience*	19.2
Lack of managerial experience	12.5
Lack of experiences in the line	11.1
Neglect	.7
Disaster	.5
Fraud	.3
Unknown	10.1
	100.0%

*not well-rounded in all phases of business

Source: The 1981 Dun & Bradstreet Business Failure Record

to their first guests, sometime before Christmas. Here's the background. You'll be interested.

Patrick and Toni Smith are from Geneva, New York, a town of about 15,000 in the Finger Lakes Region. Pat is a psychologist who was one of the top administrators at the Willard State Hospital. Since 1975 he had been responsible for the growth and development of their adult psychological services. Nine years ago he married Teunisje Van Boord, a charming lady whose parents had brought her from Holland at the age of two and plunked her down on an apple farm in Iowa. It was a second marriage for both of them. Toni had served as director of the Planned Parenthood unit in Geneva, working with a budget of over $300,000 a year.

Pat's career was taking him further away from the therapeutic practice for which he was trained and which he enjoyed into the bureaucratic problems of public institutions. His job had become changeless and challengeless, and he dreamed of ways to do something else with his life, to point it in a new direction. Pat and Toni's two younger boys, Colin and Devin, helped to focus the dream. The new life had to be lived in a good place to raise children. They examined the possibility of subsistence farming, of a ski lodge in Steamboat Springs. The better the dreams, the worse the frustrations. So Pat finally put a date on his goal: his fortieth birthday. (He made it with three months to spare.)

Looked at Vermont

Pat had always loved Vermont. Toni bought the idea of the place in the summer of 1982. By the end of the winter, they were dead serious. They were answering ads and talking to agents. They wanted a small inn with maybe a job on the side at the start. By July, the trips across New York State became more and more frequent. The looking-for-a-country-business process had stopped. Their eyes were on the Wiley Inn (built in 1926) in Peru, Vermont. Asking price: lots. Business history: sketchy. Condition: lousy. Prognosis: negative. But the Smiths wanted that inn and were determined to get it. With the help, advice, and support of a smart tax attorney in Rochester, a sharp consultant in Vermont, a progressive banker with roots on Long Island, and an understanding broker with butterflies in his stomach, they were able to pull it off.

And there was a lot to pull. The property wasn't really salable. The Wileys had built an attractive inn and a fine business based on good, old Northern hospitality. The Johnsons had bought it in the late Fifties and fine-tuned the operation for ten years more. Then it was the Vidals who prospered, retired, and sold the business to Grace Tarplin from New York, who never really got into innkeeping. Her relatives ran it (sometimes), she leased it (sometimes), it needed repair (always).

Pat put together a good, sound, business plan. But it didn't sound all that good to the first ten financial institutions he tried it on. This was the proposal: the Smiths' money would go into renovation and promotion to make the business viable; Grace Tarplin's money would be provided on a secondary mortgage on an affordable basis to prevent further deterioration of the property value; and minimal primary financing would come from a banker with about one-tenth of the confidence in the Smiths that they had in themselves. Banker Number Eleven saw the merit in the proposal and the spirit behind it, and made the move (at a far from unreasonable 11 1/4 percent, we might add). It sounds like a good deal because it is a good deal. Pat and Toni are builders—in hospitals, in social organizations, in life. That's beautiful. But Pat is another kind of builder, the kind that makes a lender a little more lenient. He's a good carpenter, a good plumber, a good electrician, things like that. Things that will make the Wiley Inn look like it did when the Wileys had it. There's a swimming pool to be patched and a tennis court to be built. The fire marshal has to be satisfied. The health department has to be satisfied. The Smiths can take care of that. That's the physical part.

The other part is psychological. You can have the best looking inn in the world but if the innkeepers aren't good at innkeeping they haven't got a business. The Smiths don't know about themselves. The banker in Burlington doesn't know about them. But we'll all find out soon. There's a reservation in the book for December 16!

The Smiths' "Balance Sheet" When They Bought the Wiley Inn

Assets	*Liabilities*
Both in thirties	Lack of knowledge about innkeeping
Both well-educated	Accustomed to forty-hour weeks
Both experienced administrators	Accustomed to delegating work
Had enough money to launch the business	Inn in poor condition, but expensive to buy
Itched for country living	
Comfortable with public	
Knowledge of finances	
Eager for a challenge	
Had ability to "sell" their idea	
Pat can do plumbing, electrical work, carpentry	

CHAPTER TWO

Why People Dream

In the third place—after sexual fantasies and musings on athletic prowess—come the dreams of having a little business in the country.

But it might be when we're in our thirties that Daydream Number Three becomes a permanent part of our lives. The first clear vision of the venture comes when payment for work we've done doesn't quite match, in our judgment, the effort expended earning it.

It's then that we begin to question all of the adages about hard work and diligence taking us to the top of some big company somewhere someday. We reserve part of our general business dreaming for those special little moments of fantasy about doing our own thing. Some people reject the recurring dreams of chucking the whole bit. Others nurture them. It seems to have nothing to do with whether a person is successful or tends toward failure. Essentially the dream grows out of four basic human motives:

It's Time To Question

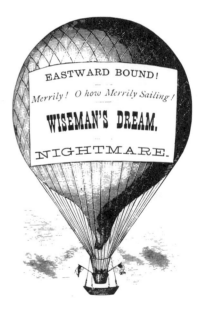

1. Escape. Everybody wants to get away from something or somebody. Some people find their jobs so boring that they do very little work. The process of moving from the desk to the bathroom to the drinking fountain to the desk to wait to start all over again can use up most of the day. Under these conditions dreaming of getting away from the desk completely is certainly justifiable. If you work in an office in the city it's almost impossible not to think sometimes about not working in an office at all—even an office in the country. So the little store keeps bobbing up in the brain.

2. Self-betterment. Most dreamers think they can improve their lot by being on their own. The American Way is to be more than your father and mother were and less than your sons and daughters. People used to talk about getting ahead. Now they discuss upward mobility. It's the same thing. Most people want to be somebody and maybe there's less competition in the country.

3. Possession. It's generally felt that owning something is better than owning nothing. Getting a piece of the action is especially tough when even your boss doesn't have any. So you dream about a different kind of action, someplace where it's quiet, away from the guy who is giving you a headache. Has anybody ever dreamed of owning U.S. Steel

all by himself? No. It's so much easier to dream of owning a little inn where Alice makes the apple pie, you make the strawberry daiquiris, and nobody makes waves.

4. Ending the frustration. The most common complaint among dreamers is frustration. Big company, little company—makes no difference. If you go to work at 9:00, frustration sets in at 9:30. We used to think that only the intelligentsia became frustrated. They were smart enough to learn quickly to hate boring work. Then along came the sixties and those who had never worked at all became frustrated! The life's values cycle brings us today to a much more serious attitude toward business, and it is really only proper for those with some tenure and experience to become frustrated. And it seems fashionable to be frustrated only after some accomplishment. But for most people a very small accomplishment can allow for a large amount of frustration. Frustration breeds dreams of a country business, the dreams heighten the frustration, and the dreams become bigger.

Two Dream Times

BEAUTY
OUTLOOKING
TOWARD
HOPE'S LAND
OF
PROMISE.

It's important to recognize that the motives for dreaming about a country business are strongest at two particular points in a person's life—early and late.

The young Horatio Alger types are in their late twenties and early thirties. Most of them have had some meaningful business experience and are finding fault either with the System or with their capacity for tolerating the System. Quite a few of them have college degrees and not a few are MBA's. There are professionals in this group—lawyers, accountants. Most of them didn't do a lot of aimless dreaming. They did a lot of careful thinking and planning. They either have some money or some good ideas about where to get some. They are at the beginning of careers that they are anxious to trade for a shot at the Good Life—maybe forty or fifty years of it.

And, of course, a lot of older men and women are experiencing an incredibly difficult period in their lives. This is a phenomenon that has only recently been recognized in men. At about the same time that the woman is surrendering her reproductive responsibilities, the man is succumbing to great concern about his responsibility to remain productive. Science finds it much easier to account for all the physiological changes that come about in the aging process than to understand the psychological shifts that are interrelated. Some men who experience the change understand it better than the scientists. At the peak of their careers these highly successful business and professional men considered change in their lives that would better suit their changed outlook. These are the dreamers who want a smaller piece of Good Life. They feel they need it to go on living for another ten, maybe twenty years.

Most of the young dreamers have been at it for a short time. They like the dream and want to stop and get reality started. The older ones have had the dream over and over and over and know that now they don't have much choice but to wake up. There are some, but not many, people in the middle, people with big-corporation blues. This malaise can set in at any age but it seems to hit like chicken pox: try to get it while you're young, pray for a light case, and establish immunity. Chicken pox or corporation blues can be very uncomfortable when you're over forty-five. The very first symptom is crossing streets to avoid pawn shop windows displaying gold retirement watches. This is soon followed by the realization that chances of your becoming CEO are less than even. There's no way up. The competing companies are worse than yours. There's no way out. There's no way!

The Big Decision

Very simply, you were born in the wrong place at the wrong time. One of God's colossal blunders. It's all true. But making up your mind to leave the comfortable corporate life behind and grope along into the unknown. . . What? With a family? Are you crazy?

And not infrequently while you're wrestling with your worries, the Big Corporation decides it has some plans for you that do not include your remaining on the payroll. In fact, some Big Corporations have been known to do this to some of their people who do not have the Big Corporation Blues. Much has been written about finding a new job, a new life for yourself after the axe has fallen. Nothing we can put down here can change the fact that severing a reasonably long and important relationship in a business—whether it's wholly your idea, completely their choice, or a mutual disaffection—is likely to be a major upheaval in your life. We can only offer the notions that (1) your contributions and accomplishments have been carved into the big stone résumé in the sky, and (2) you may be or have been the most talented and indispensable business person in the world, but let's face it, it's only business.

For almost all of the thirty-three years that I walked through a business life, I used to proclaim (or mutter, depending on the circumstances), "Someday I'll give all of this up and have a hardware store in Nashua, New Hampshire." I had never been to Nashua. I knew nothing about hardware. The phrase was my security blanket. I used these few words to relieve tension in troubled times. It was, perhaps, my mini-dream of a better world, a business in the country. And it more or less came true. And so have the dreams of many others.

A COUPLE OF FAMOUS DREAMERS

C.F. Orvis Company
Charles Frederick Orvis learned to fly-fish when he was about ten years old, back in 1841. He was growing up in the small Vermont town of Manchester near one of the most remarkable trout streams in all the

world, the Battenkill River. As he grew a little older, he started to make his own fishing rods, and his skill became more and more sophisticated. The tourist trade in Manchester was developing. People from New York and Boston were beginning to come to this new summer resort. In 1853 Charlie's brother opened what was to become the famous Equinox House. And by 1856 Charlie was able to turn his hobby into a business, the C.F. Orvis Company. He was a practical inventor and a shrewd businessmen. In 1861 he entered the mail-order business, selling tackle to people who think of fishing not as a sport but as a way of life. His daughter Mary became famous all over the world for her fly-tying ability and her book on the subject.

By the time Charlie Orvis died in 1915 he had built a substantial company. The fishing tackle business isn't exactly recession-proof, but Orvis withstood the impact of bad times and the Depression. Another great fisherman, Dudley Corkran, bought the business in 1939 and continued Charlie's dedication to high quality merchandise at a fair price. Orvis continued to grow. Corkran later found someone to carry on the traditions in Leigh Perkins, to whom he sold the business in 1965.

Today the Orvis Company has diversified, selling far more than the finest hunting and fishing equipment. This year's big Christmas catalog offers apparel, home furnishings, and sporting and gift items that reflect a country way of life. The Orvis Fly Fishing School, started in 1966, has more than ten thousand alumni. The Shooting School shows similar signs of success. So a little dream business became big. Estimates are that Orvis does over $50 million in sales. Not bad growth for something that was just a young man's hobby.

L.L. Bean

Another country businessman who became fat and happy was, of course, Leon Leonwood Bean. In 1912 he borrowed $400 and started a company on Main Street in Freeport, Maine. He sold a funny-looking, rubber-bottomed hunting boot. When Mr. Bean died in 1967 at the age of 94, the company had a payroll of 120 people and annual sales of $3 million. Now under his grandson's leadership, L.L. Bean manufactures about 200,000 pairs of Maine hunting boots and over 200 other products each year. A regular staff of 900—plus another 500 part-timers at Christmas—fills 2,200,000 mail orders annually from 8 million catalogs mailed each season. The company has no long-term debt, a return on equity of over 25 percent, and after-tax profits of around 6 percent. A respectable record for a small family-held company.

Both of these success stories are reflective of the catalog business boom. Obviously it would be impossible for a retailer in Manchester, Vermont, or Freeport, Maine, to approach these multi-million dollar sales without the help of the United Parcel Service. They started out as small country businesses. Now they're business legends located in the country.

But the ideals and abilities of the founders are still infused in these companies. They just grew about 300 times larger than the average country business.

There are hundreds of country businesses that have thrived in different ways. They're scattered all over the United States. There are businesses that exude an air of successful family ownership. Here in Vermont a couple come to mind right away. There's the fine old Basin Harbor Club on Lake Champlain, a summer resort run by the Beach family for over seventy years. On the retail side is F.H. Gillingham & Co., founded in 1886. The family's still in charge. It's a big general store in Woodstock catering to the needs of the well-off townspeople and doing a spectacular business with vacationers as well. And that's not easy to do, because the natives are usually wary of places that attract the tourist trade.

Compared to the fat-cat Orvises and Beans, the Beaches and the Gillinghams are slim and serene. Their dreams came true, not just for themselves, but for the children of their children. And those are the best dreams of all.

The Marks of Success

Six reasons why the Orvis and Bean companies are leaders:

- Associate their wares with a customer's dream of better living.
- Pinpoint their customers carefully—middle-class to wealthy, often urban but identifying with up-scale country living.
- Produce consistently high-quality mail order catalogs.
- Fill orders quickly.
- Promote use of telephone orders with credit cards.
- Maintain good customer service departments.

CHAPTER THREE

Waking Up

This is a very short chapter. Waking up can be very abrupt and very rude.

If you don't want to hear the bad part, pick up our narrative at the start of the next chapter. The things that probably never entered your dreams are these:

Work. It's not the stuff dreams are made of, but God intended us to work. Your country-store dream was about sitting around the woodstove and charming your customers. It wasn't about building the fire. Your country-inn dream was about serving the blueberry pie hot from the oven. It wasn't about scrubbing the cold kitchen floor. You may be used to a forty-hour work week or whatever. More than likely you will have to become accustomed to an eighty-hour work week. Can you work twice as long as you are presently working? Do you want to? Be honest. You can probably pay someone to do some of this work, but if you're the kind of person who is seriously considering your own business in the country, the odds are that you'll do it yourself.

Frustration, exasperation, and boredom. Your dream was of a slower pace. Contemplate, if you will, a pace that has slowed to the point where there is absolutely no noticeable trace of activity. Officialdom in rural areas can be totally exasperating. You dreamed of a new, casual kind of life. Will you settle for slow? Because that's the way it's going to be. The mails are slower—can you believe it? The phones don't work very well. The lights go out. After a year all that won't bother you, but during those first three hundred and some days, you may consume more than your share of Maalox or Marlboros or whatever your emotion-queller might be. In many areas television reception is less than good, so you'll read. But the library doesn't have the books you want. This may give you plenty of time to carve and paint decoys, if that's what you've always wanted to do.

That could be boring. The dream wasn't boring. Dreams never are!

Economic hardship. It's pretty safe to say that you will not "do as well" as you have in the past, at least not in the beginning of your adventure away from the megalopolis. While you were sleeping you never figured that you'd want a vacation away from your dream location. But you'll soon wake up to the fact that you still need a change from time to time. And you probably won't be able to afford it. Your friends from the Other Life may come to visit, and they'll tell you how lucky you are to be doing what you're doing. Then they'll get in their cars, drive off, and maybe say to each other, "But did you see how they live!" By most people's standards, your standard of living will go down. Don't say we didn't warn you.

Lack of sophistication. You don't dream about sophistication in business, you just assume that it's there. In country business it isn't. You can possibly bring a little bit of it with you but don't fill a whole attaché case. And, come to think of it, you'd better include the attaché case in the tag sale you'll have before you leave Fort Lee. You wouldn't want anyone to giggle when you get here. But bring along every last piece of common sense you have because you'll need it. Just don't let anyone know how smart you are.

Fewer challenges. You dream that you have a lot of exciting challenges and solve problems, because that's what you're good at. There are some businesses in some places where the biggest challenge you're going to face all day is getting out of that warm bed. You envisioned getting ahead by using your head. That's fine and that will happen—once in a while. Just remember, though, that many of the problems we face in the country seem to be solved by exercising the muscles in our back. "Chores" isn't a word in the cityside vocabulary. And we don't talk much about them in the country either. We just do them.

That's sort of what it's like here. We're closer to Nature's things than those who live in more populated places. Those things can be exquisite and tortuous, but we treasure them. And we tend to treasure people more, perhaps because there are fewer of them.

The Brighter Side

And on the other side of the coin...

"Ask a man who owns one" was a great automobile slogan in its time. Of course it was used in the days when the automobile manufacturer was reasonably certain that the man driving his car had a genuine pride of ownership. There are very few things around today that can fearlessly carry the "Ask the man who..." banner.

But one of them has to be a country business. Ask any country businessman about his sales and profits and, just like his citified counterpart, he'll lie. A businessman is never comfortable with the real

---

The Surprises of Owning a Country Business

Good	*Bad*
Townspeople rooting for you	The long hours
The family working as a team	How seldom you get to enjoy the "country"
The joy of the first month "in the black"	How little you know about the business
How much you learn the first month	How many things go wrong
The satisfaction of ownership	

---

numbers. When business is good, he'll tell you it's bad. When it's bad, he'll tell you it's good. He'll tell you he lies because he doesn't want his competitors to find out the truth. (And he considers his mother a competitor!) Ask him what he loves and hates about his business, on the other hand, and he'll level with you. . . often for hours.

So you can trust me when you ask, "What's it like when the dream finally comes true, when you wake up one day and you really and truly own a country business?"

It's great!

Terrifying at First

There's no way to describe the completely terrifying feeling of being on your own. The first time you put the key in the door and open up whatever it is you bought, a weight sinks from somewhere in your throat to a point just north of the middle of your stomach. And the biggest wonder in the world is, *what the hell am I doing here?*

What you've got is simply a very minor symptom of independence. You're not responsible to anybody anywhere except the stockholders of the bank that holds the mortgage on your business, and you probably don't even know them. But you do have a boss—otherwise you wouldn't be where you are. You're the boss, and hopefully you're going to be good at it. Or you won't have the job very long. You're on you own and it is incredibly satisfying experience. When the phone rings it's going to be for you. Maybe you could have some of this same terrifying/satisfying feeling if you'd bought a dry cleaners on Queens Boulevard. But you're not on Queens Boulevard; you're in the country. It can be clean and beautiful and fresh and breathtaking.

You made up your mind to buy a business in the country because that's where you want to be. You planned thoroughly, searched carefully, sought expert advice, and used your business ability as best you could.

A Complete Change

With any luck you'll have a business that will change your life completely.

You'll be totally immersed in your community, not just living there but making your living there.

You'll earn enough money to live on but not enough to worry about.

You'll enjoy the satisfying feeling of being an insider, of doing something that's needed—something probably important, possibly indispensable.

And with a lot of luck, you'll know a real sense of peace.

There's nothing more to ask for from owning a country business. And nothing more to get. If you want to make it big, you've been dreaming down the wrong street. This isn't Wall Street or Broadway or North Michigan Avenue or Sunset Boulevard. You've opted for Main Street and it doesn't go anywhere, really. It just stays there in Smalltown, U.S.A, and it's your new home. And that's the good part of the dream.

CHAPTER FOUR

Should You Really?

So you know all about the dream. Dreams are free. Country businesses cost a lot of money. You've got to wake up from your dream, grasp the reality of the whole thing, and then ask yourself, "Is it for me? Can I handle it? Is it worth it?" At this point you can understand the good parts and the bad parts of the dream of a business, but let's make sure you've come to grips with what country life is all about because your business will be part of your new surroundings.

The Physiology of Country Life

Doctors who practice in the boondocks tend to shrug off my queries about physiological differences between the patients they see and those around the larger cities. The layman, however, perceives definite differences, insignificant perhaps but obvious. In the absence of fact, I speculate as follows:

Country People are More Health Conscious. Most of us take some pride in the fact that we live in the country. Our air and water are cleaner than your air and water. Therefore we are healthier than you are. And we intend to stay that way. We are more "into" our health, our bodies, and how we feed them than you are. A lot of the stuff we eat we grow. And if we grow it, it's good and it makes us more healthy than the stuff that you eat and God knows who grows it.

Part of this attitude we've always had. It's Nature's way of compensating for our lack of money. But this attitude was nurtured and heightened in the early 1970s when some very unusual people with strange thoughts about life in general and food in particular came to live, for a while at least, on and frequently off our land. A lot of communal customs rubbed off on country people, and probably the most significant elements of the culture they left behind are those in the health and nutrition areas. We may not eat better (and feel better as a result), but to convince us of that would be utterly impossible.

Work-related exercise we take for granted: chopping wood. Non-work related exercise—running, walking, climbing, hiking, swimming—we also take for granted. Horses need exercise, too. That's why we ride them.

Country People Live Longer. It follows that if we say we're healthier we'll live longer. I believe that the statistics don't show any significant difference between the number of years country people put in versus city people, but country folk just seem to be around longer.

For one thing they are much more a part of the landscape than in the cities. There aren't very many out-of-home facilities for the care of the aged. We see a lot more grannies and gramps on Main Street than you do on the Boulevard. Everyone around seems to have a relative in his or her nineties. (Of course it's often the same relative, but you do hear a lot about them.) And then consider that a great many retired people move from the city to the country. The country lifespan may actually be shorter, but if that's true, you've got to explain away an awful lot of old people out here.

How Long Have You Been in the Country?
(Look at strangers, and you can tell by these signs)

The Signs	*Just Arrived*	*1-2 Years*	*5 or more years*
Shoes	$200 hiking boots	L.L. Bean boots	Workshoes
Trousers	Designer jeans	Jeans (worn)	Surplus pants
Winter coat	Fur-trimmed parka	Ski jacket	Hunting coat
Hat	Irish fishing hat	Ski cap	Fluorescent hunting cap
Car	New station wagon	4-wheel drive pickup	1972 Chevy
Favorite sport (summer and fall)	Tennis	Jogging	Deer-hunting
Favorite sport (winter)	Downhill skiing	Cross-country skiing	Snowmobiling
Serves when entertaining	Smoked salmon, white wine	Homemade bread, home-raised vegetables, home-pressed wine	Six-pack
Favorite topic of conversation	Beauty of country	Improvements needed	Neighbors (not there)
Favorite political cause	Stricter zoning	Improving roads	Cutting taxes
Summer activity	Entertaining friends from city	Vegetable gardening	Sitting
Livestock	Two Lab. Retrievers	Two goats	14 cats
Landscaping at home	Evergreens	Edible plants	Tire with pansies
Person you'd like to be like	Thomas Jefferson	Robert Rodale	Your plumber
Financial Aim	$1 million by age 50	Enough to Retire by 65	This month's mortgage payment

Alcoholism Is a Larger Problem. The awful truth is this: there are fewer people here than there. And alcohol can be an effective, temporary cure for the symptoms of isolation. But unless all you people in the cities come out here, the isolation will never go away. And for a lot of us neither will the alcohol. We are accustomed to feeling that things are more severe in the country than in the city: nature is more brutal, jobs are scarcer, crops freeze, animals die. So we probably feel more tolerant toward our heavy drinkers than toward the city lushes. But our problems and your problems and particularly their problems are the same. One serious admonition: if you have a drinking problem, your chances of solving it are infinitely better in an urban setting than in country solitude. It isn't that we don't want you; it's just that we can't help you.

Country Weather Is More Severe. New England has its famous winters; the Southwest has its famous summers. The floods and the tornadoes and the winds and the rain and the dust. The ice, the lightning, and the thunder. The sun, the sand, the sea. These are the things we call weather and for many, many years people haven't been able to do very much about them. Our inability to predict them is only surpassed by our inability to cope with them. They wreak havoc on our bodies. Nature can make you very uncomfortable and, in large doses, she can kill you. One things about country life: lots of times you have more Nature than you need. Nobody's going to call you a sissy if you don't like it. Not to your face, anyway.

The Psychology of Country Living

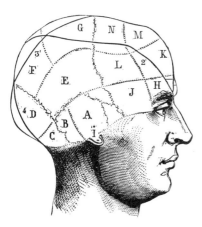

You've got an urban mind-set and you need a country mind-set? Okay. Today we're in a position to offer you a 20 percent credit allowance on your old mind-set, if you'll just latch onto our new mind-set, no questions asked. You say you won't change? I say you will. You say you can't? I say you must. If you decide to buy a business in the country you will need a strong mind (in addition to a strong body), a mind that can and will do two things.

You Need a Mind that Adapts Quickly. A whole bunch of new and different situations are going to come at you so fast that you'll think you're in some sort of experimental multi-media shock treatment. I know, I told you everything moves slowly in the country. It does, but you're being uprooted and dumped in a totally unfamilar atmosphere. If you can adapt quickly to a wholly new surrounding, you're halfway there.

You Need a Mind with Good Staying Power. So you've adapted. Now stay with it. You'll have to. Everything is going to go wrong. That's known and accepted. But if the mind doesn't want to hold still, you'll start flailing about and all the good adapting you did will be wasted. If you've got more than your share of stick-to-it-iveness, you're almost all the way home.

So there's your new mind-set. You're rolling with the punches and hanging in there. Just remember: your opponent is tough. He's Mr. Country Living at his worst.

There will certainly be a least six things that will be quite different in your life:

New Attitudes And Mores

A Simpler Life Style. This can mean different things to different people in different parts of rural America. Most everybody would agree, however, that a simpler life style means that you change the way you look. Dress clothes—a jacket and tie or a dress and stockings—are pretty much for church only. Now if you aren't at church and you see people who are dressed up, they might be coming from a funeral or they may be doctors, lawyers, or strangers. Not only will you look different in work clothes but your home will be furnished in a much more simple way. Your car or truck will be simpler. We're not talking about a casual life style; that means wearing sport clothes to non-sports events and that's for suburbia. We're talking about a simple life style; that means work clothes, work shoes, pickup trucks, serviceable furniture. Simple isn't drab and dreary; it's just plain, clean, and functional. . . and maybe not all that clean. All pretense is out. That's the way it is.

Interest in Small Things. You'll find yourself getting excited about birth, for example. Not of people, but of pigs. And goats and sheep. You'll get excited about the mail—third class mail. Minor road improvements. A fence. New teeth. Bingo. That's all there is; there isn't any more. You'll get excited about these things or else you won't get excited. And if you don't get excited about things in the country, you'll wither up like a prune and people won't like you any better than they like prunes.

Time Isn't of the Essence. There's a rumor that there's Standard Time in most of the USA, and that in the rural states we have Sub-Standard Time. That's a uniquely uncomplimentary way of telling us that our time-frame has come apart at the joints. Time just goes by. Punctuality is unknown. A guy calls you three days after he promised to, bubbling with self-satisfaction. A psychiatrist would say that we have an absence of time anxiety, which he would call a plus. But, bluntly, the urban-trained businessman tends to go bananas—at least for a while. Then he gets into the picture with the falling-apart time-frame around it, and he accepts it—because he has to.

The Meaning of Time

Country people are reluctant to take to heart the fact that everything moves more slowly here. So we don't compensate in our estimates of time. We say the house will be built in three months when we mean four and a half. We say we'll be there in an hour when we mean more like two. Some things have to get done before the frost or the rains or whatever, and those are the things that get hurried along. But things where Nature is not involved. . . no. When you're on country time—Substandard Time— figure about 50 percent slower than Standard Time and you won't be disappointed. But don't miss the bus. Sometimes it's on time.

Self-Reliance Is a Big Deal. Self-sufficiency, self-reliance, and all that. It's one of the most important things we have to offer out here. Or rather, that you have to offer yourself. Whether this is part of the back-to-earth movement or the cause or the result or the chicken or the egg isn't significant really. Whether it makes you feel good inside to grow your own food and fuel isn't an issue. If you aren't self-reliant and you move to the country, you'll become self-reliant or you'll move back to where you came from. It's that simple. Self-reliance is a fact of country life. We have to be self-sufficient because there are so few people here. And that fosters a trait that not everybody knows about...

We Share. If we pick blueberries, somehow instinctively we pick more than we need and give the rest away. In this simple, open, agrarian life, it is totally natural to share what we have—our berries and our fish, our homes, our bread. I have some; I want you to have some. And this means that. . .

Neighbors Are Precious. There's a premium on neighbors because there aren't very many of them. We get to know our neighbors pretty well. Sometimes we know too much about them and we have to share, of course. Malicious people would probably call this gossip. That does happen. Of course there's gossip in the cities, too. But there are so many people to spread the gossip that it's just a light covering. There's no two ways about it: the rural areas are gossip-intensive. If you are going to be a successful country businessman or a country business woman, we can only admonish you to let the gossip move from one side of your head to the other without a detour through the mouth.

Don't Retreat

When new people come to the country, a few retreat inside themselves and that's sad, because they miss one of the few great advantages that little places have over big places. That's people working closely together. House raisings are a perfect example. People get together (with a lot of planning done behind the scene) and in an incredibly short

In-laws and Outlaws

If you won't take my advise and let the gossip stop with you, take heed:

A goodly number of people in a small town are related. The relationship may go back five generations, but those individuals involved know the relationship—and there's a strong tendency to protect "family."

Result: You've heard something about Mary McCoy. You start to tell Harriet Hatfield the juicy bit about Mary, and you notice a certain set to her chin, a certain determination. So you back off the story as gracefully as a pig doing a dance.

And next day you find that Harriet's brother, Harry, married Janet Jones, a first cousin once removed of Mary McCoy, and everyone in town—except you—knows it.

piece of Sub-standard Time they build somebody a home. Then they have the party of the year.

Or bartering. That's working together without money and it works. Or governing. In small towns everybody wants to get into the act. So we have the Town Meeting.

The self-sufficiency and the neighborliness are not a paradox. Country people rely on themselves so they can afford to love their neighbor. There's no dependence. Just plain, honest respect. We don't always like our neighbors, but if they're sick, or their dog dies, or their roof falls in, somehow we're there so fast that it's obvious our feeling about time doesn't count when people do.

Loneliness: This Is Where It Is

There are times when no matter how much of a people person you are, you're going to be lonely. Sometimes, of course, it will be self-induced. Every area has its own "quiet place" where you can hike maybe a mile or so and there will be the most beautiful pond or quarry or stream or field in your world. Not another human has been there for a week or a month. It is a fine day and you are as alone as you'll ever get. You'll probably talk to yourself, most likely in a whisper. The whisper back will help you solve a problem or two, and that kind of loneliness is sheer perfection.

The other kind of loneliness is the result of living day after day after day in relative isolation. A shrink might call it "rural emotional depression." This is the kind of loneliness that you share. Two can be as lonely as one. It's a fact of country life that there are fewer people around. You become selective in your relationships and tighten your circle a little bit. As you become more picky and choosy, your circle of friends becomes smaller and smaller. If you work at it, you can tighten it until it chokes you. This is self-induced loneliness too, but you don't know it until it's too late. Country places don't have a monopoly on loneliness by any means. It's just that you have to be real careful. In a very small town you can run out of people to reject before you know it. Once terminal loneliness sets in, you can have smiles all over your body and, chances are, nobody will even notice them.

Cultural Separations

The country doesn't always separate you from people, but it can, and probably will, separate you from the kind of people you're used to being around. If and when you move from an urban to a rural area, you will immediately be conscious of the absence of what you consider "like-minded" people. Over a period of time your intellect has developed a need for a variety, volume, and frequency of certain stimuli. Sometimes you don't know what these things are until they aren't. If you like opera and ballet you are reasonably conscious of that and come to understand very quickly that it isn't going to happen where you're going. You may not realize, though, that you were given a mind that has to have an occasional shot of provocation to generate any good thoughts at all. Maybe you were never aware of those little inputs by your friends and business buddies. Then you'll be in the country and suddenly feel that your brain has gone to seed. Just face the music and dance to the tune that you'll be moving your mind from its accustomed watering holes to new and

What's Doing?

Don't think of the country as culturally dead. You'll find it not dead, but different. The major difference may be that you'll pay others to entertain you less frequently; more of the time you'll find your own entertainment.

Here are some of the social and cultural opportunities:

- Hometown affairs, plays, band concerts, school activities.
- Politics, serving on town, county, and state political committees, running for office.
- Public radio and television.
- Clubs, from veterans' organizations to reading clubs.
- Country events, such as holiday parades and church suppers.
- Money-raising activities, for all the national drives, plus local events to raise money for church repairs, uniforms for the band.
- Your own entertaining, such as dinners, barbecues, swimming parties, touch football, canoe trips and hiking, outings for the kids.
- For many newcomers to country living, the challenge is not how to get involved, but how to save enough time for yourself.

different ones—where the quality of water will certainly be different and there may be occasional droughts.

There is a tendency to rush off to the country to get away from Uncle Charlie. Two things have been known to happen: (1) he can follow you or, hard to believe, (2) you can miss him. Country people often have a lot of family around them, and this can heighten the feeling that you've cut your cousins off when you didn't really mean it. It can be emotionally disturbing if you are part of a closely knit family group. Often your family disapproves—vocally or sotto voce—about your packing off for the wilderness. Maybe they feel some rejection. Psychologically this can cause visits by the Four Horsemen of Gloom: Worry, Stress, Distress, and Tension. If you think for even one minute that you will worry about leaving a parent or someone who is dependent on you, financially or otherwise, you probably will spend hours and hours worrying about it. Worrying at long distance is the worst kind of worrying there is. Don't bring this kind of worry with you. We've got enough waiting for you without that one.

Many family trees, of course, have branches that don't seem to be attached to the tree at all. Even if the climate in your part of the country is fit for human consumption only one week of the year, that's the time that Kate always get her vacation. Your place may have been in last place on your kin's visiting list when you lived near the city, but now that you're near a body of water, everybody wants to visit you. So maybe those old, severed family ties will get knotted again. Just remember, it's your family. Or very much more likely, your spouse's!

So much for the changes that you can anticipate in your mind and body when you move away from It All. Probably there's no way of knowing for sure whether your life in the country will be better or worse than what you're used to. One thing is certain, though, it will be different.

Buying a business may be a pleasant—and hopefully very rewarding—experience. But if I ever told you it was going to be easy, I lied. This is the most important thing to know because either you start to live with it right now or it will haunt you the rest of your natural business life. All kidding aside, *buying your own business will be the most severe test that your business ability will ever withstand.*

And now I want you to carefully letter a motto for your wall as follows:

MOST PEOPLE IGNORE ALL THEIR BUSINESS SENSE AND COMMON SENSE, BUY WITH THEIR HEARTS AND NOT WITH THEIR HEADS—AND LIVE TO REGRET IT.

Entertaining Visitors

Helen and Scott Nearing, the noted homesteaders, had a constant flow of visitors who longed to learn the secrets of country living from the masters.

Scott understood, and believed he knew the best way to teach them. He put them to work, hoeing in the garden, building stone walls, splitting wood.

If visitors become a problem, taking up time you should devote to your new business, try Scott's method.

Keep that plaque up there in front of you at all times. Somehow prospective buyers get a strange feeling that business isn't business in the country. A feeling that everything is simple and uncomplicated and that nobody cares. That's just plain wrong. Country business people aren't sharp dressers but, as individualists, they usually have a more finely tuned business sense than the well-turned-out city troops.

People also think, for some reason, that a country business is going to make them happy. Even the most successful business won't bring much happiness if some happiness isn't there to begin with. If you're unhappy in Plainfield, New Jersey, chances are excellent that you'll be slightly more unhappy in Plainfield, New Hampshire. You've dreamed of escape from work and frustration and worry, but you've got my word that if your dream does come true, you'll have more work, more frustration, and more worry than you've got now. You say: "Okay. You mentioned that before and I nodded, but I can't really accept the premise that there's any real difference between a business in one place and a business in another."

COUNTRY BUSINESSES ARE DIFFERENT

Get ready for five key things that make country businesses harder work, more frustrating, more worrisome, yes, and riskier by a respectable amount than the same kind of business—same size and all that—in the area you're familiar with.

1. *Small Means Small.* The typical grocery store in Vermont—there are only about 800 of them—does approximately $260,000 worth of business a year. And that figure includes the supermarkets and chain outlets.

Also, while we're talking small, consider how much money you've got a chance to make. One business broker's rule of thumb is that, in the country grocery business, gross profit on sales is about 20 percent, with a 10 percent net. This means that a successful grocery store owner might be in a position to pull down $26,000. But that $26,000 might very well include use of living quarters, food, auto expenses, mortgage payments, and other items. So your actual cash income may be minimal. Small certainly doesn't mean big. It may not even mean comfortable.

Most country businesses are small because there are relatively few people to do business with. That, of course, makes a country business very appealing, but it can significantly restrict your opportunity for growth. Population growth expectancy can make a business more valuable than the same size business in another area with stable (or declining) numbers of prospective customers. On the whole, country businesses are small—maybe a lot smaller than you thought—and growth possibilities may be severely limited. These are the things you'll be checking out about a specific business before you check out of your home town.

2. *Good People Are Hard to Get.* That's a popular platitude no matter where you hail from. But in the country your so-called labor force is small. And the quality is going to be a lot lower than you bargained for.

There are other things you didn't reckon with. You just assumed that people will want to work because they don't have enough money. And that's wrong. Country people often won't work for someone they don't know. So, you think, sure it takes time to get known in the community, and I won't have any trouble getting someone when they get to know me. Well, country people frequently won't work for someone they don't like. After they've come to know you they may not like you well enough to come to work. So the ridiculously small work force may also be recalcitrant. Something to consider when you consider giving up your cozy corner office?

3. *Things Are Hard to Get.* In the country, distribution pipelines get mighty thin. Supplies of products and services decrease significantly the farther away you get from the metropolitan areas. As the highways narrow, the distribution system that we grew to know and love in our urban lives becomes more and more shaky. If you're accustomed to analyzing patterns of distribution in your business (or someone else's), you rarely think of product availability ceasing altogether. And yet it does; it has to. Consider the possibility that products and services—those you want or depend on—just won't be there.

There's another thought, too. Even where products and services are available, you can't necessarily get them. Distributors who service the more remote areas usually maintain low stock levels. Often you won't get what you order. Maybe something else instead—who knows? Out-of-stock conditions are unbelievable.

Can You Grow?

The Big Problem(s)

As labor costs and gasoline prices remain high, more and more suppliers are placing minumum-order requirements on their customers. Quantities that a small business can use efficiently are, in many cases, no longer to be had. Distributors from sizable towns are giving up good customers in small places because of their inability to service them at anything approaching a profit. So the country businessman turns to more local suppliers who are smaller, whose equipment is more outdated, and whose employees are more independent. Sometimes you get a feeling when dealing with small service companies that there is no company. . . just people working together who blame everybody else when something goes wrong.

And when the product you want is available in the quantity you can use at a price your customers might be able to afford, the obvious happens: Rural roads take their toll. The likelihood of a truck breaking down increases in direct relation to your degree of need for what it is carrying.

4. *Things Are Hard to Get Done.* Repairs take a lot longer in the country than they do in urban areas. Sometimes it is literally impossible to get someone to do a simple job. Of course, first of all the person has to want to do it. Secondly, he has to want to do it for you. Thirdly, if whatever you need done takes some kind of a part that the person doing it doesn't have on hand, the same conditions will apply to him that apply to you in the section above. Except that he's used to not being able to get things, and you're still tearing your hair out. The madder you get about not being able to get things done the harder it's going to be to get people to do things for you. There's no way out of this vicious cycle. Some say that if you can't fix your own equipment, it's a sure sign that God didn't mean for you to have it!

5. *Your Personal Life Isn't Your Own.* The last of our quintet of things that make small country businesses different from small city businesses is surely the most significant. Very simply stated, there's no separation between your business life and your personal life. This can be good and it can be bad, but it can't be avoided. In the country, for example, you can have a sign on your door that tells when you're open, but people will think of that as a rough guideline, pretty much for total strangers.

The good part of this is that, in many cases, your customers are your friends and your friends are your customers. In many small towns there aren't enough people to have friends and customers; so you'll just have to get used to both being both.

Just One Life

If you're a merchant, your merchandise should be available to your friends around the clock. If you're an innkeeper, you can't very well turn off your hospitality as you would your light. If your goods and your time aren't your own, what is? Maybe nothing. And that could be bad. If you're in the habit of closing the business door at five o'clock and opening the door to your house at six o'clock and living two fairly separate lives, forget it. The two lives come together in the country and never the twain shall part.

These are the considerations you'll have to make about moving away from It All. I've tried to point out that things may change a great deal by your going off in search of a business in the country, but I doubt that you're going to change very much.

You can't escape from yourself, from the problems that life has given you. But maybe you can find new solutions to those problems. Essentially, buying a country business will be a trade-off. You'll give up a lot of disinterested bosses for one very interested one. Structure for freedom. Sham for honesty. Status and money for an absence of same. You may give up a business life and a social life for one that is work and pleasure combined.

And if you've traded lots of things for a simple life in which you're never sure what is work and what is fun, then you've traded as well as a man ever could.

CHAPTER FIVE

Elements of Success

When everything that doesn't matter is sifted out, there are three major elements that are absolutely essential for success in operating a country business. They all seem to be of equal importance. Each one is pretty obvious. What may not be so obvious is that you need more of each key element for success in the country than you do in the city. Here's what we mean.

Your Business Judgment Must Be Excellent

You don't need any business judgment at all to be in business. You probably consider the people in the offices on either side of you absolute nerds. But you need more business ability to be successful than you do to be a failure. And I contend that you need better business judgment in the country than you do in the city to be eligible for the comparable level of achievement.

The reasons are simple. In the country you're on your own; you're out in the open, naked, exposed. You're doing your own thing and anybody can watch. There's no admission charge. Step right up and watch this city slicker make a fool of himself before your very eyes! There's no hiding, no covering up, no room for error.

How often have you put a relatively important piece of paper in a bottom drawer simply because you don't know what to do with it? How often have you seen your company compatriots camouflage some considerable boo-boo? So you say to me, "That's the way it's done here. That's what it's all about!" I say, "That's not what it's about hereabouts."

Making Decisions. The amount and quality of data on which you can base intelligent decisions may come as an incredible shock to you. Mostly you will have nothing to go on. If you have anything, it's probably misleading. So if you've been in a business where you need to be surrounded by a lot of numbers to be comfortable, you'd better start saving sevens to bring along with you. Many country spots are short on sevens.

If you like numbers, you will have them after you start accumulating them. And you may have some from the previous owner or owners that may or may not be helpful. What you will find in rural areas usually is an absence of other numbers to make your numbers meaningful. Most Chambers of Commerce do not collect data with which you can make comparisons of your business progress versus the competition. The trade associations that do have figures available have them for businesses that don't reflect your size operation.

More Problems. I've pointed up the fact that country businesses present a lot more problems just because they're in the country, so I think a lot more business ability is required to solve these problems. Unfortunately, there is no test for business ability. (Everybody is responsible for business successes, and nobody takes credit for the failures. So all of us must be pretty damned good.) If you have any doubts about your business judgment, why not ask a few of your peers what they think? If you dare, and care. You can always tell them what you think of them, so the conversation won't be a total waste.

Your Personality Had Better Be Fantastic

Business transactions proceed at a much slower pace in the country, so you'll spend a lot more time just talking to people. You'll be talking about crop conditions, catfish, frost heaves, and minnows. About fire trucks and fireflies and stable flies and bucktail flies and caddis flies. You'll be talking about different kinds of soil. In the first two months you'll learn more about the part of the country you're in than you ever thought possible. Come Month Three and you'll be telling strangers of the new things you know. Before long you'll be opinionated.

Of course talk fills voids everywhere. In the country though, there isn't much to talk about; so the way you talk is a lot more important than in the city. You might find yourself talking slower, sometimes repeating variations on your theme. Your manner, your attitude are going to be important, because what you'll be saying won't be. There's no cram course you can take that will teach you how to talk in the country, but it's safe to say that brushing up on your Nietzsche at this time is not indicated.

Don't Be a Character. In the suburbs sometimes a personality that doesn't exactly sparkle can sneak by. But in Lovelock and Plentywood there are few large cocktail parties and almost no member-guest golf tournaments to help hide your mean and horrible side. A less-than-attractive personality will stand out across an uncrowded room. Some more or less well-meaning people who decide to come to Rural America think that the solution to their problem personalities is to create characters and play roles. And that's just about fatal for the actor. . . and the audience. Any put-on is a put-down. And you're dead.

You see, one of the real joys of running a country business is that no matter how difficult it is, no matter how hard you have to work, for the first time in your business life you can be yourself and not have to worry about the consequences! You can be someone who is 100 percent you, and you can sleep nights.

Any Doubts? If you have doubts about your personality, slow down a little bit in your search for a country business. I know of a dentist who bought an inn, a very successful business, not too long ago. He ran it for a year and watched his sales decline significantly. He thought about it for a while and finally figured out why. By the nature of his profession, his past conversational encounters had been limited to talking to one person at a time, and that person usually unable or unwilling to respond. In small-group social situations around the inn—the key to a fine host's success— he was so ill at ease that he appeared rude. Steady guests quit on him; first timers never came back. His innkeeping days came to an abrupt end, and sadder but wiser, he went back to what he knew he could do and do well. His dentistry will always be less painful, I hear, than his attempts at hospitality.

If you want to check your personality, ask a couple of your neighbors what they think. Tell them to be honest. Otherwise you won't move away.

Your Luck Should Be That of the Irish Plus Some

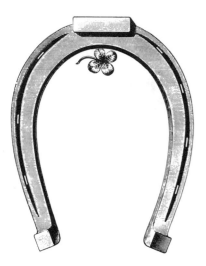

There's no question that a successful country businessman owes a lot more to the fates than his city counterpart does.

Many people don't know this, but Lady Luck is the daughter of Mother Nature and they work together. Most country businesses depend to some degree on a vacation economy. The weather is going to control some part of your success. If you need snow or rain or sun or cold or heat or wind and if you don't get it, your business will suffer. Maybe a whole lot; maybe a little; maybe somewhere in between.

It was late April in 1979. My wife and I were in Ireland and we had driven from Rosslare Harbour west through Tramore and Dungarvan to spend the evening in the beautiful town of Kinsale in County Cork. I left our room to fetch ice. Actons Hotel was suffering proudly under an occupancy rate of about 20 percent. The Emerald Isle had been through its worst winter in memory. There was snow, of all things, and spring tourists were mighty late arriving. The handsome lad in the lounge responded to my comment about the scarcity of guests in the establishment. It was abundantly clear from his manner that he spoke for the management. As he looked out over the magnificent harbour he told me in the softest brogue in all of Ireland, "Wul, it's ah weather business."

He was no more than twelve years old.

We Waited. All of the next winter in the Green Mountain State, we waited and waited and waited for the snow to fall. Mostly it didn't, and the skiers, who mean so much to Vermont's economy, stayed away in droves. Cross-country skiing centers never got to groom their trails. Inns were empty; restaurants closed down. A quiet hung over the land that was strangely bare. On beautiful, moonlight nights folks gathered by bonfires at ponds and, would you believe, ice skated? We clustered and drank cocoa and hot buttered rum. On New Year's Eve we sat by the flames, watched our breath, and talked about the snow coming next week.

Those of us with businesses held our breath and thought about the snow not coming. When it was over and the snow didn't come—it was the worst winter in fifty years—the SBA office in Montpelier had a record number of disaster loan applications on hand, big businesses like the Stratton Mountain-Bromley Mountain complex were selling ownership to conglomerates in order to get capital to survive, and little country businessmen were tossing in their towels. So often I think of my young friend in Kinsale. 'Tis a weather business.

Worst in 50 Years

There's more to luck than whether it snows or if the sun shines. People coming to your place to vacation, to see the sights or whatever, is fine. But sometimes people leave your place. The mill closes down, the new highway passes your door, only it's a mile away. Safeway opens a twelve-checkout unit two miles from your "mom and pop." This is the kind of impossibly bad luck you can understand. The whole charisma of a place can change in a couple of years. It happens all over the country. A spot is popular, a weird mystique grabs it, and, boom, it's a ghost town. No reason, no rhyme other than a funeral dirge. Whole towns go up for sale.

Of course there's plenty of good luck around, too, but you don't have to be warned about it. Most people get their fair share of good and bad, but some people's shares seem to be unequal. Your luck may change. It's like the weather. There they go! Lady Luck and Mother Nature, walking hand in hand down the road. They're talking about somebody . . . somebody who is thinking about buying a country business.

So you're smart and charming and lucky. Congratulations! Now let's see if you can pass a simple test that can offer some notion of how well you might succeed in a country business of your own.

The first part of the test is going to suggest how well you and your family can adapt to country living. Following are a slew of things people run up against in life. You'll want to know how you respond to these life elements—either positively or negatively and how positively and how

Adapting To Country Life

negatively. The scale goes from zero (Can't Live With) to 100 (Can't Live Without). Fifty is the neutral point, a shrug of the shoulders. Put a little pencil dot where you feel you rate for each item. Make a light mark so you can erase it and the next person in your family taking the test won't be influenced by your stand. Okay, here you go. Remember: this is how you think you can adapt to country living.

Country Life Test

	Can't live with							Can't live without			
	0	10	20	30	40	50	60	70	80	90	100
Southern drawl											
Extremes in temperature											
Fresh garden vegetables											
Shotguns											
Environmental issues											
Used clothing											
New England accent											
Daffodils											
Fishhooks											
Snow											
Material goods											
Peasants											
Potluck suppers											
Stockings											
Slaughtering lambs											
Volunteer fire department											
Cadillacs											
Bears											
Conservative Republicans											
Pheasants											
Nearby neighbors											
Bare feet											
Spiritual things											
The Federal Government											
Justices of the Peace											
Kerosene lamps											

	Can't live with							Can't live without			
	0	10	20	30	40	50	60	70	80	90	100
State police											
Plush carpet											
Suspension bridges											
The United States Forest Service											
Dogs											
Chopping wood											
Gossip											
Baking bread											
Oil burners											
Bare floors											
Covered bridges											
Electric lights											
Yacht clubs											
Liberal Democrats											
Local government											
Mosquitoes											
Mountains											
Pickup trucks											
Pig slop											
Wood-burning stoves											
Grange halls											
Constables											
Plumbing											
Dead cats											
Water pumps											
Tall drinks											
Fly swatters											
Tall buildings											
Muddy rivers											
Tall stories											

Thank you. We'll talk about what we think the pencil dots mean after you have completed the second part of the test, the part that has to do with running a country business.

Understanding Country Business Test

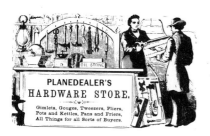

Following are ten sticky situations that owners have faced in small country businesses. Some of them may happen once; some of them come up again and again. You'll encounter problems like these no matter what kind of business you have because they're all common to the country-style operation. Here they are:

1. Seven months ago you were safe on Staten Island. You now have the hardware store in Statenville, Georgia. The previous owner had quite a few items without prices on them so there could be a difference between what people living in Statenville paid and the cost to folks from nearby communities. How do you solve this delicate little dilemma? Do you go along with the custom of customizing the price? Or are you for one-price stands?

2. The inn in Rising Sun, Indiana, is finally yours. More than anything right now you need a new busboy. The pimply son of a prominent local physician has been bugging the daylights out of you to get a chance to work at your place. His father has offered to pay the kid's keep. And it will mean quite a few extra dinners. Your own son is now fourteen and would like to help out. So?

3. Dotty Doty is a nice old lady in your village and everybody loves her dearly. People have been asking you why you don't sell doughnuts with your coffee; Dotty is very much more than willing to make them twice a week. So you do succumb. The doughnuts, alas, are dreadful—hard and sometimes burned. You've got one customer who really likes them, but otherwise zilch. There's another three dozen coming Tuesday. Where do you turn?

4. While we're on the subject of colorful local characters, you have a problem extending credit in your cash market. The old owner was tough about allowing people to pay next Tuesday for hamburger bought today. He didn't. Will you?

5. Meanwhile back at the inn. One of the local farmers suggests that you might want to trade vegetables for other victuals in the form of dinners for him and his wife. His greens look great but how good will he look in your dining room?

6. You've been unlucky and you need money to make some changes in your Curriluck, North Carolina, printing business. After you prepared what you thought was a good presentation, the bank in town has turned you down—and you've borrowed there before—because of two bad quarters in a row. You can skimp and scrape and take some money from your brother-in-law or approach the new bank in a town nearby. (You did their announcement letterheads.) You're hard pressed for a new press. How do you get it?

7. In part of New England there's a time of year when those parts are the absolute pits. The Rockresort Woodstock Inn in Vermont calls it Serenity Season, but for the rest of us, April and May are Mud Season.

Many businesses close down. The man you bought the store from did, but the man he bought it from didn't. You'd like to get away, but maybe you should stay. What will you do?

8. Would you believe your restaurant roof leaks? You did a little asphalt patching on your house back home but maybe you won't be so hot on a tin roof. You're really pretty busy, the water's coming in, and George's price seems fairly high. So?

9. Yours is the small grocery store in the small town just six miles from a town a little larger where they put in a very large IGA supermarket. You've stopped making any money and it looks like the super's there to stay. Are you going to raise your prices or cut your costs or cut your throat?

10. Where else? You're in Circle, Montana. Everybody in town likes Clara. She's been working for you for six months and everything's been fine. You've been paying her $500 a month and now she wants a $50 raise. You're in Montana; you're not made of money. What to do?

Finished? All right, let's see what you've got.

Test Answers #1

First, what's your adaptability rating? There were fifty-six things I asked you how you felt about on a scale of zero to one hundred. Low scores reveal low tolerance; high scores, a real craving. The middle is neutral—you can go either way, you're completely adaptable. Many of the items may conjure up fairly strong country associations but most can be found in both rural and urban areas. So a total score of 2800 (56×50) represents maximum adaptability. You might want to give or take 1000 points either way. Be wary of anything under 1800 or over 3800. Maybe you've got some prejudices you're not aware of. But if you're in the middle you could probably be happy living just about anywhere.

Obviously you don't have to add up your score. Just look at the pencil dots. If they hang pretty much to the middle of the page, that's fine. Occasional zigzags are okay. But if you've made clusters on the right or left, you'd better look at each listing and think about why you responded the way you did. If you can't live with a lot of the things you associate with country living, maybe you shouldn't associate yourself with the country.

Businessmen and businesswomen may like all kinds of different things, but being adaptable to varying conditions under which business is done can spell the difference between a lot of success and none at all. But business must be businesslike all over the world, and we shouldn't make any exceptions for geography. That's why the answers to the ten questions about familar business situations should be the same anywhere. If you let the green grass fool you, you shouldn't have. It's the green bills we all take to the bank.

Test Answers #2

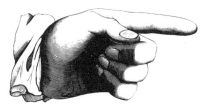

Here are a couple of insights from a few insiders. The consensus of five country businessmen on the ten sticky test situations is this:

1. Two-price stores went out with one-horse shays. Take a handful of items that sell well to the locals and make a big thing out of cutting prices on them. Let the rest of the items in the store (now that it's yours) find the right price level—one competitive, fair price for everything under your roof. High or low prices can put you out of business over the long haul. Two prices can put you out of business overnight!

2. Your son is the one that's rising. If you're not fair with your own family, God help your customers! Everybody will expect you to run a fine family business—and respect you for doing so. Nobody likes a social climber, especially when business is involved.

3. The doughnuts may be cut and dried, but the solution isn't. If you hurt Dotty's feelings, you can reduce the "good will" entry on your financial statement to a minus number. Tell her business is a little slow, cut her back to a dozen a week, display the doughnuts prominently, and inform your customers that they're really "unusual tasting"—taste is very subjective. Let your lone buyer know that his doughnuts are presently in short supply. If he doesn't take all you've got, there's probably some tight-lipped fellow who lives ten miles away and raises pigs. This way everybody's happy and you're out the absolute minimum.

4. It says "cash market" on the sign. One of the reasons you had to pay so much for the store was that the older owner didn't have any debts. Be nice and firm about not extending credit—in that order.

5. There's no way you can lose on the meals-for-produce deal, if you're reimbursing your supplier at wholesale. Many of your diners would be interested in seeing your vegetable man. If he's sort of a type, the vegetables will probably taste better. If he's too much of a type, suggest he come early before anything runs out. Farmers eat early anyway.

6. My crafty cohorts suggest this. Talk to your brother-in-law and the new bank about the money you need. Then take 50 percent of it from each. Your relative should be relieved that he doesn't have to come up with the whole amount. And the bank will be pleased to have a conscientious new customer . . . who can handle some printing at cost.

7. This looks like a have-it-and-eat-it-too opportunity. Take a shorter or cheaper vacation than you'd planned. Use the money to pay someone to handle your business on a short schedule. You ought to break even and you'll get a lot of brownie points for being open—and for offering your substitute some pin money.

8. Let George do it! Give him a due-bill for slightly more than his estimate and let him eat it off. You'll get a good roof and a good deal.

9. Make a few changes look like a lot. Offer some things the supermarket can't: homebaked bread, homemade salads, sandwiches, coffee-to-go, a few fancier foods. Make something on these items; raise

your prices slowly on other things. Compete against their weaknesses, not their strengths. Offer new and different and better services. Don't cut back; move ahead.

10. Make Clara think she was a mite pushy about the raise. After all, you'd planned on an increase—and 25 percent more than she had in mind—after nine months. Just a little while longer, Clara. This makes you sound perceptive and philanthropic and a real pal. You save $37.50 on the deal, which ought to finance an enjoyable evening in Circle for you and your wife or, depending on the situation, Clara!

Advice: business is business no matter where it's done. The chances of getting ripped off and killed while doing it are a lot slimmer in the country than in the city. Insurance costs—and a lot of other incidentals—are lower. The probability of success is iffy, but if you have good business judgment, a personality that comes with a healthy outlook on life, and an open mind about open fields, then there's no reason why you shouldn't try your luck at doing business in the country.

A List to Check

You've got to check the three things that will make some difference. Try it on your doctor, your marriage counselor, and your banker. Then come ahead.

Check Your Health. Just how high is your blood pressure? How's your heart? Ask yourself—or better yet ask your doctor—how your body is likely to respond to the strains and stresses described in Chapter 4. Think of the type of work you'll be doing. Packing cases are heavy. How do you feel about lifting eighty pounds from the floor? Again and again and again? Sweeping the floor is easy; shoveling snow isn't. Whatever you think you'll be doing physically, double it. Don't count on somebody helping you. He didn't show up today; his back hurt. Don't lie to yourself. A tired innkeeper is a lousy innkeeper. And lousy innkeepers don't keep their inns very long.

Check Your Marriage. Are you and your partner in life ready for splitsville? Then be very serious about this one. A strange environment on top of closer-than-you're-used-to-living conditions tend to bring out the worst in both of you. You've probably never worked with your spouse before. Do you know anything about how he/she works? You may appear to be a really super gent in your big, old pond; but shrink your work to country-business size and how will you react? Easy to live with? A pussycat? A little temper tantrum here and there? More and more. Can your wife or husband handle it? You're calm and cool in the temperate zone. Are you calm and cool when it's twenty below outside for two solid weeks?

Up here we call the creeping disaffection that is associated with a husband and wife working together Innkeepers' Disease. No matter what kind of marriage you have, you are going to find new strains put on it. Before you give it all up for the New Life, ponder, if you will, the possibility of a separation. The incidence—there are no figures, but I see it happening all around me—of divorce among people who buy country businesses is startling. My hunch is that in most cases the bonds were doomed before the deed was signed. Many folks seem to feel that a shaky marriage has a better chance of firming up where there is less pollution in the air. No. A country business will cause marital problems to surface if they exist undetected. Awareness of a potential hazard can often regulate its happening. If your marriage is on the rocks in suburbia, just remember it'll be on boulders hereabouts.

Check Your Wallet. Now you tell me! Right, it's going to cost a lot more than you think. We're not getting into any specifics but you certainly had better have a good feel for the ballpark. A small business can cost you anywhere from about $10,000 for a small gift shop to well over a million dollars for a posh resort. Think about where you'll live, how much cash you'll need, what amount you can borrow—you won't want to finance more than two-thirds of the purchase price (and the financer may opt for a whole lot less).

Country businesses come with lot of different price tags on them. A smart man once remarked that most people who are unhappy with a business in the country realize too late that they've bought it a size too large.

It's absolutely vital to have enough money in reserve to be able to make the business you buy what you want it to be. You don't want to find yourself—like so many, many others who've gone down the same pike—stuck with somebody else's business. And stuck you'll be if you don't have the money to make the changes that will make it really yours. Make up your mind right now not to get into a situation later on that can make you miserable for the rest of your life. Promise me you won't try to spend more money than you've got—you'll be under a lot of pressure to do just that—and I promise you you'll be happy.

Or pretty happy.

CHAPTER SIX

Doing Your Homework

The time you spend now looking at the ceiling in your den or at the dining room table, or wherever it is that you do your best thinking, is time you'll save later on when you're actually inspecting business locations. Since the places you'll eventually visit are probably going to be a considerable distance from your home, the more you use your head and plan ahead, the better.

You say, "What am I sitting around here for? I should be out there looking at businesses!"

And I say, "Not yet! Right now you're a patsy, a pushover, an easy sale. And it's no time to throw yourself into that den of wolves out there in rural America who, it just so happens, have just the right business for you."

PREPARE YOURSELF

Buying your country business is likely to be the most exacting experience of your life to date. You want to be tough as nails, sharp as a tack, and smooth as silk. Just remember the nails, the tack, the silk—basic ingredients in a casket. If you don't want to be tough and sharp and smooth (or it's too much trouble or a lot of bull or whatever), you'd better put your dreams of owning a country business to rest right now. This chapter and the one that follows are designed to make you as good a country business buyer as possible before you buy. Remember that a lot of us out here in the two-billion-odd acres that make up the "country" became good country business buyers *after* the sale. You're in a position to profit from our mistakes. And believe me, we made them. Later on, when you're driving around looking at business after business and not seeing your dream yet, think about the mistakes those owners made.

If you do your homework carefully and plan your search, you will make fewer mistakes in the actual buying process. You won't have any more smarts when you finish these two chapters than you have right now, but you'll be able to use every one you have to better advantage.

Skill Needed

Essentially you need more skill to buy a business in the country than in the city. The casual passerby might think that it's really easier to buy a country business—oh, you know, they're not really businesses, just sort of pastimes for the semi-retired or the retired-in-mind only. Not really serious businesses. (Tell that person to get lost!)

Listen to what he's saying, though. It's an attitude that tourists have about country businessmen. To many of them we are a bunch of bumpkins in a race of rubes. If we were born here, we were dumb at birth. If we came here, it was because we weren't good enough to hack it where they come from. But vacation here they do because they like our trees, our leaves, our grass, our water, or our mountains, the fish to catch and the animals to shoot. They like the country. And they like it well enough to take parts of it back to the city—their tans, their fish, their deer, their vegetables, their postcards and memories. They think we're stupid.

Of course there are others—and droves of them, bless their souls—who love our land as we do. When they go home they take with them their envy of our opportunity to live here always, of our way of life. They think we're smart.

And we really are smart. So you have to be very smart when you try to buy a business from one of us. The reason for someone selling something apparently desirable—like a charming old country inn—has to be thought through much more deeply than the given reason for transferring ownership of a seemingly less desirable business—like a car wash in Walla Walla, Wash.

Big Differences

The three big differences between buying a rural and an urban business are:

1. There are fewer businesses to choose from. There are about 8,500,000 small businesses in the United States. Let's say that 10 percent of these are for sale. Maybe you're looking for a restaurant in suburban Cleveland. There should be about 300 to choose from. In the broad categories—retail outlets, small manufacturing plants, hotels/motels, eating places—representation of businesses per thousand population should be reasonably consistent in both rural and urban areas. So if you're looking for a restaurant in Presque Isle County, Michigan, you'll have to take your choice from three!

Usually the wider the selection, the simpler the choice. This is partly psychological and partly practical. Emotionally you like to see a lot of opportunities before you buy. Consciously or unconsciously you now have the chance to make good comparisons and you can take the best of what's offered. Practically, when you're making up your mind between a small number of alternatives, you may knowingly or unknowingly be picking one of several bad choices. This may sound silly, but whether it's businesses or bananas, the fewer there are, the greater the risk of getting a rotten one. If the risk of failure is high, the skill required to select is greater.

2. Opportunities are widely scattered. Hellangone is an incredibly large area and the businesses you're likely to be interested in are scattered all over it. The few businesses to choose from are far between. It is not at all uncommon for someone looking for a business in New England to travel 250 miles between looks. It can be as exhausting as it is exasperating. But the danger of running out of places to look at is not nearly as great as the danger of running out of perserverance.

So not only do you need more skill looking for a business in the country than in the city, you need more stamina.

3. Comparables are hard to come by. In the residential real estate market, professional appraisers use comparables to arrive at fair market values. A four-bedroom colonial on a half-acre lot at 64 Hillside Drive in the same condition as the one at 79—give or take the powder room and the corner lot—is going to command a comparable amount of cash. Fine. But now we're comparing hardware stores that have sold within the last year. They're both in Oregon. Both say they netted about the same amount of money on sales of $360,000 annually. One is in Heppner and the other's in Hood River—about 100 miles apart. Are they comparable?

That one might be relatively easy for a thoroughly experienced appraiser of business property. But how about the instance where the guy wants to buy a small woodworking business in northern Maine that turns out specialty items? Or a snowshoe factory? These properties might require an appraiser who is hard, or maybe impossible, to find. And can he be trusted?

As you become accustomed to the complexities involved in buying a country business, you'll probably start to worry more about having to look at a lot of different things—wanting a drug store and taking a grocery store, that's different!—and the possibility of getting into a business you don't really want, and the probability of paying too much for it. Don't underestimate them: these are excellent worries. But they can be avoided if you determine your needs and develop a complete plan of action before you start looking at businesses for sale.

Utter simplicity: you must decide what you want or you won't know when you've found it. The old "I'll know it when I see it" routine is okay when you're looking for a place to lie on the beach, but for buying a business, it's utter stupidity.

Analyze Your Priorities

The first way to start narrowing things down is to look at your needs for personal and business happiness. Our experience strongly indicates that people looking for country businesses are part "where" oriented and part "what" concerned. As a prospect you're a mixture of "what" and "where." If you think your priorities are 85 percent southern coast of Maine, 15 percent type of business you buy, you're pretty heavily a WHERE person, and you will be looking for a country business in quite a different way than will the next fellow who is mostly a WHAT man. He's going to get himself a charming country inn and, if it's the right kind of place, it doesn't matter too much where it is. (Of course, in a few minutes he'll draw geographical boundaries which will be fairly restrictive, but right now he votes as a WHATer.)

Let's take on the WHERE people first. They're easier to handle because they have definite preferences for certain sections of the country. They grew up there and want to go back, or their uncle has a home somewhere and they don't care much for the uncle but what a place to settle down! Or they're familiar with the area because they were there on vacation. It's hot or it's cold or it's pretty or the people are nice. No matter. That's where the business should be. Now we can start honing in.

Can we pin it down to a region of the country? The Plains, the Sun Belt, the Northwest? Fine! To a state or two? Now we're getting somewhere because states have things for you, things you can hold in your hand, look at, read, savor. These are things that will help you make your decisions about buying a country business.

Send For Information

If you can confine your interest to two or three or four or five states out of our fifty, you're on your way. Each state has a Department of Commerce, Agency for Economic and Business Development, or some office or people waiting to help. There's a list of these state development agencies and their addresses in the Appendix.

Different states send out different kinds of information. Most states are heavily involved in tourism and will want you to have their official

Valuable Information

One of the most valuable pieces of information to have is the United States *1980 Census of Population and Housing*, Summary Characteristics for Governmental Units *by state* (series PHC80-3). This gives the population, housing, social, employment, and economic data for county subdivisions—towns, districts, and community areas. Here you get the federal government's estimate of population, median age, households and families, total housing units (a check on second homes), year-round housing values, all kinds of housing characteristics, vehicles, non-English speaking people, those living in a different state five years ago, high school graduates, employment, data on the labor force, median incomes, etc. A document well worth the $5.00 or so it costs. Get exact price from Data User Services Division, Bureau of the Census, Washington, DC 20233, and order from the Superintendent of Documents, U.S. Government Printing Office, Washington, DC 20402, any U.S. Department of Commerce District Office, or any Government Bookstore.

highway map (which is probably better than any other map anywhere—after all, it's their state), brochures of the various vacation attractions, and sometimes a lot more. They'll send you a list of the local Chambers of Commerce. (Or you can get one from the state Chambers—along with a lot of other helpful information. See Appendix.)

Often if you mention that you're interested in buying a business in their state, they'll include information on the economic research data they have available. You may think this is just for executives of big corporations who are interested in plant relocation and cheap labor supply—real businessmen. But if you're not a real businessman, stop reading this book right now! If the state has information available that can help businessmen decide about relocating a factory, get it. You're a businessman relocating your family!

One state that has assembled an incredible amount of data is Florida. The state has current and historical economic and demographic statistics with comparable state and national figures for each of the sixty-seven counties. You can get:

per capita income
personal income by source
employment and unemployment statistics
labor force participation
number of jobs by industrial division
average wage and salary income by industrial division
distribution of income by industrial division
number of jobs by manufacturing group
average wage and salary income by manufacturing group
value added in manufacturing
population change
migration and natural change
age, race, and sex distribution of the population
educational attainment of the population

This information costs $9 per county, and you get all data revisions for two years. Florida has a fact sheet called *Suggested Sources of Information for Developing a Basic Economic Development Collection*, and another fact sheet listing associations of interest to business and industry.

This, of course, is a lot more than the person searching for a small business in the country is likely to need to know. But a lot of it will be quite helpful to you when you start actually looking for a business or at a specific business in that state or county or town.

Once you know what data are available, you can decide what would be most important. You can write or call sources or go visit them, depending on how much time you have and how far away they are. At this particular stage, the market research unit of a state's Department of

Commerce (or whatever fancy name it goes by) is a very valuable source of information that no big businessman would think of passing up and few small businessmen think of. You don't want a lot of unnecessary information now, but you do want to be in a position to get data down the line when you do need them.

Shortening Your Sights

Maybe you're getting to a point, or you've been there for a while, where you can focus more closely on the geography, the WHERE. Great. It's the same general quest for knowledge, but you can talk to people who know more about a smaller area. A good thing to have is a local phone book. The service representative at your phone company's business office can arrange to get you directories for any area in the United States. The information in the yellow pages is well worth the couple of dollars it will cost. What banks are there? Who are the lawyers, the accountants? How many grocery stores serve the area? Where are they? Let your fingers do the walking. The more information you have about your area of interest, the more respect you'll get from area people, whether they're business brokers, folks with a business for sale, or just plain citizens who might (be careful) become your neighbors. Subscribe to the local newspapers. Find out what's happening. Read the ads—businesses for sale are often listed.

If you're a real WHERE person—almost 100 percent, say—you may have already picked out a town or two or three where you want to put down your stakes. There are more than 26,000 small towns in the country, and if you've picked a few, beautiful! Or maybe you haven't picked them yet, but you will when you know more about them. (A lot of help here comes from the folders and brochures that the state travel and tourism offices—usually down the hall and working closely with the economic development group—have sent you. Customarily these promoters break down their states into regions with lures for each one. They are spending their state taxpayers' monies to make each area appear more attractive, perhaps, than God intended it to be; so don't expect every place to look like paradise when you get there. But these free booklets are excellent if you've never been to a particualar place, and they're fine memory refreshers if you have.)

If your interest is high on the area, it's high time you talked—by letter, phone, or in person—to the people who know the place like the back of their hands: the Chambers and the service organizations. If you are going to buy a business in a town, the man to know is the president of the Chamber of Commerce. He'll get to know you after you've bought the business. Just a matter of timing. . . and your shirt. Others who you will also come to know are the Rotarians—from a business standpoint—and the Kiwanis, Lions, and Elks, from the community life point of view.

The local Rotary group can be particularly helpful if you are a Rotary member.

FOR THE NOWHERE PEOPLE

Even though you say you want a general store in a small town and don't really care much about where it is as long as it's a good place to live, there are few folks who don't have some WHERE in their WHAT-WHERE makeup. But for those people who couldn't care less where they are as long as they're doing their WHAT, here are some places that keep coming up when people dream about having a country business. If you really don't care where your business is, you might as well go where the real WHEREs want to go. This should maximize the resale value of the business you buy.

Here's the consensus list from people we've talked to:

Places Where People Want to Buy a Country Business

New England	South Atlantic	Middle Atlantic States	Rocky Mountain States
Maine	Virginia	Pennsylvania	The Rockies—
Maine Coast	Shenandoah	Pocono Mountains	particularly in
New Hampshire	The Highlands	Bucks County	Montana, Idaho,
Vermont	West Virginia		and Wyoming
Massachusetts	The Potomac	*East North Central*	
Cape Cod	Highlands	Michigan	*Pacific States*
Berkshire Hills	North Carolina	Upper Peninsula	Washington
	The Outer Banks	West Michigan	Oregon
	Great Smoky		California
	Mountains		Northern
	South Carolina		California
	The Grand Strand		
	The Low Country		

These places were chosen not only for the natural beauty of the areas and the life style but also for the demonstrated opportunity to make a pretty good living there.

True Where People

A true, 100 percent WHERE person may be looking for a semi-retirement business—a comfortable activity in which to invest a certain amount of money, live off quite peacefully, take into consideration all the tax advantages, and be a lady or gentleman of some leisure if not luxury.

Service Clubs Will Help

If you've spent most of your life in metropolitan areas, you may be unfamiliar with the Chambers of Commerce and the service clubs. But don't just sit there scratching your head. These men and women throughout Small Town, U.S.A., are a truly amazing source of information and help. From these people you cannot only get information on what types of businesses are available, but what to expect from them. Living conditions, schools, social organizations, where to fish. These folks are the leading business-people, the first families of wherever; they own the town. Three months from now you may be asked to join one or all of these organizations. How come you're not more friendly when you need them most? To ignore the free advice that these groups have for you and the interest that they have in you is true ostrich behavior. And yet we estimate that more than 90 percent of the people looking for a business never go near these organizations. A lousy business broker will tell you that you don't want to get mixed up with those guys. A good business broker will get you mixed up with them. He's one of them!

That kind of thing is fine for keeping you off the streets and out of the bars but admittedly it's a retirement business and not a business business. There is a distinction. What the man with the gold watch does now isn't very important. He's already done the WHAT so he might as well do the WHERE where he wants to. But for the watchless fellow who wants a business to support his family, not his ego, the WHAT is very, very important. He should be doing something he likes and/or is good at. Otherwise he probably won't be doing it very long.

Now For the WHATs

Most people looking for country businesses, of course, are a mixture of WHERE and WHAT, so to be as knowledgeable as possible, you've got to start getting a line on your WHATs. You'll be getting information on your future business from trade sources at both national and local levels. And there's all sorts of information available about all sorts of businesses. You'll have to sharpen the focus on your business binoculars. To help you do that we're putting down forty-eight businesses with a few facts about each and where to find out more at zero or reasonable cost.

This is quite different from what you went through to satsify your WHERE curiosity. That was a matter of getting some knowledge for now and finding out where the rest could be gotten when and if you got around it. This is getting as much information as you can right now about a kind of business to help you figure out whether that's your kind of business. A person who has thought his future life through and comes to a fairly common conclusion that he is split right down the middle (poor fellow!), 50 percent WHERE/50 percent WHAT, will want to know a little bit about quite a few different places and quite a lot about several different businesses. Usually where you'll go is a choice of the senses—the some like it hot, the seashore versus the mountains, and so on. These are the pretty pictures in your dream. Usually what you'll do there is a choice of the intellect—the things you reason will make some money. These were the fancy numbers you saw when you dreamt. Usually. There are times when this doesn't happen and those are big problem times. There are a number of French Foreign Legionnaires who, yes, fell in love with an unbelievably beautiful business only to find during the affaire that it had an unbelievably ugly bottom line. You'd better believe it!

Country Business Analyses

If you want to know what kinds of businesses there are in the country, just look in your classified phone book. All sorts of businesses exist, everything from accounting practices to yarn shops. But that doesn't tell you anything about any one of them. I've put down figures for certain businesses that are found in rural areas and that the U.S. Department of Commerce counted in its 1977 Census of Retail Trade and Service Industries. (There are many small wholesale, manufacturing, and construction businesses in the country, but meaningful statistics about these are difficult to come by.)

The following information is included in the table:

Customer Base: This is what the Census Bureau calls inhabitants per establishment—the number of people the average business serves.

Average Volume U.S.: From the Census data

Average Volume Rural: I took figures for Vermont, the most rural state of the 50.

Rural Customer Base: Vermont

Median Volume Rural: This represents my estimate (%) of the median sales. When they figure *averages* it's the total volume divided by the numbers of businesses. In a category where a major portion of the sales is from a small percentage of the outlets, the average is going to be significantly higher than the *median* or *typical* business. Among grocery stores, for example, 77.3 percent of the sales volume is done by 19.7 percent of the stores. These are the big supermarkets, the major chain operations. My guess is that the typical rural grocery store does about 45 percent of the statistical average store.

Estimated Gross Margin: This is my considered judgment for the typical rural retailer.

Kind of Business	Customer Base U.S.	Average Volume U.S. 1977	Average Volume Rural State	Rural Customer Base	Median Volume Rural State (% of average)	Estimated Gross Margin
RETAIL BUSINESSES						
Building lumber, building materials	7,366	$854,616	$788,712	4,254	$315,485 (40%)	30%
Paint, glass, wallpaper	18,286	206,046	186,438	9,834	149,150 (80)	35
Hardware	8,057	230,119	212,510	4,720	170,008 (80)	35
Nurseries, lawn and garden supply	13,761	115,499	73,435	10,262	66,092 (90)	30
General merchandise variety stores	12,265	408,295	274,522	7,045	219,618 (80)	35
Food, grocery stores	1,191	826,228	574,207	722	258,393 (45)	20
Bakeries	10,706	115,548	84,481	8,742	63,361 (75)	60
Automotive, auto and home supply stores	4,538	273,890	215,228	4,673	182,944 (85)	40
Boat dealers	32,509	396,642	112,000	23,603	112,000 (100)	25

Kind of Business	Customer Base U.S.	Average Volume U.S. 1977	Average Volume Rural State	Rural Customer Base	Median Volume Rural State (% of average)	Estimated Gross Margin
Trailer dealers (recreation and utility)	40,735	553,053	103,273	21,457	103,273 (100)	20
Motorcycle dealers	33,374	309,998	216,043	20,524	151,230 (70)	25
Gasoline service stations	1,207	319,996	258,426	874	180,898 (70)	18
Apparel, men's and boys' clothing	9,396	306,098	217,485 (estimated)	10,978	184,865 (85)	40
Women's clothing	3,978	251,204	181,757	4,583	145,406 (80)	40
Family clothing	9,887	373,666	319,737	5,900	271,776 (85)	40
Shoe stores	7,641	202,583	157,446	8,429	141,701 (90)	40
Furniture, home furnishing	2,580	245,979	176,860	2,538	150,331 (85)	40
Household appliances	12,141	269,698	164,167	8,742	131,334 (80)	30

Kind of Business	Customer Base U.S.	Average Volume U.S. 1977	Average Volume Rural State	Rural Customer Base	Median Volume Rural State (% of average)	Estimated Gross Margin
Radio and TV	8,610	212,776	115,200	4,969	103,680 (90)	35
Music stores	15,577	209,015	132,880	18,882	126,236 (95)	40
Eating Places	776	202,600	147,679	596	132,911 (90)	55
Drinking places	2,273	82,099	87,164	3,688	82,806 (95)	45
Miscellaneous drug Stores	4,299	467,952	266,150	3,371	212,920 (80)	35
Liquor stores	4,805	292,363	466,449	4,817	248,509 (85)*	20
Sporting goods/bicycles	6,762	147,702	116,773	3,006	104,799 (90)	30
Book stores	16,758	144,667	68,000	8,139	52,200 (90)	40
Jewelry stores	6,249	159,182	89,754	6,841	85,266 (95)	50
Hobbies, toys, games	11,493	95,363	47,116	6,841	44,760 (95)	45
Cameras, photo supplier	37,575	206,412	135,615	36,313	128,834 (95)	30
Gifts, novelties	6,260	75,564	53,523	2,744	50,847 (95)	45
Fuel oil dealers	19,976	648,274	692,227	3,688	623,004 (90)	20
Florists	7,255	81,703	59,689	7,738	56,705 (95)	55

	Customer Base U.S.	Receipts/ Establishment U.S. Average	Receipts/ Establishment Rural State	Rural Customer Base
SERVICE BUSINESSES				
Hotels* (12,538 in U.S.) 25 guest rooms or more	N/A	$1,401,668	$495,696	N/A
fewer than 25 guest rooms	N/A	52,835	72,227	N/A
Motels (39,323 in U.S.)	N/A	199,241	109,909	N/A
Sporting/ Recreational camps (5,303 in U.S.)	N/A	52,234	59,105	N/A
Trailer parks (13,549 in U.S.)	N/A	33,723	19,189	N/A
Laundry and cleaning, coin-operated	8,917	44,608	33,741	8,994
Photographic studios, portrait	5,832	31,946	12,535	3,803
Beauty and barber shops	817	19,892	17,272	893
Management consulting	1,504	58,017	21,590	1,396
Equipment rental	7,394	174,385	40,985	7,431
Sign painting shops*	N/A	104,226		N/A
Telephone answering services*	N/A	129,593	48,909	N/A
Automotive repair shop	1,081	82,820	50,074	943
Electrical repair shop	4,123	68,250	39,486	4,351
Reupholstery/furniture repair	8,788	29,071	17,789	6,355
Motion picture theaters	18,310	220,537	78,500	9,660
Bowling alleys	28,037	213,401	130,130	21,000

*Establishments with payrolls

NOTE: For the service business there was no reason to calculate the receipts/establishment for the rural state, and because of a wide discrepancy between various types of operations, it would be impossible to arrive at a typical margin of profit.

The numbers in that large table are intended to give you some kind of notion of what different kinds of country businesses are like and how big they aren't when you compare them to the average U.S. business. The Customer Base figures are interesting. Sometimes you need more people to support a country business, sometimes fewer. This seems to depend on the kind of business and on other factors such as demand and prices charged.

This is an example of the information available in libraries. There's also a lot of specific data you can get about businesses by contacting the national, regional, or state associations. There's a list of the national groups in the Appendix. Some are very helpful; others not so. Some give material away; some sell it. Some make it available to any interested party; most reserve it for members only. Find out what's out there. Many associations have developed ratio analyses which break down operations figures by size of business so you can determine what sort of dollar profit you might anticipate. Some have training programs. Some will do site evaluation work for you. If there's an association in the state you want to reach, get in touch with its director. He knows a lot, so the better you know him the better off you are. It's amazing how few people trying to find out about a certain kind of business actually make contact with the people who know the answers. So many people go on guessing wrong when it's so easy to stop guessing entirely.

Sharpening your focus

This section is the getting-to-know-yourself-better-than-you-probably-want-to part. It's the thinking it over . . . and over and over. Begin by writing down all the specifications you'd like your new life in the country to meet. Make lists. Put dates on them. You'll be glad you did. This way you can look back every week or so and see what kind of progress you're making. Set up file folders. Maybe for places you'd like to live and for things you'd like to do. Try these on for size:

Life Style Needs

scale of living
interests
"fitting into the community" things
schools
clubs
distances
living conditions
living quarters—buy, rent, build, part of business

Make up your own custom checklist of what you expect your new life to be like. But be sure to make three columns: Would Really Like to Have, Can Probably Get, Might Settle For.

Now do the same kind of thing for

Business Requirements

How much money do you need to live on?
What about resale potential of the business?

You should add to this list, but don't take away either of those questions. Again: Optimum, Mean, Minimum.

Now that you're starting to put your thoughts down on paper, it's not too soon to revise and rethink. Get your spouse to make the same kind of lists you're making. Check your list with that one. Do that little exercise very early on and keep doing it. It may save your marriage and your sanity. No surprises now...or later. Everything's right out there on the kitchen table. Oops, maybe it isn't. Maybe you should start a new business rather than buy an established one. (Our posture on this—that's consultant talk for "I guess"—is that it presents a higher degree of risk. It's doubly difficult to tackle a new environment and a new venture at the same time.)

This is the kind of thinking you ought to be doing in both rings at the same time, the WHERE ring and the WHAT ring in the country business buying circus. And sometimes it does become a circus, trying to imagine yourself not doing what you do, not living where you live, but packing up and going off to follow the elephants! Just remember that it won't always make sense, that there'll be times when nobody in the whole world can tell you whether you're doing the right thing; when one minute you're 100 percent sure and the next you're 100 percent scared, times when you need encouragement and there isn't any. Make sure that on every list there's space for small stairs going down so you can get off the bandwagon.

While the mail is being sorted and the phone isn't ringing, take some time to figure out what you can put into your New Life. You're making lists of what you'll be taking out. Now how about thinking about. . .

Your Country Business Input

Two things: buying power and brain power. The first is easy. Buying power is simply how far your money will take you.

First, figure out how many dollars you now have and how many more you can accumulate by converting things into dollars—such as real estate, personal property, and investments. We will call that money. You should set aside 30 percent of your money in your Untouchable Fund, in reserve to convert somebody else's business into your business, as a cushion for living costs, for unforeseen expenses, things like that. Okay, that leaves you with 70 percent of your money or your Spending Money.

About Borrowing

Your Spending Money may be sufficient to buy the kind of business you want. It may be a semi-retirement business like a farm or a small inn that would be wonderful for tax purposes and the Good Life. Or maybe you have a fair amount of capital. Great! But let's say you're more or less typical and your Life Style Needs and Business Requirements require an income-producing business that will cost more than your Spending Money. Consider borrowing money. There are a lot of crazy—not really crazy, just somewhat unusual—ways to finance your business, but down the road, sooner or later, very likely a bank will get involved. And banks tend to be conservative in fiscal matters. You will not see money lying around on counters as you see merchandise on display in other stores. It is kept for safekeeping in something called a safe. Often, you will find, the attitude of the bank in regard to your worthiness of renting a certain amount of their money and your attitude on the same subject may vary considerably. In the purchase of a typical country business your situation will most likely be something like this:

Money (100%)

Spending Money (70%)

(Money to buy the business)

PLUS

Borrowing
(Possibility of 60% of Cost of Business)

EQUALS

Amount Needed to Buy the Business

Untouchable Fund (30%)

Do-you-need-that-much? Is-that-all-I-can-get? Here's the way I come out and the way you're probably going to come out. Financing a country business is a two-way operation. Under non-robbery conditions what comes out of that safe has to go back in, say 115 percent of it. There are exceptions, but most country businesses do not generate enough profit before debt package payments to justify more than a 60 percent mortgage. This represents a sizeable commitment on the part of the lending institution and is an indication of their confidence not only in your ability as a businessman but in the suitablity of that particular business to your talents. Sixty percent means that the bank thinks the business is a viable one and that you seem like a solid citizen. Monthly payments on a 60 percent mortgage may be a lot to handle. You'll have to work this out against expenses for the specific business under consideration. Just remember it won't be nearly as much as it would if you'd gotten the 80 percent you dreamed about.

For your figuring convenience there's an Amortization Chart here, but for right now do it this way—15 at 12%: Fifteen years at 12 percent. That comes to $12.01 per thousand.

So . . . let's say you scrape the bottom and come up with $100,000. That means you've got $100,000 × 70 percent or $70,000 for spending money. If a bank will lend you 60 percent of the cost of the business, and your $70,000 is the other 40 percent, this means you can buy up to a $175,000 business, with the bank furnishing 60 percent of that, or

Mortgage Amortization Chart

This schedule shows the monthly payments necessary to amortize a loan of $1,000 at different interest rates for various terms. To figure your monthly obligation, find the payment in the interest rate column opposite the term and multiply by the number of thousands in the mortgage.

No of Yrs.	10%	10½%	11%	11½%	12%	12½%	13%	13½%	14%
5	21.25	21.50	21.75	22.00	22.25	22.50	22.76	23.01	23.27
10	13.22	13.50	13.78	14.06	14.35	14.64	14.94	15.23	15.53
12	11.96	12.25	12.54	12.84	13.14	13.44	13.75	14.06	14.38
15	10.75	11.06	11.37	11.69	12.01	12.33	12.66	12.99	13.32
16	10.46	10.78	11.10	11.42	11.74	12.07	12.40	12.74	13.08
17	10.22	10.54	10.86	11.19	11.52	11.85	12.19	12.53	12.88
18	10.00	10.33	10.66	10.99	11.32	11.67	12.01	12.36	12.71
19	9.82	10.15	10.48	10.82	11.16	11.50	11.85	12.21	12.56
20	9.66	9.99	10.33	10.67	11.02	11.37	11.72	12.08	12.44
21	9.51	9.85	10.19	10.54	10.89	11.25	11.61	11.97	12.33
22	9.39	9.73	10.08	10.43	10.78	11.14	11.51	11.87	12.24
23	9.28	9.62	9.98	10.33	10.69	11.05	11.42	11.79	12.17
24	9.18	9.53	9.89	10.25	10.61	10.98	11.35	11.72	12.10
25	9.09	9.45	9.81	10.17	10.54	10.91	11.28	11.66	12.05
26	9.01	9.37	9.74	10.10	10.47	10.85	11.23	11.61	11.99
27	8.95	9.31	9.67	10.05	10.42	10.80	11.18	11.56	11.95
28	8.88	9.25	9.62	9.99	10.37	10.75	11.14	11.52	11.91
29	8.83	9.20	9.57	9.95	10.33	10.71	11.10	11.49	11.88
30	8.78	9.15	9.53	9.91	10.29	10.68	11.07	11.46	11.85
35	8.60	8.99	9.37	9.77	10.16	10.56	10.96	11.36	11.76
40	8.50	8.89	9.29	9.69	10.09	10.49	10.90	11.31	11.72

Mortgage Amortization Chart

No. of Yrs.	14½%	15%	15½%	16%	16½%	17%	17½%	18%
5	23.53	23.79	24.06	24.32	24.59	24.86	25.13	25.40
10	15.83	16.14	16.45	16.76	17.07	17.38	17.70	18.02
12	14.69	15.01	15.34	15.66	15.99	16.32	16.66	17.00
15	13.66	14.00	14.34	14.69	15.04	15.40	15.75	16.11
16	13.43	13.77	14.12	14.48	14.83	15.19	15.55	15.92
17	13.23	13.58	13.94	14.30	14.66	15.02	15.39	15.76
18	13.06	13.42	13.78	14.15	14.51	14.88	15.26	15.63
19	12.92	13.29	13.65	14.02	14.39	14.77	15.15	15.53
20	12.80	13.17	13.54	13.92	14.29	14.67	15.05	15.44
21	12.70	13.08	13.45	13.83	14.21	14.59	14.98	15.37
22	12.62	12.99	13.37	13.75	14.14	14.53	14.91	15.31
23	12.54	12.92	13.31	13.69	14.08	14.47	14.86	15.26
24	12.48	12.86	13.25	13.64	14.03	14.42	14.82	15.21
25	12.43	12.81	13.20	13.59	13.99	14.38	14.78	15.18
26	12.38	12.77	13.16	13.56	13.95	14.35	14.75	15.15
27	12.34	12.73	13.13	13.52	13.92	14.32	14.72	15.13
28	12.31	12.70	13.10	13.50	13.90	14.30	14.70	15.11
29	12.28	12.67	13.07	13.47	13.87	14.28	14.68	15.09
30	12.25	12.65	13.05	13.45	13.86	14.26	14.67	15.08
35	12.17	12.57	12.98	13.39	13.80	14.21	14.62	15.03
40	12.13	12.54	12.95	13.36	13.77	14.19	14.60	15.02

$105,000. If you borrow $105,000, your monthly finance payments will be (105 × $12.01) $1,261.05 at an interest rate of 12 percent.

One way to go is to start looking for a business that's going to have $1,261.05 left over at the end of every month. That's not a smart thing to do, but it is smart to remember that under these circumstances you'll need $1,261.05 on the anniversary date of your bank loan each month or your place will be their place before very long. So much for your buying power. Now that your wallet is missing, let's look under your hat.

Brain Power

Brain power is what many people decide to leave in Bronxville. Many highly successful business people figure that the monetary contribution to their second career is all that's required. And that's the biggest insult to rural America since they took away our railroads and then tripled the price of gasoline. I will hazard a guess that if you've been an atomic physicist, the skill transfer to publishing a country newspaper may be on the low side, but I'll keep guessing that if you were a smart physicist—and for our sakes and those of our allies I hope you were—you will be a smart publisher.

But how about more than smart? Everybody's that! What specific parts of your present job are you good at? The people handling part? The numbers part? The planning part? The creative part? Say "when"; you must be good at something. Or is it everything?

How about your better half? What's he/she better at? Supplement your strengths or complement them? Now start thinking about the qualifications for the various types of country businesses. A people business? Most are, but some more than others. Hospitality-oriented businesses are heavily on the people-pleasant side, but good marketing skills are important here, too. Men who've had one career manufacturing boats might look for another running a marina. People with packaged-goods sales experience at the wholesale level ought to be able to use this good knowledge at retail. These are obvious; others aren't. Don't be any more bashful—or dumb—about your background now than you were when you put together your last résumé. It's nobody else's head on your shoulders. Take it off, look inside and see what you've accumulated up there after all these years. The basic consideration is this: What have you really got? How can you parlay that into success in a brand-new enterprise? While you're still culling facts and sorting our your life...

Get a feel for the field. Study ads in your newspapers and the ever-present *Wall Street Journal*. The Sunday *New York Times* is practically the bible here. Write to business brokers. Send for lists of businesses that are available. (The list is; the business may not be.) Read some books. Ask for some general material on buying businesses from the Small Business Administration and the Bank of America. Find out how to do this in the Appendix. Now's the time to visit with the Chamber of Commerce officers, the local residents, your (maybe) neighbors. Talk a little and listen a lot.

The closer you come to knowing what it is you want, the easier it will be to look. And if you don't have a pretty clear idea of what you want, you won't recognize it when you see it. You've got some idea what you can pay and pay back. You're going to have to find the type of business you want in the place you want to live that also fits those numbers. If you think you won't compromise, you don't have a full deck upstairs. But the better you plan your search, the more you know, the sharper your pencil, the less you will compromise, and the happier you will be when you do find the business, when you do buy it, and the longer you live with it.

Planning Your Search for a Business

CHAPTER SEVEN

The Right Country Business

This is what it's all about. A lot of people never get quite this far in the long and difficult process of buying a country business. Most people with the dream just plain can't accumulate enough money to make it come true. They recognize this fact, postpone their planning to a more feasible time, and that's great. There's nothing sadder than to see a young couple—or an old couple or a middle-aged single, for that matter—start a business on a shoestring and, despite all of their hope and courage and guts and hard work, have to watch it fray, stretch, and finally snap.

Some people look around a little or a lot and decide that a country business just isn't for them. They don't find what they thought they'd find, and they quit while they're ahead. Once in a while this is the result of an ill-planned search, looking in the wrong place for the wrong thing. But more often—particularly with people who have a good sense of where they belong and what makes them feel comfortable—it's just a matter of finding out what a country business would be like, of learning that their dream will never come true, simply because it wasn't a very real dream.

Undecided

And then there are those few lookers who simply can't make up their minds about where they want to be or what they want to do. They may hear of a business for sale from time to time that sounds like perfection and they'll tell their friends that they're going to look at it next weekend, but then there's a party that they really have to go to and after a week they make a firm decision that this time they'll really have to wait until next time when the perfect thing comes on the market. This type never exactly crowds the highways to country businessland.

Now three kinds of people have gotten off the bus: those without the fare, those who've decided they don't want to take the trip, and those who couldn't make up their minds where they wanted to go. In one sense these people are fortunate—they don't have to worry about finding the wrong business. And you, my friend, are not quite so lucky. You're still on the bus and there's an excellent chance that you, yes you, will end up buying a business that is not right for you. It's so easy to do. Thousands and thousands of people do it every year. It's easy because so many people are anxious for you to buy a business—the sellers and the brokers and the bankers and the accountants and the appraisers and the building inspectors and the termite people and the men from the title company. And not one of them really cares very much about whether you buy a business that is particularly well suited to your wants and needs. If all these people don't care very much, you'd better care a lot!

The Wrong Decision

Here's what happens when people get into the wrong business; four examples (there could easily be four hundred) of folks who obviously thought they were doing the right thing. These are not stories with happy endings, but they are must reading for anyone who is seriously looking for a country business and wants to make sure he buys the right one. There are plenty of country businesses around that nobody should buy. There are only a few that you should buy. If you can recognize all the wrong ones, it shouldn't be totally impossible to pick the right one, if it's there.

Here are four classic country business mistakes, with the names of the owners changed to protect the guilty.

Dwindling Stock

1. *A bad case of bare shelves.* Al and Alice decided to sell their home in Allentown, quit their jobs, and buy a country store in Bucks County, an area they knew pretty well. The owner was asking $129,500 for the store and the three-bedroom apartment above. Sales volume had grown to $175,000 a year, with indications of good potential increases of about 10 percent a year (after allowances for inflation) from new people buying weekend/vacation places in the charming, small town. Al and Alice knew they could realize $80,000 on the sale of their home and figured on investing about $60,000 in the business. After a couple of months of looking at other business in the area, they made an offer of $120,000 plus inventory which, somewhat to their surprise, the owner accepted readily. The contract was subject to availability of financing for at least 50 percent of the purchase price. This money—and absolutely no more—was forthcoming from the bank in town on the basis of a fifteen-year mortgage at 12 percent interest. Everyone thought it would work out pretty well.

Like this:

$175,000 Annual Sales, Year 1
   38,500 Gross Profit at 22% Margin
   24,000 Expenses Excluding Debt
   14,500 Operating Net
    3,000 Allowance For Living off Store
   11,500 Profit Before Financing Cost
    8,650 Financing
    2,850 Net after All Expenses

Over the past few months the owner had been working his inventory down to an affordable $10,000. The couple sold their house, made a $60,000 down payment, put up approximately $5,000 for closing costs, and decided to make some much-needed repairs before moving into the apartment. The new kitchen and bathroom cost another $5,000. So this was the end of their capital. But all of their expenses—health insurance, automobile, food, beer, everything—were in the budget with $2,850 for a great vacation, savings, whatever. And that was more than they'd ever had left over when they were both working.

But Al and Alice didn't see that the staple merchandise was thin, thinner than the store could stand.

Everything *seemed* to be moving along nicely for the first couple of months. Al was adding some items—even a line or two—that the store hadn't carried. Cash flow started to become a small problem and the grocery wholesalers extended a limited period, perhaps thirty days, of credit. Sales were trending down just slightly compared to the previous year, but that was to be expected until all the people in town began to feel comfortable with the new owners. The store was basically a grocery store (quaint, but a grocery store) and the grocery suppliers were beginning to tighten up. Tighten up was translated to COD. Al and Alice didn't always have the C on D day, so what should have gone into their stock went back to the warehouse.

Supplies of basic grocery items dwindled and couldn't be replaced. The charm was still in the store but a good selection of merchandise wasn't. Customers who had been enthusiastic supporters of Al and Alice at the start started to come by just once in a while. The downward spiral accelerated. After twelve months the bank stepped in and took over the store and kept it closed until they found a buyer with experience and considerable capital above the $90,000 selling price. Al and Alice had lost $50,000 because they didn't have (and couldn't get) the $5,000 necessary to bring the inventory up to what it should have been at the time of purchase. The previous owner, in an effort to make the total package—real estate, equipment, good will and inventory—more appealing, had done Al and Alice the kind of favor he would never have done for himself. Of course Al and Alice wanted a brand new bathroom in their home more than they wanted the old familiar brands in their store. Anyway, it was a lot of money down the drain.

Dwindling Guests

2. *The innkeeper who kept the guests guessing.* If a telephone operator had ever paged "Mr. Successful" in a hotel lobby, this man would have quickly taken the call. He was the epitome of the successful, professional, by-the-numbers businessman. Our Mr. Successful had brought new life, vitality, and a promise for the future into his father's substantial florist supply business in Denver. At 35, Mr. S was thought of by his Harvard

Business School classmates as one of the leading second-tier contenders (company size and type of business took him out of the major competition) for unusual recognition at the tenth-year reunion. Unlike most of his peers, however, Mr. S's analysis of an ideal life-balance always placed "familyman" significantly ahead of "businessman." This was the prime reason that he made the trip to Steamboat Springs in just a shade under four hours when he got the word that Styles Peake, the owner of Mr. S's dream ski lodge, had had a stroke and that he and his sister Gayle Meadows, with whom he had operated the business since 1955, had decided to retire. Mr. S had a brief letter of agreement from Styles and Gayle to the effect that when they chose to dispose of the property they would entertain his offer on a priority basis. Mr. S wanted the lodge because:

1. The Steamboat area is acknowledged to be an almost ideal location in which to raise children who have demonstrated more than a passing interest in winter sports activities.
2. The business gave several indications of being operated with a surprising degree of sophistication.
3. All current available data tended to show that his florist supply business was about to enter a reasonably long-term plateau and this was a propitious time to place it in the capable hands of his twin brother, to whom he was senior by just over twelve minutes.

The purchase was for cash, the price was agreed upon by buyer and seller to be the value ascertained by the leading commercial property appraisal firm in the Rocky Mountain area. The assistant manager, Inger, agreed to stay on with a salary increase (negotiated under rather unpleasant circumstances) for a period of six months.

And so the Successfuls moved into the owner's quarters, a pleasant four-bedroom ski house about 125 yards from the main lodge. Mr. S was very happy because his wife and 6-, 8-, and 10-year-old boys exhibited no evidence of unhappiness or strain resulting from the move. He was also extremely pleased to see very quickly certain areas of weakness in the business that could be strengthened—reductions in expenses for the bar, a gradual lowering in the group bookings quotas to allow for larger room sale dollar volume and, perhaps most important, a fairly sharp pruning of advertising and promotional expenses, which seemed excessive in the face of occupancy rates close to the 96 percent mark.

Okay, folks, this is what happened. In an effort to provide a totally normal environment for the children, the Successfuls figured they could afford to absent themselves for the lodge and ignore their guests during the critical family hours of 4 to 10 PM. These hours happen to coincide exactly with the critical innkeeping hours. The S's went a step further and just plain weren't around during school vacations, a time when inn activity is at its peak (or was when Styles was there). Inger ran a nice show, but it was her show—a lot more hers than it would have been if the curtain wasn't about to come down. These were her final performances and she did a nice job. . .on you know who!

Little things like the potato chips and pretzels and the sixty cocktail franks in a blanket that used to come out every night at six and had cost over a thousand dollars a year were gone. But Inger remembered—and remembered to remind people of them. In an incredibly nice way!

When the Successfuls were at the inn, which, by the clock, was most of the time, they effused and fawned profusely to make up for the fact that they had three boys who weren't supposed to be around the guests. It was more than a little much. But sales weren't. Down week after week compared to the same week a year ago. Not much: 6 percent, 4 percent, 8 percent. But the Steamboat Springs Chamber of Commerce figures—which included Mr. S's downside numbers—were plus 6 percent, plus 7 percent, and plus 5 percent for the same weeks.

Right after ski season Mr. S closed, just as Styles and Gayle had always done. But Peake and Meadows had for 11 years stayed open and given their all for the three extra days for a small group of somewhat unsavory travel agents who continued to book a constantly declining percentage of business. Not this year. No junket. Good-bye.

And good-bye Successfuls. Lucky folk. They sold the business after just five months for 11.6 percent more than they had paid for it. Everyone's back where they belong. And the florist supply business is making very modest gains, but much easier for a Successful to live with than the business losses he couldn't possibly understand. Because they weren't really business losses. They were people losses!

Lots of Errors

3. *Do you make these common mistakes in managing?* Nobody's perfect but a lot of people are better than this friend of mine who had worked summers in a filling station in New Jersey while he was going to college and ended up buying a filling station in New Hampshire—a beautiful little garage in a picturesque little village—when he and the First National City Bank pretty much simultaneously hit upon the idea of his early retirement. He'd been taking his vacations in the area for almost twenty-five years, watching different members of the same family operate the service station. He was friendly with all of them. The sons had moved to different parts of the country, and the business, he found out from some friends, was for sale. He overcame all the business-acquiring and financial obstacles in fine banker fashion and opened both bay doors and the one to the office one sunny Saturday in late May. By Labor Day he had made the following mistakes.

1. He decided to open daily from 8 to 8 and a half-day on Sunday instead of 7 to 7 and closed on Sunday.

2. He lowered gas prices 2 cents per gallon to get the more profitable repair business.

3. He extended credit to local customers.

4. He offered a free Coke with a fill-up to encourage tourist business.

5. He became a volunteer fireman to get better acquainted with his neighbors.

6. He let one of the boys go and reduced the hours of the other one until he just pumped gas when the station was extra busy.

7. He changed the hours back to 7 to 7 and closed on Sunday to get the going-to-work business he had lost and to save salary on the Sabbath.

8. He cut out the free Coke because he figured tourists would fill up anyway.

9. He had to give his mechanic a raise so the profitable repair business wasn't that profitable anymore and he raised the gas price 2 cents a gallon.

10. He refused credit to local customers.

11. He increased the hours of the boy he still had for July and August and tried to hire back the other one.

12. He hired one of the former owner's cousins for 75 cents an hour more than he'd been paying the boy he fired.

13. He changed the name of the business to his own.

14. He continued to give credit to those who had paid promptly and not to those who hadn't.

15. He decided to open half-day Sunday.

16. He quit the fire department because he was too busy.

Most of these things a stranger could see simply by looking out the car window as he drove by. Our friend's accountant was, of course, privy to the bottom of the iceberg and told him of a State Farm Insurance Agency in Nashua that was looking for three mature salesmen. Another career change was effected for our friend. The accountant bought the business and sold 49 percent of it to the mechanic and the two boys. By Thanksgiving the town really had something to be thankful for: the level of chaos at the Cross Corners Shell Station was back to normal.

4. *No room for printer's errors.* Jack didn't really have a trade at all. He had been working around San Francisco advertising agencies doing mechanical pasteup work, speedball lettering, sketches for presentations, some comprehensives, and an occasional line drawing. He had minor aspirations toward some serious sculpture. He could spec type, thought a lot about starting his own art service, and made good money freelancing around town. Sometimes he'd be in a bullpen at the same shop for nine

NOTICE! MEN, WOMEN, AND CHILDREN Are required to Appear AT THE STORE OF PETER CLEVER, ALL-SORTS ROW, And invest to the extent of their CASH! A VERMILION EDICT!

Saving the Shop

months, handling whatever hit his easel on a 60/40 split of the art costs billed to the client. Sometimes he'd pick up an assembly and have it back before the studio manager knew he'd been in. Jack is one of that band of commercial artists who go where the work is, have a great talent for getting it done and the temperament of a brain surgeon. They are unseen, unsung, and indispensable. The're smart, they're cool, and they usually like girls pretty much. (In dark singles bars they can often "pass" as being in advertising, once in a while as being creative.)

Jack picked up Jill in a little bar one night, and it was all over. The Hill Country of West Virginia is a long way from the Golden Gate in every way there is, but true love doesn't know from agates and picas, and that's what life is all about. Love, that is.

So Jack bought a fairly successful little printing operation and, with a small amount of big-time know-how and one of the great personalities of all time, had a beautiful business in less than a year. And then things started to happen. The Economy.

When the economy slows down in the United States, in West Virginia it stops. A few of Jack's good customers went out of business, others got to be a real pay problem. The town was drying up. Things got better too late to save a lot of people's dreams. Some places never make it through a serious slump. The sun shines again but nothing grows. Once or twice Jack closed his eyes and saw Ghirardelli Square.

But he opened his eyes to something new. He wasn't going to sell printing anymore. He was going to sell ideas and concepts and all the stuff he'd never been permitted to deal in in San Francisco because he wasn't creative. ("He does mechanicals.") A little dignified lettering on the van, a very classy slide presentation, a necktie and eight pounds of enthusiasm, and anybody with a sales problem within seventy-five miles was fair game. Jack went out of town, all right. . . and brought back business. Finished it up, delivered it ahead of schedule, and brought back more.

Just plain bad luck and nothing else had almost put Jack out of business. But fortunately he saw that his future didn't depend on where his press was as much as where his head was. And his heart was in West Virginia, too. After all he was born there!

BASIC HAZARDS

So these four stories tell us the basic hazards of small business operations. In the words of business, we must watch out for:

UNDERCAPITALIZATION
That means not enough money.

PSYCHOLOGICAL/TEMPERAMENTAL CONFLICT
That means not enough personality.

INSUFFICIENT MANAGEMENT SKILLS
That means not enough smarts.

NONCONTROLLABLE EXTERNAL CIRCUMSTANCES
That means not enough luck.

Jack was able to turn his luck around and stay in the same business. The other three were perfectly qualified to go into business. They just picked the wrong business. The frightening part—the thing to think about for a long time—is that *your* chances of finally ending up with the wrong business after you've done all the work and all the analysis your going to do are better than 50/50!

It is hard to say this: you will probably buy the wrong business. It is easy to say this: the fewer mistakes you make in buying a business the better the chances of it being the right business. The more familiar you are with these mistakes—your ability to recognize them at a distance—the easier it will be for you to avoid them.

The truisms. There are two mottos that you should have tattooed on your wrists, typed on index cards, or committed to memory. Maybe they should be strung like prayer beads, so you could say them before walking into a broker's office or looking at a potential business investment. The two essential pieces of wisdom are:

Don't believe everything anybody tells you.

It isn't polite to talk about lying or exaggerating or stretching the truth. When does permissible hyperbole become a deceptive business practice? You tell me. No, I'll tell you: when it could potentially cost you more than the cost of a local phone call. Just remember when you buy a business, they all get some of your money—the seller, the broker, the salesman, the attorneys, the banker, the appraiser, the accountant, and the bartender at the place where everybody but you goes after the closing. So nobody really lies, all right? Let's just say that under the circumstances total objectivity is mighty hard to come by.

Most businesses are for sale because the owners can't make a living.

You will hear that they want to leave now while they still have the strength to lug off the bags of money they have made. You will hear of incurable disease. You will hear reasons you won't believe—and shouldn't. This is the big question everybody asks. Therefore, it prompts the big lie. No business broker would ever think of an answer like, "Oh, they're just tired of running the business. It's really quite a strain." " No, that wouldn't do. "Strain" is a negative. He'll make it emphysema, hereditary emphysema!

Getting serious

Get advice from experts

Here's a guy who worked for a big company. If he needed legal advice, he called Legal. Accounting? Call Accounting. Purchasing? You bet. Me? Buying a country business? Need advice? Ridiculous! You got plenty of advice when you were spending the stockholders' money. But when you're spending your own money, how come you're so smart? You need it now more than ever. Get the best advice you can.

Answering Ads

Okay, begin. You've been looking at ads in the *Wall Street Journal*, major Sunday newspapers, trade journals. If you see something that interests you, you might as well follow up on it. Just the ones that are right on target, though. Don't waste a phone call or postage on long shots. You'll get off the track. If the owner expects a phone call, let him have it. It's going to be long distance and it will cost some money, but stay on the horn until you think you've found out everything about his business that you want to know. If you've got him there, get to know him. Tell him about you. Make him your buddy. Be sure he knows what further information you need. Don't make any commitment to visit Godknowswhere until you've had time to think about it.

If you plan to answer box numbers or blind ads, put together the details—everything you can think of—about the business you want. Type, location, anticipated volume, minimum profit requirements, the whole bit, and make photocopies. Send your specifications to the seller. (What good are they if you keep them a secret?) This may get him to tailor his reply rather than just send you the standard information he sent the others. That will be helpful. You're not interested in any business, you're interested only in the one that's going to be your business. Make the seller work. He's the one who'll be getting the money.

If an ad is placed by the owner and says "Principals Only," that simply means that he doesn't want brokers answering. He may or may not have his business listed with a broker. That doesn't make any difference to you. If the ad says "Brokers Protected" it means that both the selling and buying brokers will receive their stipulated commissions no matter how the sale is conducted. Let's say you don't reply to an ad yourself, but a broker you've talked to does, calls you, you buy the business, and he gets his commission. "Brokers Protected" encourages brokers to respond to the ad. "Principals Only" is supposed to turn them off.

Brokers Identified

In most states, if the ad is placed by a broker, it must be so identified. If only a phone number is given, the ad will probably say "Broker." Sometimes when an owner runs an ad, it will say "owner." In a big city

How to Answer an Ad

You're paying for the phone call. Find out as fast as possible. . .

WHAT is the business? Kind of business, kind of customers, size, shape, etc.

WHERE is it? Exact location. You may want to see it.

WHEN? Availability. And how long has the seller has had it?

HOW is the business doing? Specific volume, actual profits. Bottom line.

WHY is the seller giving it up? Try to get the real reason.

Make notes before, during, and after. Don't say later on that you can't remember what the seller said!

newspaper that word may have cost him ten bucks. He probably thought it was worth the money to let you know two things: that you won't have to worry about getting involved with a broker and that, because he's not paying any broker a commission, you have an opportunity to practically steal that business away from him. (You don't even know what his business is, and the owner's already trying to tell you it's a bargain!)

Brokers often run ads listing one specific business. If your antennae go up, get your specs in the mail. If the broker's ad lists several properties, don't make the foolish assumption that they all exist. This ad is run to tell you he has a lot of businesses for sale. Some brokers advertise regularly, week after week. Some never do. Some broker ads say "send for list." Some describe businesses.

While you're looking at ads, don't forget to look in the yellow pages of the phone books for the areas in which you're interested. (You didn't have them sent to you? Tsk, tsk.) Look under "Business Brokers" and also under "Real Estate." Many real estate brokers whose main business is residential sales have a commercial or business department.

Some brokers will have display ads in the phone book. There may be things that attract you in these ads, such as "specialists in selling stores" or "we handle bars and grills exclusively." This tells you something. The size of the ad, the street address, and whether the phone number ends in zeros are clues. But just remember you're interested in buying a business—not the brokerage. Enough about brokers' ads. Now about brokers.

WORKING WITH BROKERS

If you've been reading the lines up to this point, you haven't had a chance to read between them. That's good because there's nothing there. No implications whatsoever that brokers are dishonest. As a group they are probably no more dishonest than shoe repairmen. But the temptation to be less than totally honest has to be greater when one is dealing with emotions and abstractions rather than leather and nails. It is in your best interest to be interested in the business broker's business.

His business is sales. His goal is sales. His life is sales. The broker is successful when he makes a sale and unsuccessful when he doesn't. He is happy when he makes a sale and unhappy when he doesn't.

Does this make him dishonest? Of course not. It makes him sell. Ask any broker what the name of his game is and he'll tell you "listings." That's his merchandise, what he's got for sale, what makes him different from the guy across the street. The best salesman in the world can't sell what he hasn't got. Listings are much more important to a broker than customers are. There are many more customers than there are good businesses for sale. The better the listing the easier the sale. The less time the sale takes the more time he has to get more listings. (Business brokers are constantly coming into my store. They know my business isn't for sale, but they don't know when I might have a fatal heart attack. Why do they say, "Take it easy!" when they leave? Surely they couldn't mean that.)

Total awareness of what goes on in the business broker's head is a very valuable tool to have in your Buyer Beware Kit. As far as you're concerned, the broker lists businesses for sale. He works as a go-between for the seller (whom he represents for a commission that is usually 10 percent of the selling price) and the buyer. He is usually indispensable in finding a business because most ongoing businesses are wary of putting a sign in the window saying that they're going out of business. A broker is your basic source of information about what is available.

A broker is not a psychologist, even though he earned his living by making matches that hold considerable psychological implications. He may, however, strive to create the impression that he is in the unique position of being able to save the suburbanite from untold evils. Usually the broker is not an expert on any business except the selling of businesses. He may quote margins and ratios for certain businesses. He may talk markup and merchandise lines and occupancy rates. He will use whatever jargon he has available—and he can get more at the library when he runs out—to lull you into feeling that he is an expert in just the business you're interested in. This may be his method of convincing you that he's an authority. Once you come to think of him as an authority, you'll become dependent on him, you'll readily take his advice, you'll buy what he tells you to buy. He's got you hypnotized. Watch out!

How Brokers Work. Somebody wants to sell a business. He signs an agreement with a broker to the effect that the broker works as the owner's agent in the sale of the property (usually for a certain period of time) in return for compensation in the amount of 10 percent of the selling price. The broker agrees to list the business, and so forth. The listing can be "exclusive," meaning that the broker gets the entire commission, even, in some instances, if the seller is approached directly. A listing can be "co-exclusive" with another broker, in which case the commission will be divided according to the terms of the agreement regardless of which broker is responsible for the sale. Or it can be an "open" listing, meaning that the broker consummating the sale earns the commission. In some areas there are multiple listings for businesses just as there are for residential properties, which means that the listings are published and the information is shared by the subscribers to the service.

Most areas—particularly rural ones—do not have multiple-listing services, so "co-broking" is common. That's simply two brokers working together. You talk to a business broker, and you're that broker's customer. He doesn't have a listing that you're interested in but he thinks an upstate broker might. Downstate calls Upstate, you buy Upstate's listing. Downstate gets part of Upstate's commission (usually 30 percent). So brokers keep in touch with other brokers. If they don't have a listing, they might be able to share in the listing broker's commission. (What's the name of the game? Listings? Right.)

Using brokers. If the broker is always out getting listings (and earning his living) or on the phone with other brokers (and earning some more), what makes you think he has time for you? Well, he has to spend some time with customers to make sales. But, and this is a key thing to think about, the more successful the broker the more selective he has become about customers. He hand-picks those with whom he will spend his time. He will handle less desirable prospects in different ways. Less time, younger, less experienced salesmen, fewer phone calls. All the way down to absolutely nothing.

The broker separates in his mind serious customers from lookers. If you are a serious customer, make sure the broker knows it. If you are a looker, he'll find out quick enough.

Let's say you're serious. Then you should make the brokers work for you—as hard as possible. Your future depends on it. Never let him work unnecessarily or without direction. Good brokers get discouraged easily and stop working efficiently.

Use as many brokers as you can; this simply expands your opportunity to uncover the business you're looking for. Tell each broker exactly what you want. If you've got your spec sheet, use it. Give him all the copies he needs. It's like your résumé—in reverse.

EXAMINING FINANCIAL STATEMENTS

One of the terrible things you'll be looking at while you are looking for a business is the financial statement. Terrible, awesome, frightening. Why? Because this piece of paper is what can cost you your arm and your leg—if you're lucky. If you're unlucky, it could cost you your whole body.

Think of it this way: when you buy a home, let's say, it is a certain size and shape, made out of this and that, so many years old, and likely to be there as long as you will. It has a certain kind of wiring and, we hope, plumbing and things like that. And it's on a certain street in a certain neighborhood. Most of this is pretty much measurable in terms of value. Supply and demand establish that value.

Now you're buying a business. It may be a business with a couple of fixtures and pieces of equipment or it may involve a certain amount of real property—a building or two and some land on which they've been erected. Wiring and plumbing maybe. So far we're in the same ballpark. Stuff you can look at (or look in a book) and say, "Okay. That's worth about $11,000." Maybe you can't appraise the business by yourself, but there are or will be appraisers and people like that to help you. But, again, we hope you're interested in buying more than the building. You're trying to buy a way to make a living. And the value of that business, in terms of good will or whatever you want to call it, is what is so incredibly hard to determine. Additionally, the business may have one value for you and a completely different value for Al and Alice or the Successfuls. And the most complicating factor of all is often the tax situation. One owner might pay substantial taxes on a business with certain gross dollar profit, while another might pay nothing and earn credits.

Most small businesses pay small taxes because lots of expenses are

Be Firm

When dealing with brokers, look at only what you're looking for. Let me explain.

A broker would rather have 100 percent of the commission on a sale than the 30 percent received for selling another broker's listing.

So if he doesn't have what you're looking for, his instinct is to sell you what he does have. He'll use various tactics to distract and confuse, to encourage you to look at something you don't want.

What should you do?

Tell the broker, for example, "I'm interested in your three best hardware stores."

Your specs will tell him what you mean by "best." Best volume, best net, best living quarters, best fishing. Tell him you want to see a full description, photograph, and financial statement of each one.

And be firm. If he just doesn't have any hardware stores, move on to the next broker.

charged to the business—many of them justifiable. In the country, where certain types of businesses—stores, inns, farms—can provide all your living expenses and transportation and entertainment and medical insurance and education and practically everything you and your accountant can think of, a sharp, clean separation of business and personal expenses becomes totally impossible. That doesn't mean that it isn't done in the records, the balance sheets, the operating statements, and the tax returns. It's just totally impossible.

Three Sets of Books. It is said that many country businesses keep three sets of books: the real one, one for the IRS, and one for the next owner. The balance sheet is supposed to give the position of a business at a specific point in time; the income statement is supposed to show the results of being in operation for a certain amount of time. The former should show the value of the business; the latter should show how it's doing. So if you're an agent for the IRS, the owner is likely to show you a very black picture. But if you are a prospective buyer, the picture is sure to be a very rosy one. This is why the balance sheets, the income statements, and the cash flow analyses that the broker or the owner shows you are so very, very dangerous. Treat them accordingly. Remember, the broker assumes no responsibility for those numbers. There is almost always a disclaimer attached that goes something like this:

WE MAKE EVERY EFFORT TO INVESTIGATE THE VIABILITY OF EACH BUSINESS WE LIST, BUT WE CANNOT TAKE ANY RESPONSIBILITY FOR THE ACCURACY OF THE FINANCIAL INFORMATION PROVIDED BY THE SELLER.

Obviously, the financial statements that you will see early on are extremely unlikely to reflect the true position of the business. That's why you should always say your truisms before you look at any numbers.

Rules for Looking for a Business

Now is the time when businesses are going to be calling to you, "Hey! Look me over! I'm the one! Check me out!" The ads you answered will be answering your answer. Brokers will be phoning, writing, sending lists. Contacts you made with the Chambers of Commerce or the trade associations will be getting back to you. Now you're really in the business of looking for a business. So be businesslike! Plan!

You have just so much time to look at a business. Tell yourself this: if you don't find the right business in the time you have allotted—say, this year's vacation—that's okay. I've known people who figure they'll find a business they like in ninety days and end up buying a business they don't like on day eighty-nine. It's like looking for a girl to marry. Grab the best thing around before your time runs out. But there's no mating season for buying a country business.

It is very likely that you will have to set up time schedules. Looking for a business takes forever. The next one you are interested in is usually a million miles from the last one. You may think that you have all the time necessary to see everything that you're interested in, but if you don't use it wisely you may get frustrated and give up. Then you've really run out of time.

Have a Diary and Map. In order to set up a workable time schedule, you'll need two things: some kind of diary or appointment book and an official state map. The appointment book (finally you've found a use for that gift your insurance man sends you every year!) is not just for jotting down dates and things to do. It will be a permanent record of the things you did and the businesses you investigated. It will cut down the number of mistakes you make. (One fellow I know got very excited about a business a broker was describing and insisted on seeing it right away. After forty miles of boring conversation, the two of them pulled up in front of a business my friend looked at three months earlier. The second broker's description of the place was nothing at all like the one of my friend had heard from the first broker. . . but even so!) It is also good to get into the habit of filling out 5 × 8 index cards on each business that interests you. Keep these in the back of your diary.

Your other basic looking-for-a-business tool is the state map. Every state has an official map. If you didn't get one before, get one now from the tourism office at the state capital or stop at one of the lavish lavatories-cum-brochures on the interstates. Identify your area of interest on the map. Use a marker. If you can decide where you want your business, don't look at anything outside your boundaries.

People do things when they're looking for their own business that they'd be fired for doing for someone else's business. Here's how the business-buyer's mind works: "It's out of my way, but I'll just slip down there. . . hope I don't get lost. . . and look at that other property! It'll only take a couple of hours or so, and I'll get back before dark. I'm not at all interested in that business and have no intention of buying it because the ad said the volume was only $168,000. . . but maybe if I see it, I'll get some ideas about the one I'm really interested in up north."

Of course, he gets lost, gets back in the middle of the night, sees something he had no intention of buying, and gets mad. Two or three more experiences like this and he'll conclude that there just aren't any businesses for him in the entire region.

Rural areas are very big. Geography plus common sense says, "Schedule your trips, plan your visits, group your stops." Do these things. When you plan a vacation trip, you plan carefully. You want to conserve time, save money, and see everything you can. And this trip is much more important.

Looking at Businesses

You can make a mistake just looking at a business. And that first look is most important.

Be prepared, on that first visit, to gather lasting first impressions in these three key areas:

1. Visual. Ask the salesman to stay outside. Go in as a shopper or visitor. Look around. Be cool. Don't gawk. You'd like to have an objective first feel of the place. You'll never get it any other way except by going in cold.

2. Personal. Get to know the owner. The broker will probably do everything he can to prevent this, but try to get around him as best you can. This is the man who owns the business you may be going to buy. You're considering the purchase of his life's work—much more than what's on the books or on the shelves. You might be going to give him a large amount of money. He might turn out to be your best friend.

3. Financial. Just listen at this stage. But listen well. Ask only enough questions to be able to understand the numbers. Don't question anything seriously. Don't argue. Save your strength.

Shop Selectively. Save your strength and your sanity for those businesses that are your prime targets. Rural areas can be depressing. There's a lot of good, solid poverty out here. Poverty isn't pretty. A lot of the businesses aren't doing well. Some are being run by people who should have retired a long time ago but nobody came along to buy the business. Some prospective buyers see this and their dreams go bust. Often it is a man with a second wife who is somewhat younger than he is; they are starting over. And it's your classic "You're-not-getting-me-into-a-dump-like-this" situation.

Don't expose yourself, or any other decision-makers in the group, to businesses that are not what you want. You won't learn anything—except that you don't want to go broke—and your attitudes can shift. This can happen when you're tired, depressed, frustrated. Looking at one more wrong business may just turn you off for keeps. Don't risk it.

The more you know about a business the better your ability to decide whether you want to inspect it. Play the favorites first, then the longer shots. Phone calls and letters are a lot cheaper than gasoline. If you've established contacts in the area or the trade, now's the time to use them. Be very careful about depending on a broker to tell you what to see. They're inclined to gamble your time against their commission. (Be particularly wary of the man who wants you to take a long trip but doesn't want to go with you! If he wins on the thousand-to-one shot that you like the business, he'd make a lot of money without moving off his chair.)

The process of looking for a business can sometimes sort out those buyers who won't be successful when they find one. You have to be very tough and analytic—very businesslike—in your approach. Otherwise you will waste your time, your money, your patience. And you won't find anything. Or you'll go bananas and the white jackets won't let you have a business.

FRANCHISES

There are a number of good books about buying a franchise, written when buying a franchise was a very popular thing to do. The best one is probably *The Franchise Boom* by Harry Kursh, Prentice-Hall, Inc., Englewood Cliffs, N.J., 1978, (477 pages).

There are franchised business opportunities in rural areas, but not very many. Most of the desirable franchise operations already have somebody doing very nicely in them, thank you. Country franchises may be garden-supply outlets, truck renters, equipment renters, muffler and transmission shops, camper grounds, real estate offices, furniture strippers, building-products suppliers, catalog sales, and motels. Buying an established franchise business is like buying any other business except there's a third party involved who may be a good guy or a bad guy. But he can't be ignored. Starting a new franchise operation is starting a business from scratch.

If you've been a businessman—if you are a businessman—you should certainly think about the field of business counseling. One of the reasons so many country businesses are for sale is that there haven't been enough competent business counselors out there to provide the kind of advice that can save a business from financial and managerial disaster. The investment in a General Business Services franchise is a lot less than in most businesses. Check it out. (General Business Services, Inc., 51 Monroe Street, Rockville, MD 20850).

Retirement Businesses

That is pretty much a broker's phrase to describe a business that doesn't make very much money for somebody who doesn't need very much money. A selectively viable business? How's that sound? Such a business might be a very lovely inn well off the beaten track that attracts just the right number of guests—enough to qualify as a business by IRS standards, and not enough to interfere with a fabulous life style by anybody's standards. A lot of country businesses are perfect for people who don't want to make money. It's very nice to live where there are very few people (all of them great) and lots of write-offs (ditto). I hope many of you readers have a lot of money and don't need to make any more. But for the vast, unwashed majority for whom the sight of red ink is almost as frightening as the sight of blood, we will be discreet and not talk any more about semi-retirement businesses.

And all of that might say this about country businesses: it's much easier to lose a buck and a whole lot harder to make one. That's why you have to be right when you *think* you've got the right business.

CHAPTER EIGHT

The Community

Looking for a business can be a very pleasant experience. It takes you out into the country, into the more open spaces, gets some fresh air into your lungs and some new thoughts into your brain. You meet a lot of people, shake a lot of hands, crack a lot of smiles, and posture a little bit like Mr. Nice Guy.

Once your attention starts to focus on a particular business (or two or three) and your mind begins to wrap itself around the right business, it's essential that you wipe that happy look off your face and practice grimaces and teeth-gritting and all the other things generally associated with those who wear the black hats. Of course you can still be outwardly pleasant, but for a while, and for your own good, deep down inside you'd better be tough.

Now you're going to be looking at a business with sharply critical eyes. Your ears will be ready to pick up pieces of information that can be later fitted into the puzzle. You've sharpened all your pencils, turned up your sales resistance button, taken ten deep breaths, and have yourself completely psyched up. You're prepared for disappointments, eager to strip the varnish to get at the truth, ready for those soul-searching sessions with yourself that will affect the rest of your life.

But don't make the mistake that so many people do. They say, "Okay, this is a critical decision. I have to make it by myself." That, of course, is completely wrong. Deciding whether you want to buy any country business, to change your way of living, to give up what you have for something you're not sure about. Yes, that's a decision you make by yourself. You alone, the two of you, your family, the partners, whatever. The insiders, not the outsiders, come to the final grips with that one. That decision is behind you. The word was "Yes, a business." Now the question is, "How about this business? Is this the right business?" This is a decision you've never made before and are not likely to make again. You need all the help you can get. You need more help than is in this book. You need more help than is in this world. So whatever tiny little bit of help walks down the road, throw a net over it and hold it close. God sent it to you, so don't send it back.

A business is not good if there isn't a life that goes with it. So the first thing to figure out is about the community.

The Community

If you are more a WHERE person than a WHAT person, the decision about a community has probably already taken care of itself. The Lady of the House or some other incredibly dominant influence may have established exactly where you are going to live. Maybe not the house but the neighborhood. Maybe not the neighborhood but the town. Maybe not the town but the area.

A lot of the considerations about where—and how—you live will depend on the type of business you're interested in. Many country businesses have living quarters that are part of the premises. This is certainly true of hotels, motels, and inns. It is often the case with general stores and other retail operations in rural areas. You may be interested in a building that has a store below and apartments above.

So if the business you've chosen comes with a place to live (or vice versa, depending on the potential and quality of each), you're probably wondering whether, for business reasons, you should live there.

Living In or Out

Innkeepers usually live in rather than keep house elsewhere. The economics and the surroundings appeal to them. If they want to live out, it doesn't say much for the inn. But in a vacation-oriented area, inns and the like don't always have much involvement with local people. I know of a family who owns a successful lodge and has a house in a town eight miles away. They never neglect their customers, and no one seems to care that when the last guest is sacked out, the bosses take off. One of the problems that drives innkeepers up the wall is the lack of a private life. My friends have an expensive solution but it's their problem, their solution, their privacy. And more power to them.

Then there's another friend of mine who decided not to live in the apartment over his country store in a very small town. His reasons were based on space; there simply wasn't enough room for the family. His customers, however, reasoned that my friend thought he was too good to live over the store. And perhaps a little too good for their trade. Most of them had never seen the inside of the apartment so they made false assumptions about this character's character, which cost him quite a bit of business during his first year. When one of his girls went off to college, the family gave up their rented house down the street and moved up over the store. This saved rent money and tax money (my friend's posture with the IRS was that it was necessary for him to live over the store to protect is from fire, burglary, and other perils), provided the easiest commute in the history of commuting, and gave the family easy access to the hugest pantry imaginable. It also enhanced their attitude about the store. The place to work and the place to live became pleasantly inseparable and this was a major factor in placating the townsfolk and turning the business around.

Advice: if you are seriously interested in a business with living quarters and you don't think you want to live there, carefully reexamine your appraisal of the business. If you won't feel comfortable living there, will you really feel comfortable working there? This is the country, remember, not the city. People know where people live and why they live there. If you have your heart set on a fairly substantial hardware store with a couple of apartments above it, you should probably live in town but not necessarily over the store. This is not nearly as personal a business as the only-store-in-town variety we were just discussing. If you're considering a bookstore or gift shop that serves a number of communities in the area, who's to say but you where you'll settle down? The hours in such businesses are not as long as in inns, general stores, and the like, so driving a few miles makes little difference. And you may be able to develop good contacts in two communities rather than one.

Generally, though, you should think of a country business as a whole new way of life with a minimum of separation between the work part and the home part, the daytime and the nighttime. What's attracting you to the country—the family business—goes on twenty-four hours a day. Or it doesn't go on at all. More often than not you'll work and live pretty close together—maybe not upstairs/downstairs, but close. If the business doesn't have living quarters, fine and dandy. That's one less problem— and one more problem—you'll have to solve.

Have you studied the town, talked to enough people to get a really good feel for it? Are there enough people with similar interests to make life bearable until you can get interested in the things that interest them? You've checked out the schools, the activities, the whole scene? Have you asked some people in neighboring towns where they'd like to live if they didn't live where they do? Are the vibes of the very best quality? You're going to like it there, right? Sure? Okay. But most little towns don't have any one-way streets. Will the townspeople like you?

Little Separation

If you say, "Yes!" I'll say, "How do you know?" If you say, "Maybe," I'll say, "Forget the town and the business that goes with it." Until you can say, "Yes, I will be accepted by the community," sanity says don't buy a business in that community. Running a country business—keeping it out of the ground, that is—is super tough enough when the town loves you. If you think for one munute that the town is going to have reservations about you, make reservations elsewhere! There's no sure way, however, to know whether the town is going to put up with you or put you down. But most places are a little friendlier and more open than they first appear to be.

Here are a few nice neighbor situations that you can mull over while I go make a cup of tea:

Key Question: Will You Be Accepted?

• Your neighbor brings four brook trout, cleaned and ready for the pan, to your door one evening just as you are finishing dessert. You say something about having just eaten and why doesn't he take them over to Jack who really likes fish. Should you have made your eyes pop and told him that the fish would make a great breakfast for your family?

• Your neighbor tells you about a mill nearby where you can get all the scrap lumber you need for kindling for only $8 per pickup-truck load. You travel eight miles, fill your truck, come back and tell your neighbor to take what he wants. He takes less than half and leaves $4 on the seat of the truck. Should you make a big thing of insisting that he take his money back since you had intended this as a neighborly gift?

• Your neighbor offers to babysit while you and your husband go to the natural childbirth classes at the clinic. You're gone about three hours, come back at 9 P.M. and find your three-year-old happily playing with the neighbor's ten-year-old twins. You're upset about the baby being up so late and forget to give your neighbor the chocolates you bought for her at the pharmacy. Should you give them to her the next morning?

• Your neighbor's mother is coming to live with her in two weeks and you're thinking that the greatest thing all of you could do for them is to help them build an addition to their house. You get the group organized, order the lumber, a keg of nails, and a keg of beer. Should you have kept your neighbor in the dark about your bright idea?

• Your neighbor is on his way to an important meeting in New York, and realizes at 4 A.M. that the only way he can get there is to wake you up for gas. You get up, get his gas, and get mildly irritated. Should you let him know you think he's out of line?

• Your neighbor brings you several kohlrabi from his garden and suggests two or three different ways to cook them. Your Cordon Bleu cookbook, however, suggests something totally different for this esoteric vegetable. Should you enlighten your green-thumbed friend?

• Your neighbor is in a convalescent home—following a stroke—that's forty-five minutes away. You've driven halfway there when you remember you've forgotten to bring the carrot cake you had promised to bring. Should you go back for it?

• Your neighbor's blueberry muffins are of superlative quality but she always overprices them at the bake sale; frequently they don't make it to the cigar box checkout. Should you offer her what you think they're worth?

• Your neighbor is raffling off the best-looking quilt you've ever seen and you want it more than anything. You have some extra money this month. Should you buy twenty chances?

Country life isn't all carrot cake, but it does entail getting involved with things like carrot cake. Small things can become important things when nothing much is going on. You will be more aware of your neighbors in the country than you are in the city. You will also need to be more tolerant, more loving, more open, and more anxious to share, to lend, to work together.

The Answers

In the above situations my good neighbors thought the answers should be: Yes, No, Yes, No, Yes, No—all the way through. There's a fine line sometimes between being a good neighbor and being a patsy. Where does the good guy end and the sucker begin? I wish I could say, "Don't worry. Everything will be fine." But I can't. Little towns are crazy sometimes. They reject people—particularly business people with high visibility—like a body might reject an organ transplant. Nobody knows why; "They just don't fit in."

Sometimes part of the problem is that newcomers try too hard to fit in and fail at it horribly because they flail and gush and just don't settle in. Some people come to town and act like big moths around a light. Not harmful at all, just downright annoying.

Any Doubts?

If you have serious doubts about being accepted by a community— you, your wife/husband, your children—don't move in. Or if you're uneasy about the relationships all of you have with each other—don't move in. But if you feel comfortable with the people you've met, you feel good about yourself and each other as a family and you think that the town feels comfortable with all of you, come on by.

Should you have a grid of pluses and minuses on the community? It could have divisions for the social, educational, and cultural ratings of the community—with subdivisions of these categories. And across the top of the grid should be the optimal and minimal levels of your own needs and goals that you hope to get out of a community, perhaps with a rating of from zero to ten. And when you're finished with your ratings of a community, if you don't come up with an 83 percent—a solid B+— don't call the movers.

No, of course not. You either have something deep down inside that tells you this is the right place or you don't. If you don't, don't move. When you really do, then go ahead.

The Final Test

You've made up your mind that this town is it.

You'll be good neighbors among good neighbors, and you'll have warm friends and a lot of fun.

Take my advice and get out of there. Go away for a week. Take a trip. Visit people you haven't seen for a long time. Be sure to tell them about your weird idea of buying a country business. Go to places you've never been. Make it a real vacation.

Then go back to the town you may live in. Did you miss it? Has anything changed? Is it still as good as it was before you left?

If your answers are positive, that's the place for you.

So you'd like to live there. Now the most important question is whether you can make a living there. Can the business you're buying support you in the manner to which you are getting accustomed?

CHAPTER NINE

Check It Out

There's your dream, right in front of you. You're going to put this one (and maybe one or two others) under the microscope and see what happens. This will be the acid test to end all acid tests. You want to know whether you can live with this business and live off this business for the rest of your life. You may have done a few things the easy way to find this business. You may have lucked out. But if you take some shortcuts now, you may very well find yourself on the road to the poorhouse.

The first and, in many ways, the easiest part to evaluate is...

The Physical Assets

If you are renting, you may figure that you can skip this part because you're not buying real estate or any building. You're just leasing space and that's it. You're a renter. Sure, but you probably want the building you're renting to remain standing for a while. Obviously your interest won't be as intense as it would be if you were taking title, but you'd better take time to check out whatever it is you'll be leasing. You may not be buying it but you'll be living with it, so watch it! Whether you're buying or renting, check it out thoroughly.

First, the Land. Check the land. How much is there and where is it? Is it dry, wet or what? Can you grow things on it? Can cars park on it? Is it attractive, unattractive? Do you care? What's it like across the street? Who's over there? What does he do? The answers to these and other questions will mean one thing if you're evaluating what's supposed to be a charming country inn and will mean something completely different if it's a junkyard. Think about the amount of land. Is there too much? Do you have to buy all of it? Will you be able to sell some of it? Is there too little for expansion? Suppose your septic system stinks and you have to build a new leach field. (They take up more room than you think.) Is it the right kind of land? Terrain? Drainage? The soil? Soils in rural areas directly affect land development. The content, permeability, and stability of the soil as well as the depth of hard rock will tell you about septic systems, roads, and foundations.

Check the Buildings. On the land there are buildings. Buying,

Water Problems?

Country water problems break down into two categories—too much or too little.

In most rural areas there's a bit more to water than simply turning on the tap. Does the land you're interested in have the potential to yield adequate and clean ground-water supplies? The broker says the land is okay? Who says the broker's okay? Remember you're out where

Nature invented a lot of things that you may not be as familiar with as you should be. Like water. There can be none when you need it and your well runs dry. Or a lot when you don't need it and your house floats away.

If there are doubts in your mind, there are civil engineers in the phone book.

renting—it doesn't matter. What is the place like? When was it built and have Nature and all the people been kind? Nobody expects you to be a builder or an architect, unless you are one. But in the initial stages of examining the physical assets of a business, you should try to think like one.

Check the exterior of the building. Remember that the basic purpose of the outside of a building is to keep the inside dry. Look at the roof. Not from up there, from down here. Use a pair of binoculars and focus on the flashing around chimneys and vent pipes. Look for leaks. Check the condition of gutters and downspouts. Think about how much life the roof might have left. Inspect the siding. Poke at it with a penknife. Soft spots are rot, either from water or termites. Bulges could be symptoms of structural problems. Check for flaws in the foundation.

Once you're inside, look up. Are there serious ceiling cracks? Water stains? Down in the basement look for evidence of leaking and flooding. Use your flashlight. Be suspicious of fresh paint and other cover-ups. A wet basement isn't the be-all-and-end-all of your business, but it's good to know how deep the water gets, how you're going to have to store things, and what to look out for. Up in the attic search for discolored wood or rusty nails, sure signs of leaking. While you're up there check the ventilation and insulation. The question is not whether you'll have to make some repairs. It's whether you can afford to do all the work that's necessary.

Check out the heating system. Heat and hot water cost more today than they did yesterday and not as much as they will tomorrow. Remember that. Make sure the system works. Turn it on—so what if it's summer? Do you want to be surprised in September?

Ponder the plumbing. How old are the pipes and what are they made of? Copper lasts a long time, steel doesn't. Look for patches and other signs that the pipes have just about had it. If there's a well, well, check it. If the water runs muddy, maybe the storage tank's too small. Have you got enough pressure? Is the water pure? Is there a septic tank? When was it last pumped out? Greener grass or melting snow can tell you where it is. If there's anything else that tells you—like your nostrils—something's wrong.

How about the electrical system? The wiring? Are there at least three wires coming into the building? Is the amperage adequate for what's in the building? Would it be adequate for anything that you might want to add? Check the service panel for information, or count the number and amperage of the fuses. Does the business require refrigeration? Will you get hit for rewiring as soon as you take possession? Don't let it come as a shock.

A Simple Inspection. This is by no means a sophisticated inspection of the premises. All you'll be using is your flashlight, pocket knife, and binoculars—things it's smart to keep in your glove compartment until you sign a contract. If the owner or the broker or anybody else thinks you shouldn't be looking at the building as carefully as you are, you can begin to wonder why you shouldn't. The broker will tell you that this is no way to look at a business. He'll tell you that if you're interested you should put down a deposit, sign a letter of intent or an agreement to purchase the business contingent upon a satisfactory building inspection. This I consider a totally unrealistic pressuring technique. How can there be a logical objection to you—the prospective buyer and a nonexpert—taking a careful look at what you have a serious interest in buying? The broker could contend that you're not serious until you make a down payment. Your position is that you're not about to make a down payment until you're serious. If he has nothing to hide and wants to sell the business, he has to agree with you. What is this, a peep show? Do you have to pay money to look around? Forget it!

While you are looking around, it's a good time to make notes of the particular things you want inspected extra carefully when a professional does it. Maybe you'll have the inspection done by a general contractor, but you'd like to have a plumber or a heating contractor by his side. Or maybe you know enough about one area but need some advice elsewhere.

The building (or buildings) will probably contain equipment that you should go over very thoroughly. Make sure you understand exactly what is part of the sale and what isn't. I've known people who closed on a business, took possession, came in and looked all over for the leased equipment which had already gone back to the owners. (And that's something that can affect your Year I Profit and Loss Statement all right.) Find out what will be yours and what won't. If it's going to be yours, check it out. Make sure the equipment works, how it works, where to get parts, who services it, and whatever else you need to know. Write down the model numbers and other information to get estimates of the fair market value from dealers, trade journal ads, or other reliable sources. Is there any of the equipment still under warranty?

What is the percentage breakdown between the real property cost and the equipment and fixtures? Make sure you get all of this down in your notes. It will affect the depreciation figures in your tax picture. At some point you may want to suggest to the seller or his agent that separate values should be established for real estate and equipment in terms of the total package. It's the same money to him. It could be different money—from a tax standpoint—to you.

Know the Restrictions

But no matter how you spend your money, there will be some restrictions. You probably won't be able to operate the business willy-nilly, any way you want to. There will be local, county, state, and federal restrictions on what you can and can't do, musts and mustn'ts. First be sure to look into the fire safety code. I know people who bought an inn that hadn't been inspected by the state for thirty-seven years. There were thirty-six violations ranging from switch plates to boiler location. Contractually, the seller bore the expense of getting everything in order. But, naturally, the buyer had the hassle.

Check the zoning regulations. If you're thinking of doing something slightly different from what was done by your predecessor, make sure you will be able to do it. Maybe he was already doing something illegal. Check OSHA (Occupational Safety and Health Act) standards. Check local ordinances, particularly as they pertain to signs and other things that will be important to your business. Many communities have severe restrictions on the kinds and sizes of signs you can put up—even on your own property. In Vermont there are no advertising signs along the roadsides. None!

Licenses Needed

Check on the availability of licenses you will need. Food, alcoholic beverages, firearms, cigarettes, pesticides—all of these are often controlled at more than one level. Certain states have specific residence requirements. Some states specify that certain licenses are available to corporations, not to sole proprietorships or partnerships. There are numerous environmental laws in many states, and tax laws galore. Very often state departments of health and agriculture will have overlapping and, not infrequently, conflicting rules. In some places the restrictions are easy to get around. And in some cases they are impossible. Pinball and video machines and jukeboxes come under regulation (maybe not often enough). Farm products, livestock, and almost everything else that grows or moves is controlled. Prices are controlled on certain items, such as milk.

Checklist of Things to Check

What	You	Professional

Land
size _____
location _____
too much, too little _____
terrain _____
drainage _____
ground water _____
soil type _____

Buildings
age _____
roof _____
gutters and downspouts _____
siding _____
foundation _____
cracks in plaster _____
water stains _____
ventilation _____
insulation _____

Heating system
what kind _____
how old _____

Plumbing
pipes _____
storage tank _____
septic tank _____

Electrical system
wiring _____
amperage _____
refrigeration _____
air conditioning _____
Other equipment _____

Sometimes licenses and permits are not the same thing. You'll have to register, too. Your business, your trade name, your vehicles. And you'll be inspected. Sanitation, safety, and weights and measures.

Are you thoroughly confused? Good! Now you'll seek help. States are ready, willing, and able to give it. Anxious, in fact, because in exchange for the help, they collect the taxes and the fees. The office of the Secretary of State or the Department of Commerce is the place to begin. Most of the procedures are routine. The person who owns the business you're thinking of buying probably has a lot of information. But if you have plans to make some changes, he may not know what could happen. So you'd better find out!

THE GUESTS ARRIVED

Now back to the Smiths, the couple who bought the inn down the road. Well, their first guests arrived on December 16. They had stayed at the inn in the old days and were more or less looking for memories. There was a man in his fifties and his mother on the other side of eighty. Just the two people from Connecticut, two nights. It was quiet, peaceful. The guests enjoyed their country weekend, and the Smiths got their very first taste of innkeeping. It worked out well.

For one thing it was a tryout for the cook. Pat and Toni had come by Kathy Astrauckas sort of by accident. She's a young girl who had fine training and zero experience. Kathy applied for a job at another inn in the area, the job was taken, they sent her to the Wiley Inn, and, like that, she was hired. So Kathy did the meals, the Smiths ate dinner with the guests (or did the guests eat dinner with the Smiths?) and everything—not terribly demanding—was okay. But before the guests arrived there were a few moments of doubt about whether the inn would open on schedule, a week or so late, or never.

The fire marshal from Montpelier had insisted in November that a new boiler be installed, and that was done. He looked around and said he'd be back in the spring. There are still some minor things to be done after the Smiths generate some capital. Make a few improvements to bring the inn up to code, but the place has his blessing for now. The state health department has granted a full license for a year; the restaurant has a brand new Hobart dishwasher which cost twice as much as anticipated. The environmental health group is satisfied because the inn has over nine acres so that a third (there are two now) septic system could be built if needed.

I know of one inn that's in trouble. It is built on too small a piece of property to allow for an alternate leach field, and there's no more land. What does this inn do to conform with the law?

But the Smiths' Wiley Inn, right now and for the foreseeable future, is no longer a piece of expensive real estate; it's a commercial property.

Pat and Toni found that Vermont is making it easier for people to go into business and stay there. Maybe it's because of Pat's background handling people, but these state officials seemed to want to help him, to be a resource, to be cooperative, to share their knowledge about what's going on.

If the Smiths had gone out and hired a bunch of lawyers to fight the bureaucracy. . . But that's not their style. They got what they wanted. With a couple of signatures the big house became an inn.

Any Changes Ahead?

It's good to find out what changes might take place in your area that could change your business. Here's the kind of thing I have in mind:

My store is within the boundaries of the Green Mountain National Forest, which is administered by the United States Forest Service, a part of the Department of Agriculture. Down the road 1.7 miles is the Hapgood Pond Recreation Area, traditionally a very popular spot for campers, swimmers, picnickers, fishermen, naturalists, and the like.

When I was thinking about buying the store late in 1977, the pond had been drained so that siltation and other ecological problems could be fixed. I was naturally interested in its future (which seemed to be so closely entwined with my own) and was pleased when the business broker's salesman told me that his secretary had checked with Montpelier, the state capital, and that the pond would be open for the summer of 1978.

Had I been a little more attentive I would have realized that since the campground is operated by the federal government, nobody in Montpelier could be expected to know anything about it. The district ranger is in Manchester, the forest supervisor is in Rutland, and the regional headquarters is in Milwaukee, but I didn't check with these people.

Was Hapgood Pond open in the summer of 1978? Of course not. Was it open in the summer of 1979? Yes. 1980? No. A simple phone call in 1977 wouldn't have told me all of this. But I would have been a lot smarter and better prepared and less likely to have temper tantrums if I'd made that simple phone call.

Sometimes major highways get rerouted. Twenty miles of new U.S. Route 7 in Vermont, from Bennington to Manchester, has cost unlucky businessmen on the old route (now "Historic Route 7A") millions of dollars.

And old-fashioned country charm doesn't always stand in the way of progress. Progress like supermarkets and motels. If you've heard a rumor about this type of progress arriving near your new business, it's probably true. If you haven't heard such a rumor, find out why not! Check with the Chamber of Commerce on what is being planned in the town, or check with the highway department. Find out everything about the business you're after. What does it have going for it and going against it? Keep your finger on its pulse.

Inventory, particularly in a retail operation, is customarily a separate purchase. The basic reason is that inventory, hopefully, changes from week to week. You will buy it after you buy the store, usually at its wholesale cost. Look it over. Find out how much it's really worth. Make sure that you never become obligated to buy anything you don't want, such as dirty, damaged, or obsolete stock.

Financial History

Now it's time to look into the financial situation in a way you've never analyzed anything in your life. The land, the building, the equipment. They're all in place. No problem. The bankers appear ready to lend. The lawyers will legalize on call. Everyone's waiting for you to give the word. "Yes, I'm confident that I can make a good living in this business. I'm sure that buying this business is a viable investment." When it comes to the financial condition of a country business. . .

THE TRUTH WILL NOT OUT

Why not? People are basically honest, aren't they? Sure they are. And they're also basically sensible. For just a minute, why don't you play the role of the seller? You are very anxious to get rid of your business. It has been reasonably successful and you're reasonably proud of your accomplishments. There are some things that you could have done better, you know now. All you have to do is adjust a number here and there—nothing major—in the financial statement of the business to reflect what you know for sure that you could have done if you'd had 20/20 foresight. Hey, you're not misrepresenting anything to anybody. It should have been that way, right? And those numbers are completely possible, probable even.

And totally unreal! Now go back to being the buyer. You know that if you futz with one little number, you have to futz with several big

---

Insights on Inventory

For a non-retail operation, use the cost to seller. Itemize the inventory. Agree on costs. Work it out.

For a retail store, price marked − mark-up to get wholesale cost. Make sure you use correct mark-up for each category.

Think about, putting inventory on computer.

ones—and you end up with garbage. The seller has had a successful business and has made a good living. Like everyone else, he wants to appear just a little more successful than he's actually been. Not just to you the buyer, but to his lawyer and his friends. He can stand up a little straighter when he walks down the street. And you've got to be very careful not to walk into his trap.

Now think of what's going through the mind of the man who hasn't been successful. He's desperate to get rid of that business. He's been skimming like crazy, putting cash in his pocket instead of the till. He can't fool around with just a few of the figures. He and his accountant pretty much have to start from ground zero and make up a financial statement for the business. And a good one it will be.

Watch Out!

There are two more things that make life with the numbers slightly less than beautiful.

Small businessmen are by nature lousy bookkeepers. It's part independence and part rebellion against the system. Part incompetence. Part mischief. Whether the maintenance of proper accounting records is above him or beneath him is of no consequence to you the buyer. The books you'll probably be faced with will most likely resemble a dog's dinner.

Country businessmen are by nature crafty. If the seller has survived, it's probably because he knows quite a bit more about the workings of his business than you'll ever find out. "Ever" is about twelve days after you start operating the business. His records may show no personal expenses at all. No salary, maybe. He lives off the business. But how well does he live? How does his standard of living compare to, say, David Rockefeller's? Where does he live? What does he eat? What does he drink? Drive? Wear? Where does he spend his spare time? Tennis, anyone? Is the accounting procedure that allows—or allows for—this life style shrewd, sinful, or just plain sloppy? Only your accountant knows for sure.

Advice on Accounting

One very difficult judgment is when and how to get competent accounting advice. A lot depends on the condition of the business as represented by the seller, the condition of the books (what they actually show, what periods they cover, what procedures are used, and who has been keeping them, auditing them and doing the taxes), the conditions under which they'll be examined. Your own accountant may want to disqualify himself because of distance or ignorance. He may want to see more than exists. He may want to offer a qualified opinion that really may not be very helpful. But you know your accountant and I don't, so you'll have to decide whether he would be good for the job or whether a local practitioner would be better. If you go for someone in the vicinity of the business you're scrutinizing, make sure he has a good reputation and has no connection with anybody involved in the sale.

The timing of an examination of the books is a real problem. It shouldn't be a huge one when you're dealing directly with the seller and he's cooperative and eager to sell the business. The best thing here is for you to sit down with the seller, take your time, and go over everything he's got. He's showing you the inside of his business—how it works—so you can decide whether you want to buy it. He's trying to prove to you that the business is worth what he's asking for it. Okay.

A Binder, When?

But say you're dealing with a broker who's very anxious to get his commission. He wants to put you in a defensive position, to make it your job to get out of buying the business. He wants you to agree to a contract, a binder. That's the only way he can make a living. He'll say you can't go over the books until you agree to buy the business as represented by the seller. Then if you want your down payment back—and I assume you might want those thousands of dollars (the down payment is customarily 10 percent of the agreed-upon purchase price)—it's up to you to prove there's something wrong. The broker will tell you, "That's the way it's done." If you want to be done in that way, go ahead. I wouldn't.

My position on this is as follows: the seller and the seller's agent, in an effort to make a sale, have a great interest in convincing you that the business is worth the money they want for it. And you want to be convinced. It should not be a requirement of the buyer that he pay money for the chance to prove that the seller is a liar.

Any good broker will go along with this. The dividing line should be: extensive professional investigation. You should be able to look at anything you want before signing your name. If you want an accountant to perform an audit of the books and provide a professional opinion as to whether they truly reflect the condition of the business—to spend hours, sometimes days at this—that should be after you have signified your intention to buy the business. The same rule would hold for a professional inspection of the premises. The difference is between your finding out and an expert's making sure. If there's a problem with this among all those people representing the seller and lonely you, buyer beware! Caveat emptor!

Of course, you don't have to accept everything the seller says. He has been in business by himself and for himself, more than likely. But he hasn't been in solitary confinement. A lot of other people know a lot about his business and, if you go about your business right, you can find out what they know.

First people first—the suppliers. It has been said, "Good customers I can always get; good suppliers are hard to find." That's a great half-truth. Good suppliers are hard to find anywhere. They're almost impossible to find when you're in the country. You're small, hard to get to, nobody needs your business, forget it. In some rural areas, forget the "good." Suppliers, period, are hard to find. (I know small stores, incredibly beautiful old places like Pierce's in North Shrewsbury, Vermont, where the "full-line" grocery wholesaler won't deliver to his door. He has to get his order from a larger store where the truck drops it.) But somehow if you want to stay in business you find ways of getting the supplies that keep you in business. So every business that has an "open" sign in the window has suppliers. And, usually, the more they know about your business, the more business they do with you. You may not tell them a great deal about your business but every time you give them an order—or don't give them an order—they find out something about your business.

And, of course, most businessmen like to exchange information with the supplier salesmen. You may meddle with the truth in your conversation—that's the only really fun part of talking—but when you're through with the idle chit-chat and you give him an order for three cases of this and one case of that, he knows what's happening. For example, let's say you buy Budweiser beer from him and sell it to some of your customers. He knows how much you sold last year and for a long time before that. He knows how much you're supposed to sell for a place of your size, location, local buying habits. He doesn't count your checkouts or bar stools. He doesn't have to. If he wanted to he could give a very sharp estimate of your total sales volume: increases/decreases by month or whatever. This guy knows your business. So does every other wholesaler and distributor you do business with.

Get the Facts From...

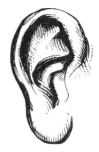

Who's Right?

The new restaurant owner was bragging that he was doing better than his predecessor.

And some people were doubtful about that.

One of them asked the produce man who had been supplying the place for years.

"If he's doing better," the wholesaler said, "then the former owner was throwing out two crates of lettuce a week."

Now these people aren't hanging out on street corners peddling little tidbits of trade talk. But they can be tracked down and, sometimes, pinned down. Find out who sells such-and-such to the place you're thinking of buying. The company and the salesman. Salesmen like to talk; so talk. Sure he's friends with the present owner, but he'd like to be friends with the new owner . . . before his competitors get all that chummy. Inns and stores and the other country-type businesses buy from an unbelievably large number of suppliers. You don't have to touch all the bases, but a couple of key queries are certainly in order.

What to Ask

What do you ask this guru, this sage? Anything you want to know. Volume, trends, location, past, present, future, guesses, opinions, cautions. You're a businessman, he's a businessman. Maybe you'll be working together. Explore, talk, learn.

But don't stop after you've talked to a couple of suppliers. You're supposed to be checking this business thoroughly, remember? How many owners in the past ten years? Who were they? Where are they? If real property is involved, the town clerk or town administrator has these records. What did they pay for it? What did they sell it for? What's the assessment? The taxes? Alcoholic beverage licenses? Other permits? What does the town know that you should know? In many cases, it won't be just the records you're interested in. It's also the remembrances. In small towns people remember a lot. Sometimes it's hard to get them to forget. And in this case—right now—you may be lucky. If the town clerk wants to talk, make sure you listen. And when you go outside, write everything down. Yes, on the 5 × 8 index cards you specifically got for this purpose.

Former owners are a fine source of information. If you can find out who they are and where they are and you don't bother to talk to them, you're not going about your business right—finding out about the business you might be going to buy. Check old employees, too. If there are skeletons in the closets, these are the people with the keys. Chances that there will be a lot of advice are very high. You don't have to take any, though. Somehow it will be colored. But find out what facts the advice is based on and make sure you've got these facts straight.

Gossip and More

There may be some people around who know too much. You'll get more gossip and rumor than you need. Just push those things aside. But don't listen selectively and hear just what you want to hear. If you do that you might as well talk to yourself and save the price of the beers you've been buying.

Often the most valuable commentators are the competitors, and they shouldn't be overlooked. Nearby competitors—the ones across the street—know a lot but may be very biased. Try to sort that out. Other businessmen in town are bound to be opinionated. They know the present owner and some of the things they think he does right and a lot of the things they think he does wrong. But it would be rare that they would know very much about the *operation* of his business because they're in different kinds of businesses. So frequently the best person to befriend is someone who has a business very similar to the one you're considering, but is outside your particular marketing area. If you don't feel comfortable doing the kind of probing we've been describing and if you're not at home with the financial projections we'll be getting into, you may want to make a formal arrangement with this man to serve as your advisor—your consultant—for a fee.

One great advantage of a consultant at this particular stage is that he knows all the ins and outs of successfully running the kind of business you want to buy. He probably knows of the business you're interested in but will want to find out a lot more about it. And he'll get the info from the suppliers and the others. You'll have to find him, check on him, allow him to work in his spare time, and pay him. Be generous, flatter him, make him feel like the expert he really is; put everything on a businesslike basis. He can save you time and money. And he can be more objective than you can.

The other big plus of a *consultant* is that you can save face. The man you're planning to buy this business from may be in a position to play a very large role in your future. If he doesn't like you, he may have more ways than you ever thought there were of funneling business away from you. So it could be good to bring along a "third person authority," an outsider, to be the bad guy. At this point you have to compare how much you really know about the kind of business you'll be getting into and how much you think you know about human nature with how much you're going to have to pay for help.

You alone or you and your helper should now be looking at the recent federal tax returns for the business you're thinking of buying. You *should* be! So maybe there aren't any tax returns. The seller and his broker don't want you to see the tax returns because they show a picture of the business that is less than flattering. They show a minimum amount of income and a maximum amount of expense and, not surprisingly, the smallest amount of taxes owed. So when you ask to see the tax returns, don't be surprised if the owner and broker are less than enthusiastic. (I know of one broker, however, who will not list a business for which he cannot readily show the current tax return. This broker is a very smart and successful man!)

HIRING A CONSULTANT

Look at Tax Returns

Remember that tax returns are different for different business structures. Corporations are tax entities and pay taxes. Partnerships (and Subchapter S corporations) file returns but the tax liabilities are passed on to the partners (or stockholders). Sole proprietorships don't file tax forms, but the profit or loss of the business is included in the owner's personal return.

If you luck out and are able to look at the tax returns, that's great! Make sure the numbers correspond with the numbers on the financial data you already have. If they don't, find out for certain why they don't! Make notes on this, don't make any mistakes about it. It's critical.

If there are no tax returns for you to look at, be very suspicious and a little philosophical. Businesses have been bought before without the buyer seeing tax returns. But without tax returns to go by, you are going to have to spend a lot more time and be a lot more careful when you figure your...

Operations Potential

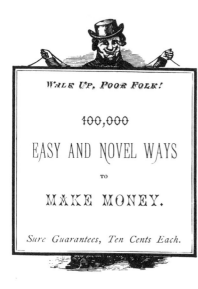

WALK UP, POOR FOLK!

100,000

EASY AND NOVEL WAYS

TO

MAKE MONEY.

Sure Guarantees, Ten Cents Each.

That's a pretty fancy title but it does describe just what we're going to do in this section. Based upon what we know, we're going to try to figure out how much money this business will make for you and whether that will be enough. (I doubt that it will be too much, although there are some special people with special tax requirements who may have to make some downward adjustments. They will have to worry about the consequences later on.) This is the single most important part of the book because you may very well have found a business that is where you want to be, doing what you want it to do. Everything appears to be absolutely perfect—except, for you, it isn't a business. You won't be able to make a living. So you won't buy it.

Decision-Making Inputs. You've got all the financial information you're going to get, probably verified by a tax return, an audit, or somebody's trustworthy judgment. You should have an income statement (or profit and loss statement or an operating statement or whatever it's called) and a balance sheet. If you don't have both of these, forget about the balance sheet and concentrate on extrapolating pro-forma profit and loss data from whatever information you do have.

To do this you'll want to consider what the market for your products and services is going to be in the near future. Apply the *marketing information* you've been able to come by that could be useful, including whatever you got from the state development agency, the C of C, the association, and your recent investigation of the business you want to buy. Will sales volume be up or down? From what? And why? You may be in a business right now where it's your job to know these things or to find them out. Or to report them in sometimes unbelievably precise detail. Perhaps the last thing in the world you want to do is guess. But a guess is better than nothing. And a good guess is better than a bad one.

Business Fundamentals Simplified (3 sheets of paper)

Balance Sheet	*Income Statement (Operating Sheet)*	*Cash Flow Sheet*
what you have what you owe	what your sales are what your costs are what your profit or loss is	what you are going to pay and when what's left over

---

If you want to take the present owner's sales figures, okay. Or adjust them. Just have a pretty good reason for making the assumptions you're making. Write it all down. If you're used to some particular form for comparative operating statements, use that one. If you prefer a blank piece of paper, I'm sure there's one around. If you're like I am and believe that forms were made to be filled out, get some forms. For now use what you can pick up at a local stationery store. Any kind of a bookkeeping record will do. There's Dome, Greenwood, Ideal, and plenty of others to choose from. Just make sure all the usual expense items are listed so you'll have a checklist.

Business Planning. Right now you're developing a business plan upon which you—and most likely some lending institution—will make a go or no-go decision. That's why all the numbers you put down should have footnotes: documentations, assumptions, or rationalizations, whatever your basis is. You may be working with historical data or making projections. As you go along you'll be using numbers, making better assumptions, refining your judgments. This projected P & L statement, along with a projected cash flow and balance sheet and the necessary explanations of the items, will become the central part of your presentation to the bank for your mortgage loan. Put that together with some sort of description of the business, the product or service and its market, the objectives, strategies, and tactics, and you have what can be called a business plan. The bank will need to know some things about your character and credit, and that ought to be it.

Books about business operation, and brokers, busybodies, and bystanders may very well try to push you into developing long documents. Probably one of the reasons you've fallen in love with the idea of a country business is that you hate long documents. What you need is a page or two of the best numbers you can assemble, notes on how you arrived at them, and that's all. The rest is all window dressing. If you think the bank wants window dressing, give them some. But find out what form your presentation should take before you waste time developing it.

Make Honest Projections

In all your financial projections, you've got to be totally honest. I'm sure the bank would appreciate it. But, more importantly, you've got to be totally honest with yourself. This is the business that's either going to make you a living or be the death of you. It's your skin, so be conservative! Don't assume you'll do better than the present owner because you're a nicer guy. Assume you'll do worse at the start. Don't assume your gross profit is going to improve. This is one of the great mistakes that people coming into their new business make. Your ratio of gross profit to sales, your margin, is pretty well set for the type of business you're in. If you don't already know it, find out from a reliable source—not the broker—what you can logically expect. You can get an idea of it from trade sources (the local association, suppliers, competitors). You probably won't be able to buy cheaper than the guy you're buying the business from. And when his customers become your customers—and let's pray silently for a moment that they do—you're not going to be in a position to charge them more than he did. So the chances of the margin changing are slim, no matter how slim the margin.

Study the Margin

And, please, look at that margin carefully. Most of the gross misrepresentations on financial statements supplied by the seller are made right on that line, "Gross Profit." Apparently it seems like a good place to take advantage of someone who doesn't know a lot about the seller's business. Sales numbers are probably pretty much in line with the real thing. And expenses are pretty easy to estimate and check. So, I'll bet that if he's going to fake a number, he'll fake a high gross profit percentage. He can make it high to make the business look desirable, even if volume declines somewhat. For the IRS he can make it low, so it appears he doesn't run the business very well. What do they expect? He isn't a genius!

But if you are going to make changes in the business—working longer hours, testing lines with better margins—make sure these are reflected in the projections (and explained in the notes). Whatever you put down should be thoroughly realistic. You won't fool anybody but yourself when you fool with the figures.

Three Situations

Here are three hypothetical operating situations for the same Maine country store in three different locations, run by three different families. It's interesting to see how the sales volume changes considerably but the net profit remains more or less the same. The store is open 8 to 8 every day. Wages are $3.60/hour, including FICA.

Situation A: Husband and wife, two teenagers helping. One employee during two-week family vacation. Minimal competition.

Situation B: Couple, no children. One employee part-time for 35 hours for 50 weeks, 70 hours for two weeks. One fill-in employee. Average competition.

Situation C: Husband full-time; wife part-time. Two part-time employees same as Situation B. Significant competition.

Good Will

Good will, as far as I'm concerned, is an archaic term. For accountants it's a line to fill in on an asset sheet. It is supposed to have something to do with the reputation of the owner, particularly in terms of customer loyalty. It is an intangible for any business, and for small country businesses that are frequently subject to things like whim and fate,

Hypothetical Operating Situations

	Situation A	Situation B	Situation C
Income			
Sales	$150,000	$200,000	$250,000
Purchase* (for resale)	117,000	158,000	200,000
	(78%)	(79%)	(80%)
Gross Profit	33,000	42,000	50,000
	(22%)	(21%)	(20%)
Expenses			
Taxes, Licenses	500	500	500
Rent**	4,800	4,800	4,800
Repairs and Maintenance	700	800	900
Gross Salaries (Employees)	600	8,000	13,600
Insurance	3,000	3,000	3,000
Professional Fees	500	600	700
Advertising	1,000	1,300	1,500
Auto	1,700	1,700	1,700
Office Supplies	300	350	400
Telephone	600	600	650
Utilities	3,000	3,000	3,000
Operating Supplies	600	700	800
Total Expenses	17,300	23,350	31,550
Net Profit	15,700	16,650	18,450
	(10.5%)	(8.3%)	(7.4%)

*Does not reflect items taken out of stock for personal use.

**Store pays rent to owners in amount of mortgage payments.

it is completely impossible to measure. It's a bookkeeping device, a way to put an artificial price tag on a particular part of the business. In one sense good will can be thought of as the value of the business over and above the physical assets, equipment, and other measurable things. You can think of it as an investment in being able to make a living.

Bankers, Lawyers, Accountants, and Appraisers

This is certainly a good time to get to know these folks if you're not already acquainted. We've discussed the pros and cons of using your own hometown accountant on unfamiliar turf. Unless your personal financial situation is highly complicated, you're probably better off with a stock purchase rather than the customary asset purchase—a local man would seem better suited.

A local lawyer is a definite advantage. He is your coach and can offer help in many ways. I would certainly ask a contact at the Chamber of Commerce to recommend a lawyer. Then have a preliminary meeting with him as soon as possible, even if you haven't definitely decided on a business. Lean on him. He's a local, professional man. Of good character and integrity . . . almost always. He's not just anybody; he's your lawyer, your attorney. A lot of his help is psychological. Once you have a lawyer, you'll feel better. He'll try to help you avoid making mistakes.

There are real estate appraisers well versed in theories and techniques, but competent business appraisers are a rarity in rural areas. That's because the sophisticated criteria that are part of an appraisal of the intangible assets of an urban business—factors for growth rate, investment risk, aesthetic characteristics, etc.—are virtually impossible to apply to a small country business.

Let your lawyer be your mentor. For financing you'll have to shop around to get what you want. Your lawyer can establish priorities here. He probably knows the banks and the bankers, and you may very well be establishing a long-term relationship with one of them. He will have more to go on than which one has the safest looking building.

Your team isn't ready to play yet, but it's good to have the lineup in hand, get a fix on individual strengths and weaknesses, personalities and peculiarities. We're not very far away from game time when each will make his contribution. All they're waiting for is for you to make your contribution—the most important decision you've ever made: Are you going to buy that business? And, here, for the first and last time...

The Buy Or Bye-Bye Checklist

In the final analysis, this is the final analysis. If you think you're going to do this only one time, put your numbers right down on the page in ink. If you feel you'll be doing the test for several different businesses, make very light pencil marks. Put your score, from zero to 100, in the boxes at the right. There are only four questions.

The Final Analysis

1. **Where?** Just how well do you like the place where you're going to live? ☐

2. **What?** Just how well do you like the business you're going to buy? ☐

3. **Can you make a living?** _____
Net sales _____
Less cost of goods _____
Gross profit _____
Less operating expenses _____
Operating profit _____
Less cost of financing _____
Profit before taxes _____
Estimated taxes _____
Profit after taxes _____
Estimated living costs _____
Balance

        If plus enter 100
        If zero enter 80 ☐
        If minus enter 0

4. **Can you afford the business?**
Total cash available
Less 30% cushion (see Chapter 6) _____
Cash available for investment _____
Cash needed _____
Balance _____

        If plus enter 100
        If zero enter 80 ☐
        If minus enter 0

Add up the total in the boxes and divide by four. If you have a score of 80 or more, go for the business. Less than 80, stay home a little longer. You and this business just won't make it. You can like the business all you want and want it all you like, but if you can't make a living, don't buy it. And if you can't afford it, don't buy it. (Don't touch that 30 percent cushion. It's there to protect you...and nobody else.)

And don't screw around with the numbers. You'll screw up your life. No sermon, no nothing. You can either make a living or you can't. You can either afford the business or you can't. I've seen too many people buy country businesses who couldn't make a living. I've seen too many people buy country businesses who couldn't afford them. Don't talk to me about life styles and hard work. Or about shoestrings and bootstraps. Talk to me about yes or no and don't waffle. This business is either for you or it isn't. If it is, great! If it isn't, so what? There are other businesses around.

CHAPTER TEN

Financing[1]

Now that you've decided you want to buy a business, you'll most likely have to buy something else that goes along with it. And that is money. It's possible that you don't need any money. You may have enough money of your own to buy a business. That is fine. No, it's a lot better than fine. With money costing what it does today, you may be richer than you realize. Say, for example, you had to go out and buy $100,000. You'll need it for a while, maybe fifteen years. Times are difficult and the best opportunity to buy that money is at an interest rate of 13 percent. That $100,000 will only cost you $227,880. That's rich!

The next thing to being rich yourself is having rich friends or relatives. How close are they? To you and with their money? If pesky Uncle Paul is perfectly willing to let you have funds and let you keep all four of your limbs, it's certainly something to wrap your mind around. I'm sure your spouse is going to tell you that you shouldn't be indebted to anyone in your family and it will all lead to bad feelings—just ask poor Uncle Peter. If your first cousin Bertha is a softer touch than First National Bank, touch her. Years ago when filthy money was dirt cheap, folks were scrambling all over their friends and relatives for loans. But now that it's incredibly expensive—well, like everything else—a lot of people feel uncomfortable about taking money from personal sources. It's sort of a "that's something they did in the old country" thing. (It was a pretty nice old country after all.) If you have a way of getting perfectly good money cheaper than what the conventional lending institutions are charging and the strings attached don't braid into a noose, go for it. It could mean the difference between having your country business—in this country—or not.

LATEST NEWS! BY Pony Express FROM THE GOLD DIGGINGS!

Conventional Financing

That takes care of personal financing. Now let's get into conventional (or perhaps, impersonal) financing. "Conventional lending institu-

1. My thanks for help in gathering information for this chapter go to Arthur N. Berry, president, Francis E. Romano, vice president and treasurer, John P. Sexton, assistant vice president, Keith R. Stanzel II, assistant treasurer, Bellows Falls Trust, Bellows Falls, Vermont; James V. Horrigan, vice president, and William J. Mahlmann, assistant vice president, Catamount Division, The Merchants Bank, Burlington, Vermont; and Jack Towsley, assistant treasurer, First Vermont Bank & Trust, Brattleboro, Vermont.

tions"—those are great words. "Conventional" has overtones of high-button shoes and starched collars. Staid. Conservative. Proper. "Institutions" has the implication of brick walls. Formidable. Strict. Demanding. Yes, and it's getting near the end of the twentieth century and bankers have been known to smile, to be warm and human, responsive. That's true out at the annual picnic. Inside the bank they become bankers. Serious. What they deal in is serious. It's money. And it's not their money. It's not Monopoly money. It's real. It belongs to the depositors. If I have my money in the bank where you get financing for your business, I would like my bankers to be very serious about giving you my money. I would prefer that they had divine knowledge about your ability to repay a loan of my hard earned. Short of that, I want them to use every ounce of their professional skill in the protection of my money. Naturally, I want you to have a loan, but I certainly don't want my bank extending it to you if there is any reason in the world why you shouldn't have it.

Depositors Protected

Banking today is, of course, a heavily controlled industry. Banks don't go bust as much anymore, which is fine with me if I put my money in them. Banks, for example, can't lend all the money they want to. The Federal Deposit Insurance Corporation, with your best interest at heart, feels that a bank shouldn't lend out more than 80 percent of its deposits. To a large extent then, the amount of money banks have for lending is based on how much money is on deposit, the amount of loans outstanding, and the degree of risk and level of profit involved in letting out more of it.

If you are the United States Steel Corporation, the chances of the bank getting its money back are slightly better than if you are Joe's Country Business. So the bank can afford to do business with U.S. Steel at a lower gross-profit margin. The price of money that banks charge their best costumers is known as the *prime rate*. It goes up and down in relation to supply and demand for money and other factors about which

What Are Points?

There's another little fillup that banks play around with. They are called "points" and they are payments by you to the bank at the time of purchase, to compensate the bank for administration.

Each point they charge you is equal to 1 percent of the amount of money borrowed. If you're borrowing $100,000, one point will cost you $1,000, and two points are $2,000. You pay the amount up front, to the bank, so if you need X number of dollars, add the point amount to it, and borrow that total.

economists write long books. It is usually the rate on which other bank services are based—like the loan to Joe's Country Business.

The rate for commercial loans is the prime rate *plus*. In the days of relatively high prime rates it could be "prime rate plus 2 percent." That doesn't sound heavy compared to U.S. Steel. Well, it's not 2 percent; it's 2 percentage points. If the prime is 11.0 percent and you're paying 13.0 percent, it's 18.2 percent more. When commercial loan rates are tied to the prime, figure a "spread" of 17 percent to 20 percent. That's the price of a money. It's expensive. Don't plan on trying to get more of it than you need. You wouldn't want to sell any of it to U.S. Steel at a loss!

How Much?

So, how much can you get? Good question. Here's a rule of thumb: A needle in a haystack is easier to find than a banker who doesn't require that the borrower have at least 30 percent equity.

The bank lends money on judgment. The strength of the borrower—his ability to repay the loan—is what counts. If they consider you a strong borrower, they will lend you 70 percent of the cost of the business. . . tops! The greater their risk, the less they will lend. The bigger the doubts about you, the smaller the loan. But you're not the only factor. The business itself—with you running it—is the other part of the equation. The greater the amount of the tangible assets, the larger the loan. The better the chances of the business being successful, the better the chances of getting the loan.

That's why it's important to put together a good presentation for the bank. They will want to see a personal financial statement. This could be one of those formal net-worth sheets or a simple list of what you own and what you owe—your assets and your liabilities. (The simpler your finances, the simpler the format.) This gives them a picture of your financial condition. The other picture they want to look at is the business—your pro-forma P & L statement. It's the same one you put together in Chapter 9 so that you could determine whether you wanted the business or not. These two financial pictures—you and the business— are essential. The rest is businessmanship. You're trying to make a sale to your first customer—the bank. Use what you consider to be appropriate selling strategy and technique. Put in a balance sheet and cash flow projections if they seem indicated. Full documentation is better than to have people guessing about practices and plans. Some history of the business. Your own résumé. Put in things that are meaningful; leave out things that aren't. Be straightforward, factual, succinct. Prepare a good, convincing document.

At many banks, loans are approved or disapproved by a committee. You may have an opportunity to meet one or two members. Your document will be your only introduction to the others. The purpose of the document, the presentation, or whatever you want to call it, is to convince the loan committee, the commercial loan officer, the president, the directors, and anybody else who might see it, that you are a good businessman, buying a good business, and it would be good business for the bank to finance this business.

What Term for the Loan?

In your presentation—your application—the term of the mortgage loan is an important consideration. The fewer the number of years over which you spread the payments, the lower the cost. That's obvious. The longer the term of the loan, the lower the monthly payments. That's also obvious. Figure out what's the best for the business. Banks will usually grant a mortgage loan amortized over a period of up to twenty years. When the prime rate soared out of sight in 1979, banks weren't too happy with their long-term, low-rate commitments. And they learned something. Like putting five-year maturities (grotesquely referred to as "balloons") into twenty-year mortgages so that the loan can be reviewed periodically. And the rate can be changed to reflect current lending practices. Or there may be a "floating" rate clause in the mortgage— floating on the tide of the prime. Essentially that's good money management for the bank and for you.

MAKING THE DECISION

Now that the bankers have everything they need, they can go to work. Essentially, they will compare the picture of your business with other businesses to see how healthy it is (or will be). They have considerable experience right in their own bank—the financial performance of their other customers in similiar businesses. Assets and liabilities, sales and profit, salaries and depreciation. And they analyze with what are known as ratios: the current ratio—assets divided by liabilities; the quick ratio—cash plus receivables/liabilities. Plus some of the others: debt to worth, cost of sales to inventory, sales to total assets, etc. They look at inventory turnover, receivables turnover in terms of days, and things like that. And they compare all this to other businesses as similar to yours as possible. They have business ratios compiled by Dun & Bradstreet. They have composite financial statements on hundreds of kinds of businesses by asset size from Robert Morris Associates, the national association of bank loan and credit officers. These are the data against which they compare your business to check its health. Very often, of course, with small country businesses, an intimate knowledge of the area, close working experience with operations like yours, and a head full of common money sense are worth more than a room full of norms. The bank uses every bit of information it has to make a yes or no decision. If your business ability is sound and you've picked a sound business, you should hear within several days that your loan has been approved. Now you're in business—with the bank.

Variable Rates

Let's face it. Banks are steering clear of making long-term, fixed-rate loans. Given the rate sensitivity of deposits today, banks feel loan rates should be variable so as to allow banks to maintain their profit. Some city and suburban banks also require the borrower to maintain "compensating balances," usually 10 to 20 percent of the outstanding loan due. (Large banks may also charge a fee on unused portions of revolving credit lines, believing that the borrower should pay some of the freight for maintaining available funds.)

Letter of Commitment

They'll send you a letter of commitment which specifies the terms of the loan. It will most likely be based on lending you a percentage of the purchase price or the appraisal, whichever is lower. This protects the bank. They may require financial reviews on an annual—sometimes semiannual or quarterly—basis so they can look at your operating statements and balance sheets. This protects the bank. The loan may be broken into pieces, one on real estate, one on equipment. The equipment loan will be short-term—five to seven years—covering the useful life of the equipment and following the depreciation schedule. This protects the bank. Now it looks like the bank is getting a lot of protection and you're paying a very high price for it. That's true. They're protecting their depositors' money. And they're protecting your money, too. It's like medicine. You don't like it but it's good for you.

If you don't think you've got good medicine, you go to a different doctor. If you don't like your loan, go to a different banker. Shop around. You do for a car and they're relatively cheap. Banker Number One isn't going to get mad at you if you talk to Banker Number Two. A good loan is good for the bank and good for you. If you don't think you've got a good loan, don't buy it. They are rather expensive, you know.

WHAT AND WHY IS THE SBA?

The SBA is the Small Business Administration, set up by Congress to strengthen the economy through the preservation of free enterprise. The SBA gives advice and money, so listen. The SBA is particularly interested in seeing money lent to stimulate business in deprived areas and enterprises involving minorities. Direct loan programs at very low interest rates exist to help in these situations. The SBA also lends to the handicapped and to people whose businesses have been displaced or affected by a disaster. And to women in small businesses. There are funds available for participation with banks in community development. Often, of course, the SBA can be helpful in getting you a loan to buy a country business through their guaranteee program.

Loan Guarantee. The SBA can guarantee up to 90 percent of a bank loan made to you. Many banks are anxious to make these types of loans. For one thing, the government assures the bank that it will be largely reimbursed if the borrower cannot meet his obligations. This reduces the amount of risk for the bank. The SBA rate is 1/4 percent to 1/2 percent higher than the commercial bank rate, so the money is earning respectable interest. (Banks usually sell these mortgages to other banks at a favorable rate and maintain a constant flow of funds.) And, of course, the SBA has very detailed forms and procedures for application and review. This gives the bank another viewpoint, another judgment on the borrower and the business. If the bank you've contacted isn't interested in an SBA guarantee, try another bank. Or get in touch with your local SBA office. Find it listed in the Appendix.

Like any federal agency, some SBA offices can be responsive to the needs of the people in the area they serve: decisions are forthcoming quickly, communications are smooth and open. However, in other SBA offices the workload frequently gets out of hand, the papers pile up, and the business of helping small business bogs down. The SBA is generally good at helping businesses in the country.

Of course, if you do get SBA financial assistance, it will most likely be tied in with a management assistance program. The SBA offers counseling and advice on spot problems and continuing bases. The publications available cover a wide range of information on general business problems plus many handbooks for specific businesses.

No Set Patterns

One thing that is clear about bank financing of a business is that there are no set patterns. The area of the country makes a great deal of difference in what kind of a reception you can expect from a loan officer. As you might expect, financing is much more liberal in the growth areas of the country. I heard just recently of a shopping center in Florida being built with 100 percent bank financing. You do have to put 10 percent down for the land! And that's without a single national lease—usually a major criteria for bank involvement. The New England banker who told me about this is not even active in the mortgage market at this time.

Different banks in the same area are going to have different postures about lending. Some banks are putting "hot money" (short-term demand deposits such as certificates of deposit) into long-term mortgages. Others aren't. Some states have laws that prevent banks from doing things that other states encourage. And everything is subject to change. Rates fluctuate, economic conditions vary, philosophies shift.

The only way to find out what's happening financially in the area of your choice at any given time is to walk into one of those banks, sit across the desk from a banker, and hit him with the query, "What's happening?" He'll tell you what you can expect. He might not have any twenty-year real estate mortgage money around but could be interested in a five-year chattel mortgage on your equipment. He might help get a savings and loan association to finance the real property. Banks like to work together. Give them a chance!

Owner Financing

High interest rates make a good business difficult to sell and a less-than-good business virtually impossible. The reason for that, just in case you hadn't figured it out, is that expensive money makes it very difficult to buy a business. So when nobody is buying a business, nobody is selling a business. And the commissionless brokers are desperate, so they start thinking. They think: "How can I get money when there isn't any?" This is known as Creative Financing. It sells businesses during times of tight money. Essentially the owner, who is anxious to sell the business, is willing to take money in different sizes and pieces and at different times than he would if he sold his business under relatively normal conditions.

When times are tough and money is tight, a broker will tell you he won't list a business if the owner refuses to participate in the financing. Owner financing is supposedly a form of guarantee for the buyer that the business is in truth "as represented," because the seller is keeping his money in the business after the sale. He is also keeping the broker's kids in shoes.

Owner financing is a fact of life. Sometimes it's the only way to sell a business. And that means it's the only way to buy a business. Here are a few variations on the theme:

1. *Second Mortgage.* It is a loan to cover the difference between the amount of the first mortgage and the purchase price. It is usually offered by the seller, but I've known cases where it was offered by an impatient broker. It can be for any term, usually short, like five years. It can be at any rate, sometimes the same as the first mortgage, sometimes lower. Whatever's attractive and necessary.

2. *First Mortgage.* The seller can hold a first mortgage at a low rate for a short term. Monthly payments might be on a twenty-year amortization basis but the note matures or "balloons" in five years when the total amount is due. This means that, at the maturity of a balloon mortgage, the person who bought the business has to obtain conventional financing from a bank at the going rate to pay the balloon. Theoretically you should be on easy street at that time. Theoretically Wall Street will have arranged a low prime for you. And there are no problems. No problems? If conventional financing is not available, the seller can take back the business or, more likely, continue the financing, probably at a higher rate.

3. *Installment Sale.* Often, of course, even when money is in good supply at reasonable rates, sellers are anxious to make installment sales to postpone or reduce the capital gains tax on the sale. The Internal Revenue Service regulations allow the seller to report income in the year of actual payment if he receives less than 30 percent of the total amount in the year the sale occurred. He simply spreads the actual proceeds of sale over a period during which he should be slipping into lower tax brackets. This is, of course, why you see so many ads for businesses reading "Only 29 percent down payment." It could be a very good deal for all parties, depending on the owner's future plans and his total involvement with our common Uncle.

4. *Wrap-around Mortgage.* This is when the seller wraps a big mortgage around a little mortgage. He takes a larger mortgage, pays his first mortgage payments out of your wrap-around payments. The deed, of course, doesn't pass to the buyer until the first mortgage is paid off. This could have advantages for sellers in certain tax situations. (You may find that there are many advantages in owner financing, many for him, some, possibly, for you. Don't let your accountant out of your sight!)

5. *Assumable Mortgage.* Some mortgages can be assumed or taken over by a buyer and some can't. Mostly those at high rates can be; those at lower rates can't. That's life! But there are some very favorable mortgages that can be assumed. Sometimes a buyer is willing to pay a significant premium for a business that has an existing, assumable mortgage. It all depends on what was happening when the mortgage was written and what's happening now.

Financing your business can be very simple or very complex. It can be a snap or next to impossible. It all depends on your financial condition and the condition of the business. Now. . . a word of caution in the world of finance: bankers, lawyers, especially those knowledgeable in the real estate area, and accountants, particularly for tax men, know their way around the jargon. You probably don't and are perfectly willing to admit it. The broker probably doesn't and isn't. Not only is he unwilling to allow that he lacks expertise in this area, he may very well try to con you into taking his advice and letting him run the show. Buyer, beware! Unless the broker is unusually skilled in the financial area, do yourself a favor and leave him out of the negotiations. I get this from bankers, lawyers, and accountants all the time. I'm just passing it along.

And now that you know a very small amount of what there is to know about borrowing money for a business, let's move right along and buy it.

Can Be Complex

CHAPTER ELEVEN

Buying the Business

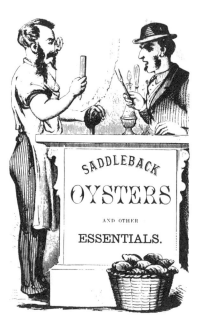

SADDLEBACK
OYSTERS
AND OTHER
ESSENTIALS.

Habendum bona fide et ux ad valorem. Ad nauseum. You have a lawyer. Ask him what it means.[1]

Buying real estate or buying a business—and it doesn't matter whether it's in the middle of the city or the middle of the prairie—is extremely difficult. The Latin words are a clue. It is difficult because you don't understand it. You don't understand it because you're not supposed to understand it. It is for the specialists to understand and the laymen to wonder about. If you knew all these things, you could be your own lawyer. If you knew all about medicine, you could be your own doctor. For now you'll have to be satisfied with being your own layman. And with all the income tax those guys have to try to get out of paying, it's surprising they have time to make a living. You're better off as a layman! Besides, you don't speak Latin.

They may make it difficult to buy a business but not impossible. Let's see what's involved.

You've thoroughly checked out the two or three businesses that interest you. This business, the right business for you, got 80+ on the acid test and you're going to move on it. You're going to BUY IT! So make an offer, formalize it, sign an agreement, pay the money, and it's yours. It's that easy. A lot of people are going to try to prove it isn't that easy, and you'll have to go along with them. But those are the steps. Everybody is inclined to get all tangled up in his underwear when he takes those steps. But they are the steps.

The offer is usually given verbally. It will include or specifically exclude certain things like inventory, equipment, customer lists, non-compete agreements, and other items. It can be accepted or rejected or a counter-offer can be proposed.

Once a verbal agreement is reached, a letter of intent or binder is signed by both parties. Buyer gives the seller a deposit which is part of the down payment (customarily 10 percent of the selling price) and agrees to

---

1. It doesn't mean anything. . . just words from the glossary of real estate terms in the Appendix.

pay the balance by a specific date, usually the date of the signing of the contract or purchase and sale agreement.

A time and a place is set for the closing (in Massachusetts it's called passing papers, which is much more descriptive). This is really the time when the deed is signed by the seller and the loan is formalized, the taxes that have been paid and the cost of the fuel and insurance that have been bought are adjusted. Fees are paid for transfers, and recordings, and registrations, and the attorneys' work. And you go away and begin a new life.

There is a certain amount of etiquette involved, and your lawyer will make sure you are properly coached and that you don't embarrass him in front of his friends. The lawyers will go back to their secretaries or wives who will routinely ask whether they had a good closing in much the same way that they inquire about a golf game.

A Different Approach

That seems to be fine for other people, but why don't you buy your business your way? Do what you want to do. It's your money; you might as well enjoy spending it. Here are five things to do that are a little bit different, guaranteed to shake up the broker and the seller and, we hope, get you the business for the lowest possible number of dollars. This is how a pro would go about it.

Take the Initiative

Don't let the broker frighten you, scare you, hurry you. He'll say things like, "This attractive young widow from Westport is just about to make an offer; so, if you've really got your heart set on owning this place, you'd better act fast." You'll say "Ho hum."

The broker can be very useful at this time because he's probably a very good salesman. Keep telling him what you don't like about the business. Don't acknowledge the good points; harp on the negative. Don't waste time arguing with him. Just keep your cattle prod at ready. Jab whenever you get a chance. The roof leaks. His margin figures look inflated. The business will never sell. Get him feeling that you'll never make an offer, that the business isn't all that great, that maybe nobody'll make an offer. Push him, bully him, make him insecure. So insecure that when you do make an offer, he'll use every bit of super salesmanship he has to convince the seller to accept it! You don't have to tell him that a slightly reduced commission is better than no commission at all. (He has already heard that from the fellow who had a bird in his hand.)

Keep Your Cool

The more cool you keep, the more dollars you keep. When you're ready to make an offer, make one. Forget the asking price; you know that it is artificially high. So a percentage of it or something like that doesn't make sense. The broker—even after you've worked on him—may feel your figure is ridiculously low. He'll tell you it would be an insult to the seller. Remember that in most states the broker is required by the regulations of the real estate commission to report your offer to the seller—no matter how low it is. So lean on him. Force him to get some kind of seller reaction.

Now here's a percentage that does make sense: your first offer should be about 20 percent less than what you've come up with as the fair market value.

Why 20 percent? I feel that if you can get a business you really want, a business that will provide a reasonable living for you for 20 percent less that it's worth, you're so lucky that I want to reach out and touch your sleeve. I also feel that if you make an offer that's less than 80 percent of what the business is worth, nobody's going to take that offer seriously. And they won't take your next offer seriously, either. The trick here (and it's as tricky as anything ever gets) is to be in the ballpark. . . but just inside! You want your offer to make the seller wince and wince harder than he's ever winced. But you don't want him to start to laugh at you.

Figure the Fair Market Value

In the Appendix there's a glossary of real estate terms. The definition of market value is: *The highest price which a buyer, willing but not compelled to buy, would pay, and the lowest a seller, willing but not compelled to sell, would accept.* That's in the abstract. And we're not. So you need a formula.

Different books have different formulae. Some compare buying a business to other investments, but that doesn't make much sense, if what you're really investing in is a country way of life. Appraisers will often combine assets and good will, which can be one thing to the seller, another thing to the buyer, and probably not much of anything at all to the accountant who is examining a small business with marginal profits. Are you ready for the secret formula?

The best formula we've come up with is this: *The worth of a business is equal to the value of the physical assets plus 175 percent of annual takeout.* Or:

$$\text{Value} = \text{Assets} + (1.75 \times \text{Takeout})$$

Annual takeout is all the non-operating dollars the business generates. It includes your salary and other benefits accruing from the business—insurance, medical payments, car expenses, perhaps meals and living quarters—as well as any profit you make. Financing costs are included, too.

The 1.75-times formula assumes that the seller's work in building the business is worth 100 percent of your first year's takeout, 50 percent for the second year and 25 percent for the third. This might be considered your payment for "good will" or the "value of the business"; it's really your investment in making a living. Look at the price that formula gives you and then think about selling the business five years from now. You should be more than sure of getting your money back.

Here's an example of a good, solid country store doing about $200,000 a year in volume. Owner, wife, and one teenager share an attractive three-bedroom apartment above the store. The value of the structure and land is $65,000 and the equipment $20,000, so physical assets total $85,000. Takeout—part of it business, part of it money, part of it the value of goods and services in lieu of money, includes:

clothing	food	rent
financing	car	telephone
heat	electricity	travel
entertainment	medical	profit
salary	taxes	etc.

and comes to $26,563. So . . .

$$\$85,000 + \$46,485 \ (\$26,563 \times 1.75) = \$131,485$$

Call it $131,000 and make an offer of $105,200.

Now here's a bookstore doing $100,000 a year with nothing to buy (exclude inventory, which has to be considered separately) except $2,000 worth of equipment. The takeout is $20,000 in owner's salary and profit so the business is worth:

$$\$2,000 + \$35,000 \ (\$20,000 \times 1.75) = \$37,000$$

The offer is $29,000.

I like the formula I invented because I invented it, and it looks like a very fair way to establish a value for a business that somebody else has built over a number of years into something you can use to make money. The assets are the assets and that's fine. If the seller invested money in a new stove or a second-hand meat slicer or a third-hand wood splitter, he's getting paid back for it. Now if he invested time and skill for which he has yet to be paid, it seems logical to value his time and skill on the basis of what you'll get out of it. Your first year he ought to get all of it back. The second year you're changing things and making a lot of your own contributions. You know what you're doing. But you're still living off his work. So half you, half him. In Year III his influence is felt but it's significantly diminished. To 25 percent.

But the definition of fair market value is the glossary's, not mine. To find out what the fair market value is, what you're really going to pay, and what he's really going to accept, you've got to. . .

Bargain

And bargain well. Many people absolutely detest the idea of hassling—particularly about money. They think it's unpleasant or vulgar or something. With other folk it's as accepted a thing to do as putting on shoes in the morning. A lot of people do it instinctively. They come in my store, hold up a loaf of bread, and ask, "How much you trying to get for this?" Can you believe that? A loaf of bread, baked in a big bakery, famous brand name, price stamped on it by the baker, and the guy thinks I'm going to play games with him? That's just plain unpleasant and vulgar!

Whether you're at your best or at your worst when you bargain, you'd better do it for your business. It's your bread (in a larger sense of the word) and it's important that, if there's to be a sweeping of the crumbs, it should definitely be in your direction. If you're a good bargainer, go to work. If you're not so good, get somebody else to do it for you. The seller uses the broker. You can use your consultant, your accountant, your lawyer, or your mother-in-law. With one exception you're paying these people to be bad guys.

For some people an acceptance of the initial offer is the end of their lives. The seller will wonder for the rest of his days whether he could have gotten more and the buyer will carry to his grave the thought that he could have paid less. That's why I like the "20 percent off" for the opener. It should produce bargaining. (If it didn't you should have tried 25 percent. Live with that!)

But mostly it will be offer and counter-offer, cat and mouse, until somebody feels like snatching defeat from the jaws of victory, and both parties, according to Hoyle, are declared winners.

Relax, have one drink and quick as a rabbit send a . . .

Letter of Intent

To the owner. Traditionally, of course, this is all done by the broker. You can wait while he figures out how he's going to spend his commission, now that he knows exactly how much it's going to be. Or you can retain your aggressive posture and set down the conditions under which you will go to contract. If you and your lawyer prepare this letter rather than waiting for the broker to do it, you have the advantage of making the stipulations rather than having to change them. Assume the attitude that it's your ball game, you're in charge, and you're getting what you want. Don't try to give the other people ulcers, but a certain air of confidence will do you a lot of good. (And it will also help to disguise that awful feeling of utter despair that invariably accompanies the first realization that very shortly you're going to own a country business.)

If you've played your role in buying a country business correctly, you are a different person now. When you were looking for a business, you appeared disinterested, distracted, aloof. When you concentrated on one or two specific properties, you were disappointed and negative all the time. You were very cool; nothing interested you. But suddenly— bang!—you made an offer which took everybody by surprise and created confusion. And now you're a tiger.

In your letter of intent make sure you state all the conditions that will be part of the contract and all of the contingencies that have to be met before signing. Financing, a final audit of the books, a complete building inspection, and anything you feel would contribute significantly to an orderly transfer of ownership should be in the letter. Stipulate that the owners won't compete for a period of time, that mailing lists are part of the sale, that the owner will provide advisory services. Put in everything you want. Put in a few things you may not even care very much about. Let the other people take them out. Don't be outrageous; just be out for yourself.

The broker's going to be more on your side now. The quicker he gets everything signed, the sooner one of the signed things is a check payable to him. Keep three steps ahead of him. Make him follow you. Get him to do what you say. (You did what he wanted.) Move. Don't let the seller screw things up. You've just about bought a business. Be the boss!

The Formalities

The lawyers, the accountants, and the bankers think that what happens between now and the day you put the deed in your pocket is the real part of buying a business. And for them it is. It's the way they make a living. But for you it's not. One part of your job is over; another is just beginning. Commencement always comes at the end.

Sure, deals fall through. Some people can't get mortgage money. But you're in pretty good financial shape. You checked that out before. And you're keeping a cushion. Sometimes professional inspections reveal that the building is falling down or that the numbers don't add up. But you looked those things over pretty thoroughly. You checked because you wanted to know if you wanted the business. So there shouldn't be any surprises. If it turns out that there is something you can't—or shouldn't—live with, don't try to. If there's a little thing in the books that was hidden, you may have to forget the whole thing. That happens. I know of a case where a good tax man found that $27,000 of "profit" on the books was a one-time refund windfall. So keep your fingers crossed until all the precincts have been heard from. And don't have a big party yet.

I think a small one is in order, though. I'll be right over.

And, by the way, congratulations!

CHAPTER TWELVE

Special Situations

Most people who don't have enough money of their own—including what the bank or the present owner or a mysterious stranger is gracious enough to provide—to buy their own country business tend to put off such a purchase, to postpone the sweet agony until their bankroll is big enough to make their bedroll dreams come true. But there is the impatient fringe who just can't wait to find out how bad their own business can really be. So for that group of masochists without money we offer the following:

The Pros and Cons of Partners

Getting together is something folks seem to want to do. Particularly when it comes to owning and operating an inn or motel. You see it quite frequently: Your Hosts—the Smiths and the Joneses, or Gene and Jan and John and Jean.

You constantly hear of two people going into business together who don't need each other's money. Two brothers sharing a contracting business. Friends or relatives owning a store. A brother and a sister sometimes. They can work well together, have common interests, similar goals. And they go their separate ways when the business closes down for the night. Maybe they're good friends; maybe they're not. It doesn't seem to make any difference. Fred is the outside man. Harry handles production. Maybe they have problems working together, but who's to know. That's their problem.

Problems Ahead. George and Harry sold their city restaurant and bought a country inn, something they'd been talking about for twelve years. Highly competent professionals, George in the front, Harry in the back. And they brought their wives, Harriet and Georgia. George and Harry didn't have to go into a new business together. The financing would have been duck soup for either one of them. They wanted to be partners because they had always been partners. From a restaurant to an inn, a simple transition. No way! Country life was difficult to adjust to, for all four people. The inn business was a longer, more involving kind of hospitality, quite different from just serving fine meals. The wives remained in the background but still had to participate in the rituals. Now bear in mind that these two fellows were skilled businessmen, long-term partners with great respect for each other's capabilities, financially comfortable, with concerned and cooperative wives. And they had plenty of trouble.

Here you are. No credentials in innkeeping. No experience in country living. Just four wonderful people with your hearts set on a lovely inn. You'd rather be just two wonderful people but the lovely inn you had your hearts set on would have set you back further than you had to go, so you'll go with these two other wonderful people. So instead of owning an inn, you'll own half an inn which is better than no inn at all. Lotsa luck!

I've heard that two couples, by pooling their resources, can make a business possible. Time and again, however, I've seen two couples make a business impossible. I know of one business which two couples ran very successfully for over thirty years. (Successfully, I'm told, because one couple worked and the other watched.) The next two couples had two divorces within thirty months. One of the two couples that came next found a way to stay with the inn; the other went off and stayed in Connecticut.

Choosing a Partner. If you need a partner because he's good at one thing and you're not, that might work, provided you're good at something. If you need a partner because you can't afford to buy a business without him, that might work, provided you're good at everything. Your partner won't do any work because he's putting up half the money. So you'll have to have the strength of a Goliath. He will be very critical of the work you're doing because you're working on his half of the business. To avoid killing him you will have to have the patience of Job. So if you are that strong and that patient, here's what you do: work a little harder at whatever it is that you do and save your money and wait a little bit longer for the business you want.

Advice from a lawyer: not buying is the next to the last option. Buying with a partner is the one after that!

Syndicates

This isn't a bad idea. Four or five people put their money together, buy a business, have somebody run it for them, and share the profits. This has merit if the business is very profitable. But most country businesses aren't!

You understand that, but how about a business that has things to offer other than money? Like vacations. Suppose five families get together and invest $20,000 each. That's $100,000. Isn't that enough for a down payment on a ski lodge in the $300,000 range? Probably. Would there be enough to hire a competent manager? Possibly. Well, then what's the problem? Timing.

If you want to invest that kind of money in vacations, you probably have children. If you have children, they probably go to school. If they go to school, they probably have vacations. If they have vacations, they probably have them at the same time as the other schools. So all the investors will want to use the ski lodge at the same time and there won't be any room for the paying guests. That's what seems to happen in reality.

If you could get the right group together, it might work. If the group thought of the business as a club rather than a traditional lodge, it might work better. The bylaws and the rules become very important. How the thing is constructed and run would make the difference between having shares in a place to live—a condominium or a beach house—and sharing a business specifically set up to take care of the needs of the owners first, the customers second.

Many wealthy people like sun and snow and hunting and fishing. Maybe you enjoy the same things but have very little money. Think about ways to make their money work for you. Not in a bad sense. In a good sense. Maybe you have time and expertise. They have jobs and need to relax. So you contribute your time. They contribute their money. Everybody's an owner. Or maybe a syndicate could work with one of the owners being the manager on a part-time basis. If you have your heart set on a country business, don't rule out group rule. Try to find a way to make it work.

An Option to Ownership

I've seen it happen. It's a bit like having a fairy godmother. Suppose this woman had run a store for a number of years and considered herself entitled to some rest and rehabilitation. She planned to stay in the village where she had made her living and wanted to make sure that the people who took over her business would be a credit to the community. She never got around to putting the business up for sale but a few of her close friends knew the situation. One of them suggested that she "rent" the business to a young couple she was fond of and let the monthly checks represent the down payment. The business was generating enough profit so they could pay her $1,000 a month, which in five years totaled $60,000.

At that time they obtained a mortgage for the balance and made the purchase. Actually a letter of agreement was the only legal document completed at the time of the "rental" understanding and the terms were completely acceptable to both parties.

Not Owner Financing. There's a lot of difference between this arrangement and owner-financing of a sale. In this case you can move in and manage a business with no investment at all. And you'll know that in five years it will be your business. Or ten years—whatever suits both parties. If you manage it badly, your godmother (and probably the villagers) won't want you to have it. But if you're good at it—and she won't let you make any big mistakes—things couldn't be better.

There is no list of available fairy godmothers looking for this kind of deal. But checking around in a few towns that you'd like to live in certainly wouldn't hurt. Don't agree to pay more for the business than it's worth just because you're able to find this rare kind of financing. You shouldn't have to. And make sure you work this all out with a lawyer before you get started. You wouldn't want to have any problems come up when it comes time to get the mortgage and make the sale of the business.

While Waiting

A lot of people plan ahead. I know a couple in St. Paul, Minnesota, who will have saved enough money to buy an inn in about four years. A family in Shreveport, Louisiana, will be buying a store in a little over a year. So while they're saving more money or getting the right buyer for their house, time is hanging heavy on their hands. What they'll do is to put their minds to work at a local college. A couple of courses in small business management, restaurant operations, retailing, meat cutting, a few other things. If you know what you know and know what you don't know, you'll find plenty of topics that are right down your alley. Get a catalog, study it, and pick out what you want to learn. And for some subjects, find a text and study. You've got libraries not far from where you live. Take advantage of them. Get smart!

Don't Be an Apprentice

Some people I've known think it's a good idea to work for a while in the kind of business that they plan to own. This clues you in on what it's like to run a store or own an inn, and you could come up with some valuable insights. This is okay if you're a teenager. But if you've decided

Another Package

Occasionally you'll find a seller who is more interested in a retirement income or salary plan than an outright sale. This could be similar to the "renting" of the business, maybe with various other benefits (medical, for instance) included. If you find a business that you can wait awhile to own and the owner is anxious to sell to just the right person at just the right time, a lawyer and an accountant can probably put together a fine package for both you and the seller. Naturally you won't find situations like these through brokers who need their commission on the sale now, not later. But if you are short on cash and hear about someone who is long on this kind of generosity, look into it right away.

that you want to buy a country business and just plain don't have the money, the best way to get that money is by doing what you do best and earning top dollar doing it. Country businesses just can't afford to pay you what you're worth. So stay in the city until you can afford to move to the country. It may take a year, five years, or ten. But stay. Don't give up everything, come to the country, take a job somewhere, and hope. Working in somebody else's business can make you lose your taste for the whole thing.

If it's a good business, you'll be yearning more than you're learning. You won't want to do it the boss's way anyway. You'll see his eccentricities, you won't approve of his style. You'll find yourself grading him. If it's a lousy business, you won't like it at all. The apprentice system went out a long time ago; don't try to bring it back. Sometimes owning a country business can be a little demeaning. Being a hired hand in one, when you don't really have to be, could be a real putdown. Don't compromise. If the time isn't right, if the money isn't there, if you haven't found what you want, don't crawl. Walk back to the second best place you can be—just where you came from!

Businesses in Resort Areas

Don't get concerned with resort area versus non-resort area in your thinking. Decide on the where and the what and develop your other specifications. If the business turns out to be in a resort area, fine. If not, that's okay too. Consider these factors, though, if a business in a resort area does appeal to you:

Living conditions make a big difference. Logic says that schools in summer resorts won't be as good as in winter resorts. If business in the area is very seasonal, consider what these population shifts are going to do to your life style. If businesses close down, what do you do when you're closed? Make sure these little things find their way into the big picture in your mind.

You may never find time to do what the vacationers do. You may be close to the slopes or the salmon or whatever turns you on. But you may never get out there. If you're trying to make a living, business comes first. You may be able to sneak off for an afternoon now and then, but don't count on it!

Season is a very big thing in your life when you own a resort area business. Everything you do revolves around what they do. The "they" are the vacationers, the tourists, the resorters, the customers, the guests, the people who make your business a business. Or your business better. In the off-season, the year-round residents are there but you'll know there are no "people" around.

You Must Wait. Whenever it is that they come, you wait for them. You clean, you paint, you stock your shelves. They are taking their vacations, their time off, and you're working harder than ever. Your world is upside down. When they go away, you go away, take a vacation or just take it easy. If you're a businessman, it doesn't take very long to get used to it. You live by it, you die by it. On weekends you ask people what the traffic is like. Are they coming? You worry about the weather when you know just how much you can do about it. You're booked, you're not booked. When the phone rings, is it a reservation or a cancellation? Did we double the beer order? As the very wise egg man says. "If you don't run out, you'll have enough."

So you live through the season. Good, bad, plus so much, a little bit off. Whatever. Then what? Do you have a six-month business? If you buy a business after the season, how long will you have to wait for some income? Do you starve in the winter or the spring? It's good to know just when you do starve. Please, if you're planning to buy a business in a resort area, make sure you see it—and take a good long look—in the off-season. See your dream business at its worst. Don't take anybody's word for anything. Can your body and mind handle living in a place when nobody else is there?

More of a Strain

There is no question that a business that is highly seasonal is much more of a strain than a steady, ongoing operation. All your troubles, your worries and fears, your time, your money—everything—it all comes at once. It comes up like a squall and disappears like a rainbow. That's when things are good. When things are bad you may not notice the seasons so much. Then you can really worry!

Time for Loafing

Seasonal businesses have their good points. You can loaf, goof off. Some of the most beautiful places in the United States get more beautiful in the fall. Indian summer. Sometimes Nature saves her best for the natives. The quiet, the peace, the slow time, chats with the neighbors, the bonfires, warmth in the coolness. These things may be there. They may be the things you came to the country to find. They may be the things that go with the business and that make the business worthwhile.

Starting a Business Locally

Country people buying a country business act just the way city people do. They make a lot of the same mistakes.

Of course, it's much easier for people living in the country to look for a business. They don't have to drive 300 miles, get exhausted, and make the decision of their lifetime before they drive back. They have the opportunity to watch businesses closely, see how they do at different times with different owners. And they hear rumors and gossip mingled with some interesting facts. They know about people retiring, moving away, getting ready to sell. They may have had their hearts set on a certain business for a long time, hear that the owner wants out, and decide that they want in.

All too often, though, they decide to act quickly—perhaps before someone from the city beats them to it—and regret it for a long time. They tend to move fast because they think they know a few things and they find out too soon that they didn't know enough. Long-term country people tend to depend on hunches when they should be calling in lawyers and accountants. They think their neighbor, the seller, will take care of them. The neighbor's moving away, remember. The seller has an inflated idea of the value of his business. It's just as inflated for a local buyer as it is for the fellow from New Jersey.

So, even if you were born two miles from the business you want to buy, move just as cautiously, do just as much investigating (it'll be easier for you than for a stranger) as if you were from another planet. You'll thank your lucky stars for it later on. It won't take you as long to get all the facts. And it shouldn't take as long for you to make up your mind. But don't take any shortcuts.

Country people feel comfortable with stores, repair services, contracting businesses—the kinds of businesses where they're more likely to do business with people they know. They don't seem to care that much about buying motels or inns, businesses in which they'd see a lot of strangers. That's why there are so many tourist-type businesses on the market. Hometown businesses are picked up—the good ones at least—by hometown people before the brokers get their cotton pickin' hands on them. This leaves the recreational businesses, the high-risk babies dependent on Mother Nature, the gift shops and souvenir stands and all the rest, getting shopworn in the business brokers' listing books.

Starting From Scratch

Starting a business from scratch can take a lot of scratch, money, that is. Figure on it costing more than buying the same business, okay? Suppose it's a motel. At today's cost of workers and building materials, it is highly unlikely that new would come in lower than old. You have your own design, but you have a huge debt.

Or take something at the other end of the spectrum. You can rent space and start a bookstore cheaper than buying an established bookstore. The difference is, of course, that the ongoing shop has customers coming in and the vacant store doesn't. The big question is, "Are the customers worth the difference?" My answer, without having seen either location is, "Probably." Now if it's a matter of starting a bookstore where there's

A Big Advantage

Country people have a big advantage buying a country business. They're there! Unfortunately, they don't always take advantage of that ad- vantage. They buy without doing their homework. Literally their homework.

never been a bookstore before, you've got to consider that the average bookstore in the United States depends on 16,758 people for its trade (according to the 1977 Census of Retail Trade). You've got to figure out whether you can round up this many people who haven't already been rounded up by another bookstore.

Avoid Vacant Stores

Beware of *vacant stores* in general and particularly general stores that have gone out of business. Brokers will be showing you properties that used to be this or that. There's probably a very good reason that it isn't this or that today—failure. Investing good money in a bad business makes little sense. Investing good money in no business makes no sense. The odds for success in any country business are not the greatest. But betting on a dead horse? The rule of thumb on this is: an established business may have its problems but they are known (or can be found out). A business started from ground zero will develop unknown (and sometimes untold) problems.

Let country people start country business, if they want to. They know where they're at. They know all the problems of living where they live. They know the weather and the people and whether the people need this or that kind of business. (At least they know a lot more about it than you do if you're from someplace else.) So if you're thinking about moving to the country and starting a country business from the ground up, don't. You'll have a lot of trouble just adjusting to country life. Don't have your business make your life more complicated than it has to be. Plan on buying a business that's moving before you move!

A Place to Look

One place to look for businesses that are still moving—although maybe they've moved in the wrong direction—is the Small Business Administration's resale program for businesses that have defaulted on SBA loans. The SBA is now trying to auction these businesses as going enterprises rather than letting the assets go piece by piece. More than 10,000 companies are now in the process of liquidation. Bargains are to be had, SBA financing is available at favorable rates—90 percent is possible—and, of course, counseling can be part of the package. To find out about these sales contact the Small Business Administration, Office of Portfolio Management, 1441 L Street, NW, Washington, DC 20416.

Very Small Businesses

Back yard businesses can bring in a few bucks. There are things you can do around the house that won't hurt anybody. And maybe keep you in beer money. These are not businesses. They are suppplemental business activity. They won't bring in enough to live on. They can make your living more comfortable. Maybe. Consider:

Food co-ops. Start with a few families. Order in bulk. Keep a small percentage to run the thing. Get to know your neighbors.

Day care centers. Country children are tied to their mother's apron strings. And the mothers don't always like it all that much. Good day care at reasonable rates is hard to find. Find out what it would take to get into it. If you can take it.

Catering. This is something besides stuff for the bake sales. Sometimes people would like to entertain their friends and still be part of the party. This isn't for the watercress sandwich crowd. But country people do like to get together and don't always want to gamble on pot luck. Weddings, whatever. Check it out.

Fruit and vegetable stands. It's very hard to get good produce in the country. It's all shipped out. Big stores, no way: it comes from headquarters. Little stores, not easy. Your old reliable fruit and vegetable stand of yesteryear has virtually disappeared from the landscape. If you've got a garden out back, put a stand out front. If nobody stops, you can stop. What can you lose?

Antiques. This is probably the only way to sell antiques in the country. In a very small way.

We know a young couple who bought a lovely Vermont home and turned it into an antique dealership. They knew a lot to begin with. They studied hard and learned more. They advertised and promoted heavily. They bought shrewdly. They sold intelligently. Randi is charming, attractive. Jake is witty, very likable. They did everything right. And nobody came to buy. They went into the antique business full time, professionally. But it's not a country business.

The showrooms on Madison Avenue, in Philadelphia and Boston and other "old money" cities, are where the action is. And there are a number of established dealers and serious collectors "in the trade" who operate very quietly in suburbia. There may be three dozen dealers in all of

New England who have a real business. For the others it's nothing but a tax break or a heartache. If you've got some spare furniture and some spare time, you can put a sign on your house and ads in the newspaper. And you'll make some money. But you won't make a living, if that's what you're after.

Think about telephone answering services, home maintenance, kennels, rubbish removal, welding. Keep going. There are a lot of other things that people do for pin money that they don't have to pin their hopes on. You've probably got a lot longer list than I do. And if you're lucky, some of them might develop into real business. But, for now, don't count on it.

Watch Out

Back-forty businesses, like horse farms and cattle ranches, are pretty much designed to take money away from you. Don't get me wrong. There are successfully operated horse farms and cattle ranches in many parts of the country. But, unfortunately, they're not little businesses for the likes of you and me. They're big businesses, some of which are operated to make money and some to lose money. Some need wealth and some bring wealth. Leave raising cattle to the big boys. Leave breeding horses alone. Horse farmers today are investigating the cross-country ski-center business or thinking of other ways to keep land developers away from the door. Produce farmers are selling out to the giants. Dairy farmers, the same thing. There's not much room for the buffalo to roam anymore. Campgrounds and trailer parks are taking over the world. Stay for the night or stay forever. The country in this country is getting smaller all the time. Better find a country business while there's still some country left.

CHAPTER THIRTEEN

It Can Be Rough

American business is huge: every business day Dun & Bradstreet makes more than 5,000 changes in its credit-rating Reference Book—that's what businesses use to check up on other businesses. Every year several hundred thousand firms are started, just about as many stop doing business, and even more change ownership. In the midst of all this, Dun & Bradstreet manages to do some tabulations about why businesses failed—businesses that went out of business owing people money.

Business Failures

In 1981 there were more business failures than at any time since 1961. (And in 1982, for which figures aren't yet complete, business failures went up to Depression levels.) For 1981 we see failure rate (per 10,000 operating concerns) highest in retail operations such as:

Infants' and Children's Wear	114
Furniture and Furnishings	84
Dry Goods and General Merchandise	78
Sporting Goods	78

...all the way down to:

Toys and Hobby Crafts	26
Jewelry	24
Women's Accessories	23
Grocery and Meat Products	21
Drugs	20
Department Stores	16

On the manufacturing side we see it go from:

Furniture	173

on down to:

Food	45
Paper	40
Chemicals and Drugs	39

By area, New England suffered the least number of business failures with 37.9, and, at the other extreme, the Pacific region showed 132.9 leaving business per 10,000. On the states: Oregon (287.1) and Washington (210.1) produced very high figures, and Wyoming (2.5) and New Hampshire (9.2) were significantly lower than average.

Success Rate

The success rate of businesses tells a slightly different story. Of all the new firms started, about one-third aren't in business by their first anniversary. After two years over 50 percent have gone by the boards, and after five years 80 percent are memories. The remaining 20 percent has pretty good life expectancy!

Country Failures

People who plan to buy a country business are often fleeing from something, grabbing at perhaps the first thing that comes along. And when it comes to business buying, the first thing that you see has a poor chance of being the thing that you should buy.

Country businesses are bought by people without much experience in running a small operation. A lot of country businesses are at the mercy of the weather. Economic recovery following recessions can be slow. Customer prejudices can be fatal.

Time to Work

So after you've bought the business you've got to do a lot more than the average person if you're going to make it work. You've got to study the business you're in and find out how your business is different from every other store or inn or bait farm or chicken ranch. You can make up for lack of experience by filling in the voids in your information.

What do you need to know about your business? Two things; everything you can find out and some things you can't. Never stop looking for information about your business. No matter how long you've been in it, you should be all-but-consumed by insatiable curiosity. If you're in a business, visit every other business like it that you can find. Talk to the owners. Make friends with these competitors. Talk to whomever it is that you're in business with—your spouse, your buddy, your cousin—about this research. Get a good dialogue going. Preserve it and treasure it.

Not Easy

Many people come to the country and buy a business, and that's about it. They think it's easier than having a business in a citified area. It's not easier; it's harder. People think they can go into a country business and it'll take care of itself. Wrong! Why did they come here if it's not easy? Because they wanted to be here and no matter if it's riskier and takes more work. That's what they wanted. A country business is not a toy. It is a very real business!

Smiths Are Doing Fine

Once again, a look at the Smiths. How did they make out at the Wiley Inn over the Christmas holidays? Well, fabulously. They were full from December 27 right through New Year's. They had four guests who booked for next New Year's. Most everybody had a good time. And the proprietors are starting to learn about themselves.

The inn provides an atmosphere to which the Smiths can relate. You remember that Pat Smith is a psychologist and Toni had been involved in social work. They see that the inn is physically structured for a large amount of interaction among the guests. The inn, with its public rooms spread out in sort of an even way, is absolutely perfect for walking around in one's stocking feet. But the theme, the focus of the new Wiley Inn, is the warmth, the coziness, the woodstoves, the way people gather, the idea of interacting without knowing it.

The guests responded to the Smiths' children. They formed a relationship. They stroked them like they were pets. The families put the dining tables together for a family-style Christmas. There was a group spirit, they were comfortable with themselves, they were together. They lingered after meals, they shared wine. The inn and the people in it are the community. It is like Pat's encounter groups.

The inn was full again last weekend.

Use the SBA

Another thing to do is to use the Small Business Administration. The Appendix lists their management assistance publications. This list of for-sale publications has been pared over the years and the good stuff remains. These you order from the Superintendent of Documents in Washington.

The free management assistance publications are much better now than they used to be. In addition to the management aids, which cover a whole raft of topics, there are the small business bibliographies which list books on a wide variety of subjects, and the starting-out series, which give the financial and operating requirements for selected businesses on one-page fact sheets. This material is available from a warehouse in Fort Worth. It's free.

Remember these publications are for all people. There is nothing specifically geared for country businesses. Most have a larger enterprise in mind. You're going to have to use the material selectively. Get to know the people at the SBA. They can be helpful.

CHAPTER FOURTEEN

Planning Your Business

Hundreds and hundreds of books have been written about small business. About the organization, the operation, the management. About the business plan, the marketing plan, the whole thing. Business courses have been taken at thousands of schools and colleges using the books that were written. Computers have been sold by the millions to those who have taken the courses and read the books.

But there's nothing to say that you're any brighter or any better equipped to run your business because you've bought

a book or

a course or

an MBA or

a computer.

A number of business brokers use business planning as a technique in selling a business. You analyze a business, work up a business plan for that business and, sure enough, you want to own it. It's your baby! You have to have it.

And I've known people who got so upset about doing a business plan for a broker that they didn't want to see him any more.

A business plan is exactly what you want to make it. If you have been in the kind of business that requires you to work up fairly elaborate plans for yourself, your clients or whomever, then you may want to do one for *your* business. Or you may be so fed up with doing plans that you don't want to do another one. Ever. You may need a business plan to get some money from a lender. You won't need it for any other reason except for help with your taxes.

If, because of your background, you like and respect business plans, fine. If you've come from a different kind of world, and you aren't into

Can Be Avoided

Conventional Wisdom

The elaborateness of a business plan is in direct relation to the number of people who are going to read it.

Outline of Business Plan

(Financial Proposal)

I.   Description of the market
II.   Description of the business
III.   Projection of sales
IV.   Start-up costs
V.   Amount of loan needed and proposed use of loan
VI.   Beginning balance sheet
VII.   Pro forma cash flow statement for the first year
VIII. Explanation of the pro forma cash flow statement
IX.   Pro forma income statement for the first year
X.   Balance sheet after one year of operation
XI.   Projection for the second year

Attachments:

Résumés of the principals
A list of the equipment needed
A list of the initial inventory
Copy of the lease
A list of prospective customers

Source: Massachusetts
Department of Commerce

writing or figuring or projecting, that's fine, too. You've finally bought a business. You are finally going to have the kind of a plan that makes you feel comfortable. Not the broker, not the banker, not the accountant or the lawyer or anybody but you. Don't think that just because you have a country business, you'll have to have a country business plan if it frightens you, or you find it distasteful or it's a bore. Sure you'll have to know an incredible amount about your business (and you'll learn more every day) but you *don't have to write it down*.

Business is *making decisions*. How do you know what to order? Look at what you ordered last week, what you had, add the two together, what you've got now, figure how much you've sold, how much to add. That's for buying and selling. You're making decisions based on what sold last week and what will sell this week. Okay. You've got it on a piece of paper, maybe in a book. Let's say the following week is Christmas. So using the *best assumptions* you can make you can look in the book at the previous Christmas and make some judgments based on new data—the weather, general condition of the business, etc.

PLANNING NEVER ENDS

Planning is not a one-time thing. It goes on forever, just as long as the business exists. You know how much business you did last year, last month, maybe last week. Is it going to get better or worse? It doesn't stop. If you're open for business it keeps right on going. Nine to five. Around the clock. It doesn't matter. Time is going by.

A lot of country businesses depend on the boss to do several different things—from being top management to sweeping the floor. If he likes to be top management most of the time, the floor gets dirty. And customers can see that. Most country businesses are oriented toward customers. Customers don't see top management. And customers can't see a plan.

Need a Computer?

Most country businesses are not laid out for *computers*. If you like a computer, by all means get one. To put an entire retail operation on a computer might take a lot more time than you'll have for a while. Inns are questionable. Computers are very helpful. They can do a lot of things. They cost money. Maybe your business is set up for one. But don't try to make one fit.

Financial Statements

Financial data are for explaining why you're where you're at. They're for your income tax and any time you need money from a bank (or any other source). For income tax, whether it's on Form 1120 or 1120S or 1065 or 1040, you will have to make two statements, a profit and loss statement and a balance sheet.

A *Profit and Loss Statement* takes the business over the last twelve months. Not very complicated. What you made, what you spent, and how much (if anything) you had left over. On the tax forms it'll look somewhat different but just don't leave anything out.

The *Balance Sheet* looks at the company at one point in time (at the end of the fiscal year for the tax folks). Your balance sheet and that for U.S. Steel look very much the same, on the left hand side, that is. The balance sheet finds its way into one of the schedules on your return.

Both of these financial statements would be footnoted to explain any irregularities that are not self-explanatory. For banks or places where you get money, you would have your actual balance sheet and your *pro forma* balance sheets (which is Latin for projected). The *pro forma* is your business plan.

Improving the Business

From the treasure trove of business lore:

The better the INFORMATION*	The smarter the DECISIONS
The easier the ASSUMPTIONS	The greater the improvement in the BUSINESS

*Country businesses generally lack good, dependable information. Substitute judgment!

Profit and Loss Statement

For Period From   *To*

INCOME

Gross Receipts or Sales
    -less returns and allowances   _____

Net Sales
    -less cost of goods or
    of operations   _____

Total Gross Profit   _____

EXPENSES

Taxes, Licenses, and Permits   _____

Rent   _____

Repairs and Maintenance   _____

Gross Salaries   _____

Employer's Share Social Security   _____

Insurance   _____

Interest   _____

Advertising   _____

Auto Expenses   _____

Dues and Subscriptions   _____

Operating Supplies   _____

Office Supplies   _____

Telephone   _____

Utilities   _____

Travel   _____

Entertainment   _____

Laundry   _____

Contract Services   _____

Miscellaneous   _____

Total Expenses   _____

Operating Profit   _____

Balance Sheet

Balance Sheet: Date   *19*

Current Assets		Current Liabilities	
Cash in bank and on hand	_____	Accounts payable	_____
Notes receivable	_____	Notes payable*	_____
Accounts receivable	_____	Payroll deductions payable	_____
Inventory	_____	Accrued expenses	_____
Other current assets	_____	Other current liabilities	_____
TOTAL	_____	**TOTAL**	_____

Fixed Assets		Fixed Liabilities	
Land	_____	Notes payable**	_____
Buildings	_____	Mortgages payable	_____
less depreciation	_____	Loans	_____
Subtotal (buildings)	_____	Other fixed liabilities	_____
Equipment and fixtures	_____		
less depreciation	_____	**TOTAL**	_____
Subtotal: (equipment)	_____		
Other fixed assets	_____	**TOTAL LIABILITIES**	_____
TOTAL	_____	**NET WORTH** (assets less liabilities)	_____

Other Assets			
Securities	_____	**NET WORTH +** **LIABILITIES**	_____
Prepaid expenses	_____		
Investments	_____		
Intangible assets	_____		
TOTAL	_____	* In less than one year	
TOTAL ASSETS	_____	**In one year or more	

Pro Forma Cash Flow Statement   September through August 19

	Sept.	Oct.	Nov.	Dec.	Jan.	Feb.	Mar.	Apr.	May	Jun.	Jul.	Aug.
Cash coming in (in-flow)												
Total cash in-flow												
Cash going out (out-flow)												
Cost of goods												
Selling expense												
Transportation												
Advertising												
Salaries												
Fringe benefits (10% of salaries)												
Heat												
Fixed expenses: Rent												
Electricity												
Telephone												
Office Supplies												
Transportation												
Legal & Acctg.												
Insurance												
Debt Service												
Miscellaneous												
Total cash outflow												
Cash surplus (deficit) for the month												
Cumulative cash flow (running total)												

Cash flow projections show how much, when, and where the money comes from. This is cash money, not depreciation or amortization, coming into and going out of the business. The cash flow projection is a very useful tool for you and, if you need cash, your banker.

The cash flow projections will be helpful in doing a deviation analysis (showing absolute and percentage variances vs. the plan) and any other kinds of estimates you want to make.

Capital Equipment List

The only other thing you will need will be a capital equipment list, particularly helpful in figuring depreciation on things you use in business but aren't going to sell: desks, typewriters, meat cutters, and lathes.

Forms of Business

Your company can be set up as a *sole proprietorship*. It's the simplest form. Just tell everybody you're in business. You'll probably have to file a form of registration with the town or city you're going to do business in. You and you alone are responsible for all the debts and other liabilities of the business. The income or loss is reported on your personal income tax—Form 1040. Not much to it.

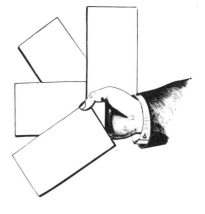

Now a *partnership* is a little more involved—but not much. It means that two or more people are going into business together and that each one is totally liable for the business as a whole and whatever the other partners do. These are *general* partners. You can also set up a *limited partnership*. This means that each limited partner is liable for the amount of money he invests in the business. And there must be at least one partner who is a general partner and thus is liable for the kit and kaboodle. An oral agreement is okay for a general partnership—but not recommended—and limited partnerships require registering with the secretary of state for your state. Income tax filing: information on 1065, you pay on your own 1040.

Corporation

Now when you go about setting up a *corporation* it's like you're creating a new person—an entity with rights and privileges and stock and stockholders. Your corporation can be sued. It has its own tax returns and meetings of the board. It has limited liability, ease of raising capital, ability to separate ownership from management, plus tax advantages and disadvantages. There's a filing fee (for the secretary of state) and an annual fee. Taxes: Form 1120.

If you have thirty-five or fewer stockholders you can become a *Subchapter S corporation*, and taxes are transferred to your personal income (1040). Information return: 1120S.

Ask Your Lawyer

Take your pick on these. They all have pluses and minuses. Some might be required for the type of business you're in. You'd better have your lawyer work on it.

Regulations and permits: There's a lot more than three. We can't take all fifty states and go down the list. But let's take Maine as an example. First of all, the *Federal*:

  Occupational Safety and Health Act
  Social Security
  Minimum Wage-Hour Laws
  Child Labor Provisions

Now State:

  Minimum Wage Laws
  Corporate Fees
  Taxes
  Pollution Controls
  Site Location of Development
  Subdivisions
  Plumbing, Sanitation, and Health
  Land Use Regulation
  Unemployment Compensation
  Workers' Compensation
  Retail, Wholesale, Trade, and Services
  Alcoholic Beverages
  Agriculture
  Commercial Fishing
  Department of Business Regulation

And finally at the *local level*:

The state of Maine has 446 towns and cities ranging in population from 24 to 65,000 plus. Various regulations and business controls are the responsibility of these local governments. The following is a general listing:

Regulation	*Local Authority*
Zoning ordinance	Planning board
Shoreland zoning ordinances	Planning board
Subdivision regulations	Planning board
Sealing of weights and measures	Sealer of weights
Building codes	Code enforcement officer
Housing code	Code enforcement officer
Mobile home ordinances	Planning board
Licenses for restaurants and other eating places	City council/select person
Licenses for the sale of alcoholic beverages	City council/select person
retail and taverns	City council/select person
amusement licenses	City council/select person

There may be other local ordinances in effect within certain municipalities. In all cases you are advised to inquire about local regulations at the city hall or town office in the community where you plan to conduct business.

The various states have many different regulations concerning the businesses and occupations that are carried on within their borders. We've gone over the requirements for the six New England land states—Maine, New Hampshire, Vermont, Massachusetts, Rhode Island, and Connecticut—and put the material together in one booklet, *Licenses, Permits and Registrations*. It lists everything you need to know and where to call to get the necessary application forms. We sell it for $6.95 postage paid. Our address is:

Storey Communications, Inc.
Schoolhouse Road, Pownal, VT 05261

Insurance

My advice is not to stint on insurance the first year or so you're in business. You may not need anything; you may need a lot. There are kinds of insurance you're familiar with, and a number you've never heard about. Trying to piece all of your insurance together is difficult even when you have a great grasp of the business. Trying to put together fire and workmen's comp and liability and property damage and death and liquor liability and general liability and bodily injury when you don't know all that much about your business is virtually impossible. Get the advice of a broker. Ask around, find out, get the help of the trade association. You could be sued for $1,000,000. The guy could win. Courts are settling more and more for the plaintiff. You would be out of business for good. In spades.

All of these legal considerations are part of your overall financial plan. Making decisions about your business is what you'll be doing from now on. You'll make them with the best possible assumptions based on the best available information. There's no magic about it. If you want to find out about your customers or prospects, you can ask them or pay somebody else to ask them. How much will it cost and you can make a decision on that one. Is it worth it? Maybe yes. Maybe no. Right now you're in the best possible position. All those people who wrote those books and all those people who taught those courses don't have much else to do because that's what they do for a living.

But you've got a country business to run. And, oh yes, if you have a chance, try to sweep the floor.

A FINAL VISIT WITH THE SMITHS

Well, the January thaw was late this year. It came in February, just before the Presidents' Birthday week—the biggest time for New England skiing. It rained and rained and rained. The temperature was in the fifties. It was incredibly bad winter weather and big brown spots started showing on Bromley, Stratton, and Magic mountains.

Reservations were cancelled. By the droves. The established inns were hit hard. The Johnnie-Come-Latelys were wiped out. And the Wiley Inn is a JCL. About $4,500 came off the business plan for February, $4,500 that Pat and Toni Smith didn't see. Never will.

But it's Easter and the Smiths broke even for their first six months. They feel they're doing well. They don't have anything to show for being in business for half a year. But Pat and Toni survived.

Oh, their brochure arrived from the printer's this week. Looks good!

CHAPTER FIFTEEN

Running a Country Business

There are lots of different businesses in the country. But by and large most people who are after a business seem to want either a store or an inn. So let's look for a minute or two at the particular problems the storekeeper faces and later on we can see what the innkeeper is up to.

If you're going to run a country store, you'll be facing a problem as soon as you open the door—from the inside. You're not from where the store is. You're from a couple of hundred miles away. Every customer who walks through that door knows it. And you know it, too. You're going to be a lot more bothered by it than anybody else.

You wake up in the middle of the night and you can't go back to sleep because you're not from Hometown. You're eating your breakfast and you worry. You get into the store and you damn near panic. You're from someplace else and all the other people are from right there. Now tonight you'll go to bed and you'll wake up tomorrow and you'll be from Hometown just like all the other folks. It'll just be a matter of how long you've been here. You came there specifically to run the store. You can't do anything about where you're from.

But right now you have an advantage. You're a little bit unusual. You're different from the folks up the road. You may talk somewhat differently. You may do things in a slightly peculiar way. If you were just like all the other people Hometowners wouldn't bother to stop in. They came along to see you because they wanted to find out what you're like. A while back you decided you wanted to buy the store because you wanted to be yourself. Don't ever try to be anything else. And stop worrying about where you're from. Worry about who you are. Think about what kind of a neighbor you'll make. And you'll probably be a fine neighbor if you do just one thing. Relax!

Now that you are willing to accept your nativity—you'll be kidded about it for a long time—there are a couple of things you can think about. The first one is:

Don't do anything about it for a while. Previous owner had two people. Keep them on and see how you come out. Previous owner has

THE COUNTRY STORE

Staffing

none. Stay at none. Chances are you'll be busier at certain times than others. Lunch time, just before closing. Weekends. July and August. Ski season. Fishing. Hunting. Find out how big the peaks and valleys really are. If you can pick and choose among those people who want to do part-time work, you've got it made. But most country stores are in areas with folks who don't want to work a bit here and a bit there. People want to work full time. Find out what the situation is where you are.

If you have people who are good workers and with whom you're comfortable, work them as hard as they'll work when you're busy. When you're not so busy, there's a problem. Talk it over with each person. Forty plus hours a week when there are plenty of customers and ten or so when there's no pressure. The "or so" depends on just how labor-oriented the area is, how many young mothers there are, and how persuasive you can be. Remember that you're going to have to put up with a lot more "seasonal" help in the off times than perhaps you want to. If you've got a built-in staff—your own kids—you're pretty well off. If you don't have them, it's just the cost of doing business. You've got to have the right people when the store is crowded. People on vacation don't want to spend all their time in the store waiting to get waited on. Here's the net: customers will leave a store if there's nobody to help them. Staff with the peaks in mind.

Buying

Now that you've got your staff all set, what are you going to sell? Your selection of wholesalers is limited. For basic groceries, gourmet foods, produce, meats, and sundries you may have to choose between a certain firm or none at all. Suppliers are few because there isn't that much business to go around. Stores are far apart. Gasoline is expensive. Labor is expensive. Making a stop is expensive. So today you'll see the less efficient wholesalers dropping by the wayside.

Distribution is based on volume. The more a distributor can offload at each stop, the better. So the distributor is offering the retailer a wider choice of merchandise. The retailer is forced to centralize his buying. Suppliers are talking 100 cases per delivery. Maybe more. Big problem.

For years small country stores were served by small wholesalers. These people—if any of them are still around—are being pinched. They are raising their prices, adding upcharges, delivery fees, maybe even charging two different wholesale prices depending on store volume.

Grocery chains do not penetrate into the less-populated country areas. But buying groups—the IGA's and the Red & Whites—are reasonably prevalent. They sell everything to the retailer. These wholesalers are more or less merchandising these stores, dictating the policy from the products to development—market analysis, store planning, equipment—to services—electronic ordering, customer pricing, security programs, sanitation. Now that doesn't sound too much like a small country store. But it's happening.

Many of the stores are going this way—buying everything from one wholesaler to get the ordering quantities up to their minimums. But the wholesaler's quality for meats, produce, and everything other than nationally advertised packaged goods is a lot lower than what the country store has been getting from the small, caring supplier. The owner can't afford the prices of the small supplier (if there are any left). And he can't afford the minimums of the large wholesaler. In long range he has two choices: go with the bigger supplier and have a pretty mediocre store. Or go with the more upscale suppliers who are tending toward more gourmet items. Your future is either upscale or downscale. It all depends on where your store is located and how much pressure there is from full-line, automated suppliers. Study the merchandise on your shelves. Figure out what you'd like to have. What basic direction? Check out the wholesalers who'll deliver. Decide.

Pricing

If you've got the merchandise, you've got to sell it. And before you sell it, you've got to put a price on it. It's just that simple. That's what retailing is all about!

MARK-UP = profit % on **BUYING PRICE**
MARGIN = profit % on **SELLING PRICE**

To get margin from mark-up $\dfrac{\text{mark-up}}{100 + \text{mark-up}}$

To get mark-up from margin $\dfrac{\text{margin}}{100 - \text{margin}}$

Remember that those average mark-ups shown in the table are *average*. They're not how you price your merchandise. They might be how you'd *like* to price it. Remember too, that, those are mark-ups, not margins. You might be a little bit higher, a little bit lower; way up, way down. It all depends on your competition.

If you are a long drive from a chain or a large independent, your store is the prime supplier for food for your town. This means you can price the items fairly and not pay too much attention to other stores in other areas.

If there's a good chain outlet or a clean and modern independent store nearby, your pricing for basic groceries must be somewhat higher than the larger outlet because you're paying more. You're stocking them as a matter of convenience for your customers. But you will be competitive on beer and wine and cheeses and soft drinks and speciality items that he doesn't buy from his prime wholesaler.

If you are near competition—say within fifteen miles—you have to figure out how you can capitalize on what other retailers are doing.

"Convenience"? On-the-spot? Fast service? Snacks and soft drinks? Are people looking for that in a country store? Is ten miles a convenience? Don't forget the atmosphere, your attitude toward the customer, the total ambiance of your place. If a lot of people prefer to shop in your store, they're going to overlook the pennies on certain items that you charge as a premium—the premium of doing business with you.

Promotion

Promoting your store is vital. But you may be surprised at the kind of media you have in your area. There may be a weekly newspaper in which you could run ads. Possibly it's a shopping news which is distributed free. Maybe radio. Promote when you have something to say—unusual merchandise, weekly specials, prices. The more personalized the medium the better off you are.

Direct mail is important. You can send out a card once a month or every other month. A Christmas card, change in hours, new lines added. Maybe it's a once-a-year thing, maybe three times a year—at the beginning of different seasons. You'll claim that you see your customers all the time and the other people are hard to persuade. Why bother? Like a good retailer, you do a lot of listening and not much talking. Direct mail is a good way to talk to your customer when he's at home with his feet up.

Average Country Store Mark-Ups

Item	Percentage (roughly)	Item	Percentage (roughly)
Soft Drinks	30	Coffee	35
Beer	20	Cigarettes	30
Wine	35	Postcards	50
Dairy	25	Gift items/books	50
Snacks	30	Bait	30
Produce	40	Gourmet groceries	40
Eggs	25	Paper goods	25
Basic grocery	30	Pet foods	25
Frozen foods	35	Sundries	45
Ice cream	30	Local products	40
Fresh meats	45	Bread and rolls	25
Deli meats	45	Fishing/ hunting supplies	40
Gourmet cheeses	45	Ammo	25
Gas	12	Clothing items	40
Candy	30	Health and beauty aids	35
Newspapers/magazines	25		

You want all your customers to shop for all their needs all the time. Try it once. See how many comments you get, how much people enjoyed getting a mailing from their own country store. Figure out how much it costs. Do it as often as you can.

Find out just who your customers are. Study the checklist or list of voters at at the town hall. Get to know the names. Figure out their relationships. Study the contests, give-aways, and other promotions that the big chains are running. They're the experts. Figure out ways of adapting these promotions to your area. You don't have to give away money. You've got a whole store full of merchandise. A pound of cheese, a pint of maple syrup, a pound of coffee. These are the things that people remember. Contests, drawings. Try to make your store the focal point of your town. Any kind of activities, charities—don't just participate, help lead. Start small. Every group gets the same thing. Whoever produces results gets more next time. Just remember, don't give the store away. You bought it to make some money—not just friends.

Handling Customers

Your customers are your friends. You don't have friends in a non-country store. You have some acquaintances who are your customers. There is a world of difference. In the country you are an absolute equal. In the city you are a couple of social steps down. You call Mrs. Hubbard, Mrs. Hubbard. In a rural area she's Ethel or Aunt Ethel. And that's just fine. But think about it. Think about how really easy it would be if all your customers were strangers or people you'd never see again. You wait on a guy and he's gone for the rest of his life. You don't have to be polite or solicitous or caring. If you weren't going to see that particular customer again you'd act very much like a robot. "Thank you, sir. Have a nice day."

But with customers in a country store, you're going to see some of them this afternoon and most of the rest tomorrow. You're going to like some a lot better than the others. Some of them you won't be able to tolerate. And nobody is going to know the difference. It's true. You're going to ask them about their grandchildren and their pigs. About how their body's working after the last operation and whether their pickup runs okay after the tune-up. And there's got to be a fair amount of difference between the tone you use for each one. You can be busy working on your income tax but you'd better stop and say "hello."

You'll be using the first names of the customers. Of course it's a lot easier to wait on the people and not remember anything about who they are or why. And that is very acceptable for stores in not-so-rural areas. When you're in a town of a couple of hundred people—or a couple of thousand—you know what's going on. You talk about what's going on.

You don't talk much about what's happening on the other side of the mountain. Your conversation is just about what's right here.

First Year Checklist

It would be a good idea to have a first year checklist. Make it up when you've been in business for a few weeks. Things you want to get done. Physical improvements. Is your store just about the way you want it or are you going to make some changes? How major are the improvements? Are you going to take it step by step? Will you need help? Changing your merchandise? These are big steps. Take it slowly.

Decide what you want to sell. Food, beer, wine, soft drinks, gas, deli meats, produce, cigarettes and candy, magazines and newspapers, clothing, hardware, health and beauty aids, kerosene, gifts, books, maps, toys, fishing supplies, worms and crawlers, hunting supplies, guns and ammo, licenses, fresh meats, game inspection station. How big is your store? How big is the market? Think it through.

General stores are pretty rare these days. Concentrate on the things that aren't all that available in stores nearby. Can your store be thought of as a prime supplier of specific commodities based on availability, quality, and price? What is your place known for? Can you bring in related items rather than new departments?

Do you have enough help? Can you get more? Where are your customers? Are you serving your area well enough? How about suppliers? Are you getting your share of customers that live within three miles? What percentage of a customer's total purchases do you get? Are you entitled to more? You can't be all things to all people. But you might be able to get 2 percent more from 100 people without any trouble. Maybe 200. That could be $25,000 a year. At the end of the first year you want to be pretty familiar with the answers to all these questions:

Are you selling the *right merchandise*? Can you make alternate merchandise available—through suppliers that you can call on—that your customers will buy? Price and quality?

Is your store functionally attractive? Do your customers enjoy shopping in it?

Do your customers have to wait to get adequate *service*? Lack of merchandise on the shelves? Long lines at check out?

Your Goal

The right merchandise at the right price attractively displayed and easy to buy. This is what you want. You will come close to your ideal in one area and maybe sacrifice in another. If you have everything right you have a perfect store. (There are no perfect stores.)

Casey Stengel said something like:

"If you don't know where you're going, you're going to end up someplace else."

A lot of people with small grocery stores figure their investment is in the store itself, in a certain way of life. They live off the store, take little or no salary, and realize a profit when they sell the business. The store, of course, provides them with a pretty fair income. Food, clothing, a place to live, auto expenses, most everything you can think of. There are a lot of people around who simply buy a store, run it well for a few years, sell it, and buy another. So whether you want to sell the store or whether you're in love with it and want to keep it, it won't matter much for the next five years.

Five-Year Plan

Do you want to make money considerably over and above your living expenses (which won't be all that easy)? Do you want to break even with a reasonably good life? Put a few thousand aside? Once you've completed your first year and you're pretty happy with the operation (or know what has to be done) you can figure out where you're going to go and work like hell to get there.

After you've got a feel for a year, do pro forma operating statements with certain variables.

See how much your sales can grow before you're in a position to add more employees.

Figure out how much an extra hour at one end or the other of the day will generate in volume. Two hours. A lot of places are open 7 to 10.

How do you get your employees? Have you got a kid in high school who won't mind studying in the store? How about Saturdays? Sundays, shorter hours?

Small stores do anywhere from $100,000 to $800,000 a year. That's quite a spread. Maybe you can double the business over a short period of time. Maybe you want to and maybe you don't.

Remember that your store has an optimum level of business. Growth, size, volume don't mean profit. Your net is going to shrink, most likely, after you get beyond a certain point in expansion. You may have to hire more people. (This is where a computer would be handy.) Depending on your location you've got to sell more groceries. You've got to keep those shelves stocked. And that takes more people.

No two stores are alike and no two profit pictures are the same. Do your five-year plan—just messing with the figures—every quarter. If you've got a good business, you'll enjoy it. If you don't have a good business, you can improve it and think about selling it.

Priorities

You'll want to stick to priorities as the time goes by. You'll want to enjoy yourself. You'll want to enjoy all those things that you came to the country for—a different life, a slower pace, an appreciation of other people and the beauty of the world around you. A little bit of success makes you greedy. You want to work harder. Your business grows. That's okay...up to a point. The point might be just where you decided to trade in the city for the country. So be very, very careful. When you wake up in the morning, look around—at the countryside—and somehow be thankful that you're sharing in it. It's a very big deal!

THE COUNTRY INN

They say it takes about five years before you can tell whether a country inn will be successful. The Charltons are in their sixth year.

Eric and Beryl Charlton had been thinking about a country business for some time...just thinking. They lived in York, Pennsylvania, where Eric was executive vice president in charge of sales for a medium-sized industrial company. They owned a pleasant farm where they raised nothing much more than three children. On their drives to vacations in Canada they often passed the Rabbit Hill Inn in Lower Waterford, Vermont, and thought that someday a business like that might be theirs. You see, Lower Waterford stands out among Vermont's little towns as uniquely beautiful. About ten miles from St. Johnsbury and close to the Connecticut River, it has an unbelievable view of New Hampshire's White Mountains.

The Charltons did what almost no country business seekers do—they went about their search scientifically. Eric's company was into decision analysis systems. In his job he worked with them every day. So he did some analyses of his own, on himself. By nature and by occupation he saw himself as a people-oriented person. Beryl had practiced nursing, a highly human-concerned profession. Because of this they rejected every engineer's dream of a hardware store and concentrated on hospitality-type businesses. They considered the advantages of restaurants but thought of the longer customer contact at an inn as significantly more desirable. So it was to be an inn, but where?

Eric and Beryl were both born in England and liked the remoteness of the countryside. They rejected moving south; they didn't want to go west. North was what was left. New York was out; so it was to be New England. Universal decision: the mountains or the seashore? Decision analysis said either. Meanwhile back at the inn—what kind, how big? Answer: in a small village where there can be local involvement; a comfortable, manageable size, twenty rooms maximum. After a bit they knew what they wanted to buy and didn't waste anybody's time looking at what brokers wanted to sell.

One fine day a broker called and said he had found their inn, a great place with twenty rooms on Route 18 in Vermont. Eric said, "It sounds like Rabbit Hill Inn." And it was. It had just been listed.

Eric feels he paid more than he should have for Rabbit Hill but (and the but is big) he assumed a low-interest mortgage. The Charltons are very happy entertaining people in their new home. Their life has changed greatly and they like that very much.

The inn has been booked to 100 percent occupancy during the summer months for the past couple of years and they like that very much, too.

They have a chef, an assistant cook, and an outside man. They have a bookkeeper who spends 20 to 40 percent of her time at the inn, and housekeepers and waitresses who work seasonally. The Charltons find that married women in the area can be called upon to work pretty much as needed. And they have an assistant innkeeper. They tend to delegate a lot of things but they're just as busy. They get repeat business from Boston and Montreal. They're able to be away when the inn closes during April and again during November. With their twenty-five kilometers of cross-country ski trails as an attraction they're back in business December 15. The place couldn't be more successful. It's a very good example of a fine New England inn.

Services

Innkeepers must decide what kind of service they wish to provide, from a full-service inn with meals and beverages, tennis courts and swimming pools, on down to overnight lodgings with a shared bath and no frills. Without any meals you're getting very close to a motel, perhaps not the way you perceive it but the way your customer looks at things. An inn is a personality—the personality of the owners. The more ways that you can demonstrate its uniqueness, the better off you'll be. The better innkeeper you'll be. A motel is nothing more than a building with beds that provides ready access to one's car. The convenience of that car is the one element that separates your inn from a motel down the street. The key is the car—the leaving, the exit, the getaway. Speed and convenience. At an inn the vital factor is staying and how much and in what ways the guests can enjoy themselves.

Repeat Business Important

Like any place in the hospitality business, an inn depends on repeat business, getting some of the same people back time after time after time. Inns don't usually suffer from convenience. They're not at the high-rental intersection of two interstates. They're off on a road that sometimes you can get lost finding. Getting your repeaters is a matter of giving them more and more of what they came for. Figure out what you can do and go from there.

While you're considering the stoves and the sinks of the place you're going to buy, you should have been thinking about the people who are going to use them. How do you *attract the right staff?* Some restaurant people—like John Donahue at the Toll Gate Lodge in Manchester, Vermont—move their workers with them. He has a winter place in Palm Beach and he moves the key people back and forth. But an inn stays in one place. When you look at an inn, find out how the present owner keeps his waitresses and chambermaids in a seasonal business. Are they

Cooking for Twenty

If you're an accomplished cook, figure on cooking for twenty people—all at different times—and maybe something will occur to you, like having help in the kitchen. Chances are you won't be able to do it alone. If you are a good cook, stay with it. Get some help. If you're not into the culinary arts, get a cook or a chef or whatever he or she calls himself or herself. Probably a chef costs more and the food tastes better. A chef and an assistant cook—you get the picture.

content to come and go as the guests do or are they always looking for permanent jobs? It's not good if they're not showing up! Be sure you know who will

wait on tables
clean the rooms,
and do some outside work.

You could do all of the above if you weren't busy doing something else. Figure out what you can do from 100 percent occupancy down to 0 percent. It's going to be better if you close—or have room accommodations for casual, off-the-road guests—rather than to offer poor service. Some localities have the right kind of prospects and some don't. You can train people but it takes a while. You may not know how to wait on tables or make a bed. Ask around.

Bar

Themes

The basic thing about serving food and beverage is that you've got to do it right. With personality. It's very easy to pour ten scotches. Pouring them into the same guy is fundamentally foolish. Watch your bar. Bar service is a fine piece of income. Make sure you keep it under control. An inn that serves its guests drinks before dinner, whether at the table or in a lounge area, is great. But large bars attract people who aren't that interested in eating. If you're serving really good food, don't run the risk of ruining it for a few people.

Most good inns have themes that make their business attractive. Decor is important, carrying one color throughout. A mixture, whatever. Make sure your guest rooms capitalize on your basic decorations—antiques, pieces here and there, unusual ashtrays, wastebaskets. Many inns make even their smaller rooms homey and inviting with decor touches that mean a lot overall. Little things that people can take away are mighty fine advertising. Soap, matches, sewing kits, shower caps, shampoos, combs, toothbrushes, shoe horns.

Another theme is activities—art galleries, cross-country skiing, fishing, anything that sets the inn apart and gives it a personality. It depends on where the inn is, what is around it, and, most specifically, what the interests of the innkeepers might be. Don't leave your brains at home when you're thinking about making people at home. Whatever interests you have probably can be dramatized throughout the inn. All kinds of artwork for sale. Plays, movies, the opera. Sports. Antiques from any period, any country. Bears and elephants. Go a little further than you'd go at home. An inn is like an exhibit area. It's home—plus.

What else you do besides the theme and the decor is entirely up to you and what's available in your community. If there's a theater nearby, build it in. If there's any sort of cultural attraction, make that part of your plan. Hikes, scenic auto tours, all kinds of nature activities. Have printed sheets that give all the information about where to go, what to do, and how to get back to the inn. If your place has cross-country ski trails and there's no snow on the ground, show the guests some movies of cross-country, lessons and tips, how to wax. And make sure you've got a few things to do for rainy days, shopping tours, things to see.

Comfort

The most important thing is to make the people who come to your inn comfortable. It means that you go out of your way about twenty-four hours a day. Physically—by making sure that what they have is what they like. Mentally—by taking care of details in advance. Little notices about credit cards, check-out time, cashing checks. Polite but firm. The inn has a policy. For guests, being comfortable at your place is being at home.

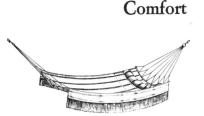

Associations

There are associations for innkeepers. Join the best one in your area. Most are affiliated with the American Hotel and Motel Association. Don't let the name bother you. Hotels, motels, and inns are all in the same hospitality boat—striving for a share of the tourist dollar for lodgings and food. Look at their membership list, check the people you know, then decide. It's not cheap to belong. But you get your Blue Cross-Blue Shield at reduced rates, plus a fair amount of help from the association. The dues are based on how many rooms and dining seats you have. If you're new to innkeeping, the association will be a lot of help. If you've been a member for a while, you have your friends. They've got figures to show that the net operating income on food and beverages might be around 11 percent of sales, and on rooms, 74 percent. These are fun to play with and you'll get some sort of feel for what you can expect. They have guides and directories and promotional literature, all of which are designed to get people there in the first place, specialized advertising in which you may or may not want to participate.

Advertising

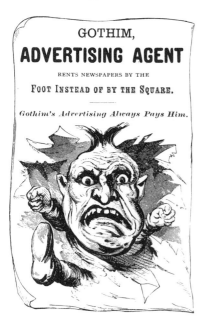

GOTHIM,
ADVERTISING AGENT
RENTS NEWSPAPERS BY THE
FOOT INSTEAD OF BY THE SQUARE.

Gothim's Advertising Always Pays Him.

Advertising for your inn is a big subject. If you're not doing well—you've bought an inn that had been closed, or something like that—build advertising into your plan of operation. Make sure you spend your advertising funds. Let your customers know exactly what to expect when they get there. If you must, increase the room rates and the meal prices to cover the ads.

There is no secret way to advertise. You pay your money and you take your choice of the available travel media in the big markets where most of your people come from. What you're going to say in the ad depends on what your theme or personality is all about...what the innkeeper is all about. You are starting to build a reputation. You are starting to build an image. The ad should reflect what the inn is. You don't want a house full of people who thought they were getting one thing and are settling for another. Be very honest. Tell them what the place is like.

Don't exaggerate. Include your prices if you think they're a good value or for snob appeal. And, above all, ask the reader to send for your brochure.

Brochure

If you own an inn, the most important piece of paper in the world is your brochure. It's what you send out to bring people in. It's also what you distribute to people who've been there to *get them back*. Your brochure is something you've invested in, $500 and up. It's something in which you've also invested hours and hours of effort. It can be inexpensive and effective. It can cost a bundle and be worthless.

If you're laying things out and seeing how they look, get some help. If you want to go to an advertising agency, go, but go with ideas. Have a pretty good concept of what you want, explain it to the people who'll be doing it, and leave them alone. When you see the copy and layout, don't pull your punches. Listen to all the explanations and then you decide. You're paying for it. You're going to be happy with it. Don't settle for what you don't want. You will live with it for quite a while. When you place it in the envelope as you're sending it out, you want to have pride in what you're letting speak for you.

It should reflect the personality of the inn. Very simple, very grandiose. One color or four colors. A simple two-fold or a large piece that opens up. Some pictures of your better-looking rooms. Line drawings. Whatever best expresses what your inn is all about. Guests will take a brochure if they've enjoyed their visit. Put it out where people can see it. You're very proud of it, right?

The brochure is a little bit like postcards. (Have some dignified cards if you want to supplement your basic piece of promotion. It's a good idea.) Guests will use the brochure to remember the time they had. And the time they had at your place is pretty much up to you. If they liked it, they'll come back. If they didn't, they won't. It's not like a store. You can buy things a hundred times and not give a damn about the owner. It isn't like a motel or a hotel when you may see the owner once or never.

If you don't get people back, there's something you're doing wrong, and you'd better find out—try a simple questionnaire in your rooms or at the checkout—and fix it. You've got the best possible way of doing research on your inn. A lot of folks don't do it because they're scared or lazy or don't care that much. You've got a captive audience that stays with you longer than almost any other businessman (except an undertaker). Make use of what the guests are saying. Right there you've got the future of your inn.

CHAPTER SIXTEEN

For the Records

Many people buy a business in the country and say, "Okay, that's it. No more records. I'm out here in the wilderness and nobody knows I exist." It's as if you're going into hiding, changing your name, your fingerprints, growing a beard. "I won't keep any records and the IRS will never find me. I'm going to steal the money and nobody will ever know." There seems to be a feeling that right on Euclid Avenue in Cleveland you will keep abundant records and somewhere around South Paris, Maine, you can run a business without keeping track of it.

Records a Must

There can be no business without records. Without some kind of a book, the business has no meaning. It can be a store full of shelves, an inn with beds and tables, a big, long bar with a happy hour, a farm for horses, or a print shop with movable type, but no book, no business. If somebody comes into your business and asks how's business, you won't even know what he's talking about.

Country businesses are difficult to run. There are many problems connected with them—some that are unique to a particular part of the world that concentrates on smallness. But to think that at the end of your long move you'll be paying less attention to numbers is completely and 100 percent ridiculous. Now you will say that it will be easier to keep up the books because business will be small. That's probably right. And you will say that you can do it whenever you want. And that's probably true. And your own method. More or less. No accountants. Well...

Work and Paper Work

There are two equally important parts of your business. The first one is the real work. That means everything you do that isn't making some sort of reference for the future. Then there's paper work, which is.

If your business has a cash register and you use it, it's an important part of your records—part of your books, your journals, your ledgers, and whatever else you may have for storing numbers and looking at them later. Your register may have one button or a whole batch of buttons, it may be manual or electronic, it may have a memory which is better than yours or it may not, it doesn't matter. It's your basic record-keeping device. You can keep track of sales on an abacus or in your head. Whatever's best for you. You've got sales checks, check stubs, cancelled checks, you've got credit memos and debit memos, receipts, petty cash slips, bank statements, and other forms for doing business.

You can do your business on a *cash* basis, which means you record the actual cash as it changes hands, or an *accrual* basis, when the promise of the transaction is made even though payment is later. Once you've got that settled, you can move on to the other great accounting mystery—debits and credits and how they apply to several types of accounts (asset and liability, income and expense, capital). There is a large amount of jargon attached to the entire accounting procedure.

Most people maintain good, accurate figures on a daily basis, summarize them monthly, and give the whole thing to the accountant at the end of the year. It doesn't cost very much to do the taxes for a small business. If your records are complete, the accountant needs about three or four hours to do the whole thing.

Good Records Valuable

The *better your records*, the better off you are. Accountants can come upon very small things in going over your files that can save you hundreds of dollars on your taxes. Small things like methods of depreciation, investment credit, income averaging, bad debts, earned-income credit, plus hundreds of items they are trained to spot.

If you've taken courses in accounting, that's great. Do a tax return and have an accountant check it over. He'll probably change something. Your accountant will give you the best possible filled-out form for whatever taxes you may be liable for. Ask a lot of people about the accountants available. Find out what their experience has been. Then decide. There's nothing more annoying than changing an accountant. It wastes your time. Pick one who is not going to jail and one who isn't likely to open a competing business. (I know someone who faced both those situations.)

Good records are valuable when you get ready to sell the business. I

Getting an Accountant

If you're going to use an accountant—most people do unless they've got some special background in this area—get to him before you do anything about setting up your books and making a lot of mistakes. Chances are he has a system designed for your type of business. You may feel the expense is not justified to get all those fancy checks, but see how much it costs.

have done a lot of consulting work for folks who want to buy a business. In many cases I can't dig up any really helpful information that tells me that the owner can make a decent living. This is just as incredible as it sounds. The owner will show a couple of sheets of analysis paper that don't add up or mean anything. The owner mumbles something about not wanting to pay taxes and expects me to figure out his meaningless numbers. He expects that somebody will come along and buy his business because that person doesn't want to pay any taxes either.

No person in his right mind is willing to bet his life's savings on a bunch of numbers he suspects. It doesn't matter what kind of an excuse is given for not having the numbers. If somebody wants the business, he wants the numbers.

I've seen hundreds of businesses for sale that lacked any way for a prospective buyer to judge them, except that the owners claimed they never paid any taxes. Taxes are not pertinent. The value of the business is vital to document. Any person who likes his business likes it well enough to show you how good it is.

Inventory and Purchasing

Depending on what kind of business you're in, you'll need records that show *inventory* and *purchasing*. Inventory can be done weekly or yearly. You can arrive at an inventory figure by knowing exactly what you've purchased and exactly what you've sold. A physical inventory means counting every piece—or sometimes it is done by teams of professional inventory experts who approximate within known limits. Purchasing records come basically out of your checkbook, posted by department in a ledger, and are available for checking sales by department.

Sales records or *fee* records (for service businesses) are something that even the most indolent, deceitful, dishonest person keeps. He may inflate them or deflate them, or change them in some way, but he knows how much he's selling. He may lie about it to himself by skimming off his cash, but basically he knows how much he made. Sales records go into a book.

Cash records are from your checkbook, your cash register, cash drawer, cash box, or whatever it may be. There are *credit records* from sales slips and the several different records involved in consumer credit and trade credit which, if carefully handled, can increase your business. There are a number of *employee records*, payroll particularly. And there are *fixtures* and *property* records on which depreciation and appreciation are based. And there may be several other records which your business needs. Basically they are simple. Just about as simple as they are for metropolitan businesses. Business records are the same in both places. But country businessmen resist keeping them. They may think of themselves as "revenooers," trying to get away with something, putting something over on somebody. But they're not, you see. They're just putting it over on themselves. Their business isn't worth diddly if they don't have the records to prove that it is!

Using the Balance Sheet

Over a period of time you will begin to pay some attention to the elements of your balance sheet. You will begin to watch your progress against yourself or against other businesses in the same industry. These industry figures are available from Dun & Bradstreet and Robert Morris Associates, both of whom are very important in the business community. You can play all sorts of games with your balance sheets like:

Current assets to current liabilities—current ratio
  (generally close to 2 to 1 is a good idea)
Current liabilities to tangible net worth
  (what's owed to what's owned—80 percent tops)
Net sales to working capital
  (low: unprofitable use of working capital. High: vulnerability to creditors)
Net profits to tangible net worth
  (after-tax profits=key measurement)
These are *balance sheet ratios*. What is good and what is bad in the various ratios depend on a number of things—most importantly, the business you're in and how successful you've been in generating a return on money, how you're faring, and how your stockholders are making out.

Operating Ratios

You should also be familiar with the *operating ratios*. At the end of each line on your profit and loss statement blank is a percentage sign. These blanks are not there for making the page look more interesting. They are there for you to fill in with numbers. Operating ratios are something you are probably a lot more familiar with than the acid test or the quick ratio that deals with assets and liabilities and equity. These are

---

Who Keeps the Books?

You're a grown person. You will have to decide who does the *bookkeeping*. It depends on your business, how much you like numbers, whether there's anybody available to "do the books," how much they cost, and how good they are. I do my records daily and see my accountant once a year.

Bookkeeping is easy if you're set up to handle all the input and have a line or a space for everything to go into.

things you can judge, like your margin, advertising costs, rent, car/truck, utilities, insurance, accounting and legal expenses, payroll, and what's left over.

This is where the trade associations look at the operating results of their members—by large or small, different areas, types of business, different ways to doing things—and report back a composite to their group. You can compare your results based on one month's experience with the whole national average of people who are in the same business. It's really very helpful to know what the other guy is doing. Look at yours and look at his. What are the reasons you're too high or too low? Look at your gross profit versus the average. Are you making enough money up front before you start taking things away from it? Operating ratios are vital to your business. Make sure you have something that tells what you're doing.

Accounting Methods

You may get involved in *aging the receivables*. This means figuring how long accounts have been on the books—thirty days and up. More plainly—how long people have owed you money. Excess of past-due accounts could indicate poor management.

Amortization means the gradual retirement of debt by periodic payments or proration of expenses written off over time.

Appreciation is the increase in value of a fixed asset to market value. It is usually not used for financial statements, but *depreciation* is. It is the concept that all fixed assets (except land) deteriorate or wear out. The asset's value goes down over its useful life. An inventory valuation is made in one of three ways: average cost; first in, first out; and last in, first out. The last two are pretty much for department stores or manufacturers. Average cost applies to most retail operations.

Learning About Accounting

There are lots of things you should know about accounting and you do know them if you've gone to school, taken courses, and become certified. Those of us without benefit of that education tend to have trouble with the nomenclature, the columns, proving, and trial balances. Like any of the professionals, accounting is filled with certain words that keep outsiders out. A good, simple book on accounting is very worthwhile. A good, simple accountant is a godsend. Make sure you understand what he's talking about. You're the one who goes to jail.

CHAPTER SEVENTEEN

Go for It

There's a new way of life for the thousands and thousands of people who have come to the country. The space is wide open. There are no crowds, no lines, no waiting. There's no frustration, a lot less anger, little or no fear. Strangers smile at you, often say hello. Your neighbors will stop on the street and talk.

Relaxed? Not really. Relaxed means a loosening, and life in the country was never uptight. There's no good way to describe what it's like. It's not the same for all places and all people. But it's simpler, easier, to the point. We don't strive to keep up with others. Possessions mean less. You work a lot harder for what you get, and you don't get much. What you do get can be complete peace!

And, let's face it, it's worth every dollar you have. The ability to get away from what you've been doing and start over again. That's what's so incredible. A new beginning. A second chance. People want to change their identities, to try it one more time. That's what the country offers them. A big, huge arena in which to start life all over. To do what you did wrong the right way. To live better. It takes every ounce of energy you can come by. You want to do it perfectly. There is no room for compromise. You go all out or you go back to where you came from. It is attitude. You're taking all your money and all your guts and putting them down on a very large gamble. No business is a sure thing, and country businesses are less than that. Keep your fingers crossed. You're due for a shot of luck!

The Frühaufs

Not long ago an article in the magazine section of the Cleveland *Plain Dealer* told how a number of northeastern Ohio families packed their bags and came to Vermont to buy businesses. Ed and Loretta Frühauf came after twenty years in Mentor, Ohio, where Ed had been a research chemist for Lubrizol Corporation. They bought the Reluctant Panther Inn in Manchester, opened it in May 1980, and have been doing beautifully ever since. They are building an image of their place with fine gourmet cooking—like quail baked in spicy wine sauce—and realizing a 20 to 25 percent return on investment. The inn accommodates twenty-two people, is booked for peak season well in advance, and everybody seems to be happy.

Barbara Mouat

Barbara Mouat, also from Mentor, who opened an inn in Manchester the same month, first met the Frühaufs in Vermont. Mouat bought the handsome Worthy Inn, an 1889 building that accommodates a hundred people. She has shown a 15 percent ROI since she took over the place. Jazz groups and barbecues, four-course meals and a casual, homey atmosphere are offered—and welcomed.

The Thornburns

From Pennisula, Ohio, we have the Thornburns, Ron and Mary Louise, who saw and wanted the Inn at Weathersfield (in Perkinsville). Ron had been a marketing analyist with B.F. Goodrich and then vice president at Southfield Publishing Company before the move. Mary Louise worked for travel and insurance agencies. The place had been vacant, and had no furnace, an old septic system, and bad floors. They bought the inn for less than $85,000 and spent more than that making it a home for beautiful period antiques. It has six guest rooms and a dining room—and style.

The Phillipses

Barbara and Harold Phillips came from Solon and settled in the town where they'd camped for eight summers, in Cavendish. Harold had been a surveyor in Ohio. He began work full-time at his cabinet-making hobby once they moved to Vermont. Barbara has an antique shop in the front of their gristmill. They don't miss Solon.

Mike Amunssen

Mike Amunssen was vice president of Central Data Systems in Akron when it was bought by Itel and moved out of state. In July 1975, Mike and Gerry moved out of state, too, to Ludlow. They acquired an inn, named it the Winchester, acquired another down-the-road inn, the Timber Inn, and now operate both of them. Successfully.

These are just a few of the people who've come from the Cleveland area to southern Vermont in the past few years. Let's take a look at the neighborhood. What's been happening lately on Vermont State Highway 11 just a couple of miles from my store?

The Kandahar, a twenty-two room modern inn, has tennis courts, a swimming pool, a spacious dining room, and quite a bit of public room area. It is now being run by the Walt Bitlers and the Richard Drexles. They have a lease with an option to buy the inn in a couple of years. The owner is Doug Melville; a man from the steel industry who bought the place about four years ago and plans to return to Pittsburgh. The inn is attractive but it's big and needs a good staff. They have it.

Down the road about a mile is the Bromley Sun Lodge, purchased by Floyd and Carol Hunter of North Conway, New Hampshire. Erwin and Cheri Dostal had been operating the inn since it opened the doors in 1976, and sold it to the Hunters. The lodge is one of the largest hotels— 51 rooms and a 125-seat restaurant—operating right on a ski slope. The new owner was with the Eastern Slope Inn in North Conway, and Attitash Mountain Village in Bartlett, New Hampshire, and the Viking Hotel in Newport, Rhode Island. He has had many years of hotel management, marketing, and consulting experience. Floyd is active in Hunter Associates, a consulting firm, serving the hospitality industry in New England.

A New Market

Chad and Susanne Bessette from Phoenix, Arizona, have just completed work on their new Bromley Market, leased with an option to buy. They have a small convenience store with apartments above.

A little further this way is the old Estelle Best estate of 525 acres which was sold not long ago to Bromley Mountain for the development of the eastern slope for skiing. The investment in the property will allow the corporation to duplicate its condo arrangement at Bromley Village totalling close to 300 units. Lifts and a base lodge are independent of the existing operation.

About three miles down Route 11 is the Nordic Inn, purchased recently by Judy and Tom Acton from Connecticut. They bought it from Inger Johanssen and Phil Pagano, who had built the place into a fine restaurant with six guest rooms and a maze of cross-country ski trails. The Actons, with Phil serving as a ski instructor, are continuing the operation. No previous hospitality experience for the Actons.

We follow the road into Londonderry. There have been a couple of changes at the shopping center. Casey's Pub has been opened by Morey and Karen Oliver, owners of the Londonderry Hardware, and Ron and Joanne Prouty. Reports on the food and the profits are good.

Bruce Grass is the owner of the West River Associates, Inc., Business Clinic on the second floor of the annex to the plaza. He does all kinds of work for small businesses and recently got into financial development.

Carol and Don Anderson, originally from Connecticut, who own the Londonderry Twin Cinema, just recently opened the Equinox Twin Cinema in Manchester. Reports are that both theaters are doing nicely.

Bill Austin now manages the Londonderry Gulf outlet. Bill has been here about twelve years, and was from Stamford, Connecticut. He sold the Londonderry Auto Service a short time ago.

Lanny West bought Londonderry Auto. He has gotten expert mechanic Kirk Goodwin to run it while he pays attention to his Pepperidge route.

Merrill's Restaurant is back in operation with Mary Merrill at the helm. Breakfast and lunch enthusiasts are back, too.

TOMTIT,
DEALER IN
WIND INSTRUMENTS,
HAUTBOYS,
WEATHERCOCKS,
JEWSHARPS,
AND
PENNY WHISTLES.

B & B Repair Service and Mini Mart, which is pumping Mobil gasoline, recently bought out an old service station about five miles along Route 11, just over Andover line. It's owned by Ben and Butch Jelley.

Lee and Beth Davis from Ohio bought the Simonsville Inn, changed the name to the original Rowell's Inn, and are doing a bed and breakfast business in beautiful nineteenth century surroundings. Six rooms ready, more to come.

And just before you get into Chester there's the new Cranberry Inn, an attractive, old sprawling place, dating from 1816. It is presently a bed-and-breakfast operation. Andy and Sharon Papineau are from Rhode Island.

Those are a few of the changes that have taken place in businesses along a twenty-mile stretch of highway in Vermont. They range from places like the Bromley Sun Lodge to a one-man consulting outfit like West River.

Many Moves

Country businesses tend to change more often than others. Take Morey and Karen Oliver. They started with a theater, then moved over to the hardware store, and now have a shared interest in Casey's Pub. The Andersons have a new movie house. Lanny West sold his market in Winhall a couple of years ago for what was reported to be well over half a million dollars, bought the Pepperidge route, gave half of it to his father, now keeps an eye on the garage. There's a lot of movement. If you're into something good, you stay with it, maybe add on, start something new. If you're doing something you don't like, there are ways to change. People who buy a country business are the kind of people who want to be very happy doing what they do. Not just a little bit. Not just, it'll work out sooner or later. But now!

This is the end of a book of advice about country business. There really isn't anything more to be said. If you've got the right business in the right place, it's perfect. You're one of those who were searching for a different life and you've found it. It's really no big deal to anyone other than you. But making yourself a part of that big move to the little town takes immense courage, a thorough understanding of what you want out of life, and a hope and a prayer that you'll get it. I've known lots of people who've come to the country and stayed—and a few who've gone back to pick up their lives as they were before. Good luck to them. They need it. Somehow life here didn't match their expectations. I don't think it was our fault. They just weren't made for the country.

But if you think you've got half a chance—maybe a little less than half—don't wait too long. Just make up your mind to go for it.

I don't think you'll ever regret it.

FINIS

Appendix

STATE DEVELOPMENT AGENCIES

This is where the WHERE people can get information—facts and figures, government-oriented data.

Alabama Development Office
c/o State Capitol
Montgomery, AL 36130

Alaska Department of Commerce & Economic
  Development
Division of Economic Enterprise
Pouch EE
Juneau, AK 99811

Arizona Office of Economic Planning &
  Development
17 West Washington
Phoenix, AZ 85007

Arkansas Industrial Development Commission
State Capitol
Little Rock, AR 72201

California Department of Economic & Business
  Development
Office of Business & Industrial Development
1120 N St.
Sacramento, CA 95814

Colorado Division of Commerce & Development
1313 Sherman St., Room 500
Denver, CO 80203

Connecticut Department of Commerce
210 Washington St.
Hartford, CT 06106

Delaware Department of Community Affairs &
  Economic Development
Division of Economic Development
630 State College Rd.
Dover, DE 19901

Florida Department of Commerce
Division of Economic Development
Collins Building
Tallahassee, FL 32304

Georgia Department of Industry & Trade
Post Office Box 1776
Atlanta, GA 30301

Hawaii Department of Planning & Economic
  Development
Post Office Box 2359
Honolulu, HI 96804

Idaho Division of Tourism & Industrial
  Development
State Capitol Building, Room 108
Boise, ID 83720

llinois Department of Business & Economic
  Development
222 South College St.
Springfield, IL 62706

Indiana Department of Commerce
1350 Consolidated Building
115 North Pennsylvania St.
Indianapolis, IN 46204

Iowa Development Commission
250 Jewett Building
Des Moines, IA 50309

Kansas Department of Economic Development
503 Kansas Ave.
Topeka, KS 66603

Kentucky Department of Commerce
Capitol Plaza Office Tower
Frankfort, KY 40601

Louisiana Department of Commerce & Industry
Post Office Box 44185
Baton Rouge, LA 70804

Maine State Development Office
Executive Department
State House
Augusta, ME 04333

Maryland Department of Economic & Community
  Development
2525 Riva Rd
Annapolis, MD 21401

Massachusetts Department of Commerce &
  Development
100 Cambridge St.
Boston, MA 02202

Michigan Department of Commerce
Office of Economic Expansion
Post Office Box 30225
Lansing, MI 48909

Minnesota Department of Economic Development
480 Cedar St.
St Paul, MN 55101

Mississippi Agricultural & Industrial Board
Post Office Box 849
Jackson, MS 39205

Missouri Division of Commerce & Industrial
  Development
Post Office Box 118
Jefferson City, MO 65101

Montana Department of Community Affairs
Economic Development Division
Capitol Station
Helena, MT 59601

Nebraska Department of Economic Development
Box 94666 - State Capitol
Lincoln, NE 68509

Nevada Department of Economic Development
Capital Complex
Carson City, NV 89710

New Hampshire Office of Industrial Development
Division of Economic Development
Department of Resources & Economic Development
Post Office Box 856
Concord, NH 03301

New Jersey Department of Labor & Industry
Division of Economic Development
Post Office Box 2766
Trenton, NJ 08625

New Mexico Department of Development
113 Washington Ave.
Santa Fe, NM 87503

New York State Department of Commerce
99 Washington Ave.
Albany, NY 12245

North Carolina Department of Natural and
  Economic Development
Division of Economic Development
Box 27687
Raleigh, NC 27611

North Dakota Business and Industrial Development
  Department
523 East Bismarck Ave.
Bismarck, ND 58505

Ohio Department of Economic and Community
  Development
Box 1001
Columbus, OH 43216

Oklahoma Department of Industrial Development
600 Will Rogers Building
Oklahoma City, OK 73105

Oregon Department of Economic Development
317 South West Alder St.
Portland, OR 97204

Pennsylvania Department of Commerce
Division of Research & Planning
632 Health and Welfare Building
Harrisburg, PA 17120

Rhode Island Department of Economic
  Development
One Weybosset Hill
Providence, RI 02903

South Carolina State Development Board
Post Office Box 927
Columbia, SC 29202

South Dakota Department of Economic & Tourism
  Development
620 South Cliff
Sioux Falls, SD 57103

Tennessee Department of Economic & Community
  Development
1014 Andrew Jackson State Office Building
Nashville, TN 37219

Texas Industrial Commission
714 Sam Houston State Office Building
Austin, TX 78711

Utah Department of Development Services
No. 2 Arrow Press Square, Suite 200
165 South West Temple
Salt Lake City, UT 84101

Vermont Agency of Development & Community
  Affairs
Economic Development Department
Pavilion Office Building
Montpelier, VT 05602

Virginia Division of Industrial Development
1010 State Office Building
Richmond, VA 23219

Washington State Department of Commerce &
  Economic Development
101 General Administration Building
Olympia, WA 98504

West Virginia Department of Commerce
Industrial Development Division
1900 Washington St. East
Charleston, WV 25305

Wisconsin Department of Business Development
123 West Washington Ave.
Madison, WI 53702

Wyoming Department of Economic Planning &
  Development
Barrett Building, Third Floor
Cheyenne, WY 82002

STATE CHAMBERS OF COMMERCE

This is where the WHERE people can get more information—lists of local Chambers of Commerce, business oriented data, etc. The state Chambers of Commerce are supported by funds from the local and regional groups and act as clearinghouses for information on a statewide basis. Addresses for those states that have Chambers of Commerce are listed below.

Alabama
468 S. Perry St.
Montgomery, AL 36101

Alaska
310 2nd St.
Juneau, AK 99810

Arizona
2701 East Camelback Rd.
Phoenix, AZ 85016

Arkansas
911 Wallace Building
Little Rock, AR 72201

California
455 Capitol Mall
Sacramento, CA 95814

Colorado
1390 Logan St.
Denver, CO 80203

Connecticut
60 Washington St
Hartford, CT 06106

Delaware
1102 West St.
Wilmington, DE 19061

Florida
Box 5497
Tallahassee, FL 32301

Georgia
1200 Commerce Building
Atlanta, GA 30303

Hawaii
735 Bishop St.
Honolulu, HI 96813

Idaho
Box 389
Boise, ID 83701

Illinois
20 North Wacker Dr.
Chicago, IL 60606

Indiana
Board of Trade Building
Indianapolis, IN 46204

Kansas
One Townsite Plaza
Topeka, KS 66603

Kentucky
Versailles Rd
Frankfort, KY 40601

Louisiana
Box 3988
Baton Rouge, LA 70821

Maine
477 Congress St.
Portland, ME 04111

Maryland
60 West St.
Annapolis, MD 21401

Michigan
501 South Capitol Ave.
Lansing, MI 48933

Minnesota
480 Cedar St.
St Paul, MN 55101

Mississippi
Box 1849
Jackson, MS 39205

Missouri
400 East High St.
Jefferson City, MO 65101

Montana
110 Neil Ave.
Helena, MT 59601

Nebraska
424 Terminal Building
Lincoln, NE 68508

Nevada
Box 3499
Reno, NV 89505

New Hampshire
57 Market St.
Manchester, NH 03101

New Jersey
5 Commerce St.
Newark, NJ 07102

New Mexico
Box 1395
Gallup, NM 87301

New York
150 State St.
Albany, NY 12207

North Dakota
Box 2467
Fargo, ND 58102

Ohio
17 South High St.
Columbus, OH 43218

Oklahoma
4020 North Lincoln
  Building
Oklahoma City,
  OK 73105

Oregon
220 Cottage St. N.E.
Salem, OR 97301

Pennsylvania
222 North Third St.
Harrisburg, PA 17101

Rhode Island
206 Smith St.
Providence, RI 02908

South Carolina
1002 Calhoun St.
Columbia, SC 29201

South Dakota
Box 190
Pierre, SD 57501

Tennessee
505 Fesslers Lane
Nashville, TN 37201

Texas
1004 International Life
  Building
Austin, TX 78701

Vermont
Box 37
Montpelier, VT 05602

Virginia
611 East Franklin St.
Richmond, VA 23219

Washington
Box 658
Olympia, WA 98507

West Virginia
Box 2789
Charleston, WV 25330

Wisconsin
111 East Wisconsin Ave.
Milwaukee, WE 53202

Commonwealth of Puerto
  Rico
Box S3789
San Juan, PR 00904

U.S. Virgin Islands
St. Thomas & St. John
Box 324
St. Thomas, VI 00801

St Croix
17 Church St.
St Croix, VI 00820

TRADE ASSOCIATIONS

This is where the WHAT people can get information on specific businesses. Many of the national associations have state and regional groups. Check them out.

Antiques
National Association of Dealers in Antiques
7080 Old River Road. R.R.6
Rockford, IL 61103

Appliances
National Association of Retail Dealers of America
Two North Riverside Plaza
Chicago, IL 60606

Automobiles
National Automobile Dealers Association
8400 Westpark Dr.
McLean, VA 22101

Bakers
Retail Bakers of America
Presidential Building, Suite 250
6525 Belcrest Rd.
Hyattsville, MD 20782

Barbers & Beauticians
Associated Master Barbers and Beauticians of
    America
219 Greenwich Rd.
PO Box 17782
Charlotte, NC 28211

Bars
National Licensed Beverage Association
1025 Vermont Ave. NW
Suite 601
Washington, DC 20005

Beauty Culturists
National Beauty Culturists' League
25 Logan Circle, N.W.
Washington, DC 20005

Bicycles
National Bicycle Dealers Association
29023 Euclid Ave.
Wickliffe, OH 44092

Booksellers
American Booksellers Association
122 East 42nd St.
New York, NY 10017

Building Materials
Western Building Materials Association
PO Box 1699
Olumpia, WA 98507

Campgrounds
National Campground Owners Association
c/o W.G. Crumrin
Martinsville, IL 62442

Ceramics
National Ceramic Association
PO Box 39
Glen Burnie, MD 21061

Chimney Sweeps
Chimney Sweep Guild
PO Box 1176
Portland, ME 04104

Dairies
National Dairy Association
6300 North River Rd
Rosemont, IL 60018

Department Stores
National Retail Merchants Association
100 West 31st St.
New York, NY 10001

Druggists
National Association of Retail Druggists
1750 K St. N.W.
Washington, DC 20006

Florists
Florists Transworld Delivery Association
29000 Northwestern Highway
Southfield, MI 48037

Gas
National LP-Gas Association
1301 West 22nd St.
Oak Brook, IL 60521

Grocers
National Association of Retail Grocers of the
  United States
PO Box 17208
Washington, DC 20041

Hardware
National Retail Hardware Association
770 North High School Rd.
Indianapolis, IN 46224

Hobby Industry
Hobby Industry Association of America
319 East 54th St.
Elmwood Park, NJ 07407

Home Furnishings
National Home Furnishings Association
405 Merchandise Mart
Chicago, IL 60654

Hotel and Motel
American Hotel and Motel Association
888 Seventh Ave.
New York, NY 10019

Innkeeping
National Innkeeping Association
122 East High St.
Jefferson City, MO 65101

Jewelers
Retail Jewelers of America
1271 Ave. of the Americas
New York, NY 10020

Liquor Stores
National Liquor Stores Association
1025 Vermont Ave. N.W.
Suite 1104
Washington, DC 20005

Lumbermen
Northeastern Retail Lumbermen's Association
339 East Avenue
Rochester, NY 14604

Northwestern Lumbermen
7300 France Ave. South
Minneapolis, MN 55435

Marinas
National Marina Association
3711 Great Neck Court
Alexandria, VA 22309

Menswear
Menswear Retailers of America
390 National Press Building
Washington, DC 20045

Music
National Association of Music Merchants
35 East Wacker Dr.
Chicago, IL 60601

Recreation Vehicles
Recreation Vehicle Dealers Association of North
  America
3251 Old Lee Highway
Fairfax, VA 22030

Restaurants
National Restaurant Association
311 First Street, N.W.
Washington, DC 20001

Shoes
National Shoe Retailers Association
200 Madison Ave
New York, NY 10016

Skis
Ski Retailers International
717 North Michigan Ave.
Chicago, IL 60611

Sporting Goods
National Sporting Goods Association
717 North Michigan Ave.
Chicago, IL 60611

Television and Electronics
National Alliance of Television and Electronic
  Service
Associations
5906 South Troy St.
Chicago, IL 60629

Theaters
National Association of Theatre Owners
1500 Broadway
New York, NY 10036

Small Business Administration Field Offices

Alabama
908 South 20th St.
Birmingham AL 35205
205/254-1344

Alaska
Federal Building
701 C St. Box 67
Anchorage, AK 99513
907/217-4022

Box 14
101 12th Ave.
Fairbanks, AK 99701
907/452-0211

Arizona
3030 North Central Ave.
Suite 1201
Phoenix, AZ 85012
602/241-2200

301 West Congress St.
Federal Building Room 3V
Tucson, AZ 85701
602/792-6715

Arkansas
PO Box 1401
Little Rock, AK 72203
501/378-5871

California
1229 N St.
Fresno, CA 93712
209/487-5189

350 S. Figueroa St.
6th Floor
Los Angeles, CA 90071
213/688-2956

1515 Clay St.
Oakland CA 94612
414/273-7790

2800 Cottage Way
Room W2535
Sacramento, CA 95825
916/484-4726

* Regional Office
880 Front St.
Room 4-S-33
San Diego, CA 92188
714/293-5440

* 450 Golden Gate Ave.
PO Box 36044
San Francisco, CA 94102
415/556-7487

211 Main St.
4th Floor
San Francisco, CA 94105
415/556-2820

Fidelity Federal Building
2700 North Main St.
Santa Ana, CA 92701
714/547-5089

Colorado
*Executive Tower Building
1405 Curtis St.
22nd Floor
Denver, CO 80202
303/837-5763

721 19th St.
Room 407
Denver, CO 80202
303/837-2607

Connecticut
One Hartford Square W.
Hartford, CT 06106
603/224-4041

Delaware
844 King Street
Room 5207
Lockbox 16
Wilmington, DE 19801
302/573-6294

District of Columbia
111 18th St., NW
Sixth Floor
Washington, DC 20417
202/634-1818

Florida
400 West Bay St.
Room 261
PO Box 35067
Jacksonville, FL 32202
904/791-3782

2222 Ponce De Leon
Blvd.
5th Floor
Coral Gables, FL 33134
305/350-5521

700 Twiggs St.
Suite 607
Tampa, FL 33602
813/228-2594

701 Clematis St.
Room 229
West Palm Beach
FL 33402
305/659-7533

Georgia
* 1375 Peachtree St. NW
5th Floor
Atlanta, GA 30309
404/881-4943

1720 Peachtree St. NW
6th Floor
Atlanta, GA 30309
404/881-4325

Federal Building
52 North Main St.
Statesboro, GA 30458
912/489-8719

Guam
Pacific Daily News
Building
Room 508, Martyr and
Chara Sts.
Agena, GU 96910
671/477-8420

* *Regional Office*

Hawaii
300 Ala Moana
Room 2213
PO Box 50207
Honolulu, HI 96850
808/546-8950

Idaho
1005 Main St., 2nd Floor
Boise, ID 83702
208/334-1096

Illinois
219 South Dearborn St.
Room 438
Chicago, IL 60604
312/353-4528

Illinois National Bank Bldg.
1 North Old State
Capital Plaza
Springfield, IL 62701
217/492-4416

Indiana
501 E.Monroe St.
Suite 120
South Bend, IN 46601
219/232-8163

New Federal Building
5th Floor
575 N. Pennsylvania St.
Indianapolis, IN 46204
317/269-7272

Iowa
210 Walnut St.
Des Moines, IA 50309
515/284-4422

373 Collins Rd NE
Cedar Rapids, IA 52402
319/399-2571

Kansas
Main Place Bldg.
110 East Waterman St.
Wichita, KA 67202
316/267-6311

Kentucky
Federal Office Bldg.
PO Box 3517
Room 188
Louisville, KY 40201
502/582-5971

Louisiana
Ford-Fish Bldg.
1661 Canal St.
2nd Floor
New Orleans, LA 70112
504/589-6685

500 Fannin Street
Federal Bldg. &
Courthouse, Room 5 B04
Shreveport, LA 71101
318/226-5196

Maine
40 Western Ave.
Room 512
Augusta, ME 04330
207/622-6171

Maryland
8600 LaSalle Rd
Room 630
Towson, MD 21204
301/962-4392

Massachusetts
* 60 Batterymarch St.
10th Floor
Boston, MA 02110
617/223-2100

150 Causeway St.
10th Floor
Boston, MA 02114
617/223-2100

302 High Street
4th Floor
Holyoke, MA 01040
413/536-8770

Michigan
477 Michigan Ave,
McNamara Bldg.
Room 515
Detroit, MI 48226
313/226-6000

Don H. Bottum
   University Ctr.
540 W. Kaye Ave.
Marquette, MI 49885
906/225-1108

Minnesota
610 C-Butler Square
100 North 6th St.
Minneapolis, MN 55403
612/725-2928

Mississippi
Gulf National Life
   Insurance Bldg.
111 Fred Haise Blvd.
2nd Floor
Biloxi, MS 39530
601/435-3676

100 West Capitol St.
New Federal Bldg.
Suite 322
Jackson, MS 30201
601/969-4371

Missouri
* 911 Walnut St.
23rd Floor
Kansas City, MO 64106
816/374-3316

1150 Grand Ave.
5th Floor
Kansas City, MO 64106
816/374-5557

815 Olive St.
Room 242
St. Louis, MO 63101
314/425-6600

731 North Main
Sikeston, MO 63801
314/471-0223

309 North Jefferson
Springfield, MO 65806
417/864-7670

Montana
301 South Park Ave
Room 528,
Drawer 10054
Helena, MT 59601
406/446-5381

Nebraska
Empire State Building
19th & Farnum St.
Omaha, NE 68102
402/221-4691

New Jersey
1800 East Davis St.
Camden, NJ 08104
609/757-5183

970 Broad St.
Room 1635
Newark, NJ 07102
201/645-3683

New Mexico
Patio Plaza Building
5000 Marble Ave. NE
Albuquerque, NM 87110
505/766-3430

New York
99 Washington Ave.
Room 921
Albany, NY 12210
518/472-6300

111 West Huron St.
Room 1311
Buffalo, NY 14202
716/846-4301

180 Clemens Center
   Pkwy.
Room 412
Elmira, NY 14901
607/733-4686

35 Pinelaw Rd
Room 102 E.
Melville, NY 11747
515/454-0764

* 26 Federal Plaza
Room 29-118
New York, NY 10007
212/264-7772

26 Federal Plaza
Room 3100
New York, NY 10007
212/264-1766

100 State St.
Room 601
Rochester, NY 14614
716/263-6700

100 South Clinton St.
Room 1073
Federal Bldg.
Syracuse, NY 13260
315/423-5382

North Carolina
230 S. Tryon St.
Suite 700
Charlotte, NC 28202
704/371-6111

215 South Evans St.
Room 206
Greenville, NC 27834
919/752-3798

North Dakota
PO Box 3086
Fargo, ND 58102
701/237-5131

Ohio
1240 East 9th St.
Room 317
AJA Federal Bldg.
Cleveland, OH 44199
216/522-4194

85 Marconi Boulevard
Columbus, OH 43215
614/469-6860

550 Main St.
Room 5028
Cincinnati, OH 45202
513/684-2814

Oklahoma
200 NW 5th St.
Suite 670
Oklahoma City, OK 73102
405/231-4301

333 W. Fourth St.
Room 3104
Tulsa, OK 74103
918/581-7495

Oregon
1220 S.W. Third Ave.
Room 676
Federal Building
Portland, OR 97204
503/221-5209

Pennsylvania
* One Bala Cynwyd Plaza
231 St. Asaphs Rd.
Suite 640
West Lobby
Bala Cynwyd, PA 19004
215/596-5889

One Bala Cynwyd Plaza
231 St. Asaphs Rd
Suite 400
East Lobby
Bala Cynwyd, PA 19004

100 Chestnut St.
Room 309
Harrisburg, PA 17101
717/782-3840

1000 Liberty Ave.
Room 1401
Pittsburgh, PA 15222
412/644-2780

Penn Place
20 N. Pennsylvania Ave.
Wilkes-Barre, PA 18702
717/826-6497

Puerto Rico
Federal Building
Room 6991
Carlos Chardon Ave.
Hato Rey, PR 00919
809/753-4572

Rhode Island
40 Fountain St.
Providence, RI 02903
401/528-4586

South Carolina
1835 Assembly St.
3rd Floor
PO Box 2786
Columbia, SC 29201
803/765-5376

South Dakota
101 South Main Ave.
Suite 101
Sioux Falls, SD 57102
605/336-2980

Tennessee
Fidelity Bankers Bldg.
502 South Gay St.
Room 307
Knoxville, TN 37902
615/251-5881

211 Federal Office Bldg.
167 North Main St.
Memphis, TN 38103
901/521-3588

404 James Robertson
  Pkwy.
Suite 1012
Nashville, TN 37219
615/251-5881

Texas
Federal Building
Room 780
300 East 8th St.
Austin, TX 78701
512/397-5288

3105 Leopard St.
PO Box 9253
Corpus Christi,
  TX 78408
512/888-3331

* 1720 Regal Row
Room 230
Dallas, TX 75235
214/767-7643

1100 Commerce St.
Room 3C36
Dallas, TX 75242
214/767-0605

4100 Rio Bravo St.
Suite 300
Pershing W. Bldg.
El Paso, TX 79902
915/534-7586

222 E. Van Buren St.
Suite 500
Harlingen, TX 78550
512/423-4533

2525 Murthworth
#705
Houston, TX 77054
713/660-2409

1205 Texas Ave.
Room 712
Lubbock, TX 79401
806/762-7466

100 South Washington St.
Room G-12
Marshall, TX 75670
214/935-5257

727 E. Durango St.
Room A-513
Federal Bldg.
San Antonio, TX 78206
512/229-6260

Utah
125 South State Street
Room 2237
Salt Lake City, UT 84138
801/524-5800

Vermont
87 State St
Room 204
Montpelier, VT 05602
802/229-0538

Virginia
400 North 18th St
Room 3015
PO Box 10126
Richmond, VA 23240
804/771-2617

Virgin Islands
Veterans Drive
Room 283
St Thomas, VI 00801
809/774-8530

Washington
* 710 2nd Ave.
5th Floor
Seattle, WA 98104
206/442-5676

915 Second Ave.
Room 1744
Seattle, WA 98174
206/442-5534

651 U.S. Courthouse
PO Box 2167
Spokane, WA 99210
509/456-5310

West Virginia
109 North 3rd St.
Room 301
Clarksburg, WV 26301
304/623-5631

Charleston National Plaza
Suite 628
Charleston, WV 25301
304/343-6181

Wisconsin
500 South Barstow St.
Room 89AA
Eau Claire, WI 54701
715/834-9012

212 E. Washington Ave.
Room 213
Madison, WI 53703
608/264-5205

517 E. Wisconsin Ave.
Room 246
Milwaukee, WI 53202
414/291-3941

Wyoming
PO Box 2839
Casper, WY 82602
307/265-5550

Regional Office

SBA DEVELOPMENT CENTERS

University of Arkansas, Little Rock, AR 72203
501/371-1971

California State University, Chico, CA 95929
916/895-5938

California State Polytechnic University, Pomona,
 CA 91768
714/598-4210

University of West Florida, Pensacola, FL 32504
904/476-9500 ext. 425

University of Georgia, Athens, GA 30602
404/542-5760

University of Maine, Portland, ME 04103
207/780-4420

St. Cloud State University, St. Cloud, MN 56301
612/255-3214

University of Missouri, St. Louis, MO 63121
314/553-5621

University of Nebraska, Omaha, NB 68182
402/554-2521

Rutgers University, Newark, NJ 07102
201/648-5627

The Wharton School, University of Pennsylvania,
 Philadelphia, PA 19104
215/243-4856

University of South Carolina, Columbia, SC 29208
803/777-5118

University of Utah, Salt Lake City, UT 84112
801/581-7458

Washington State University, Pullman, WA 99164
509/335-1576

University of Wisconsin, Madison, WI 53706
608/263-7794

Howard University, Washington, DC 20059
202/636-7178

GLOSSARY OF REAL ESTATE TERMS

These are some of the words and phrases used by people whose business it is to buy and sell real estate. They're from the *Real Estate Salesperson's Law Booklet* published by the Division of Licensing Services, Department of State, State of New York.

Abstract of Title—A summary of all of the recorded instruments and proceedings that affect the title to property, arranged in the order in which they were recorded.

Accretion—The addition of land through processes of nature, as by streams or wind.

Accrued Interest—Accrue: to grow; to be added to. Accrued interest is interest that has been earned but not due and payable.

Acknowledgment—A formal declaration before a duly authorized officer by a person who has executed an instrument that such execution is the person's act and deed.

Acquisition—An act or process by which a person procures property.

Acre—A measure of land equaling 160 square rods or 4,840 square yards or 43,560 square feet.

Adjacent—Lying near to but not necessarily in actual contact with.

Adjoining—Contiguous; attaching, in actual contact with.

Administrator—A person appointed by court to administer the estate of a deceased person who left no will; i.e., who died intestate.

Ad Valorem—According to valuation.

Adverse Possession—A means of acquiring title where an occupant has been in actual, open, notorious, exclusive, and continuous occupancy of property under a claim of right for the required statutory period.

Affidavit—A statement of declaration reduced to writing and sworn to or affirmed before some officer who is authorized to administer an oath of affirmation.

Affirm—To confirm, to ratify, to verify.

Agency—That relationship between principal and agent that arises out of a contract either expressed or implied, written or oral, wherein an agent is employed by a person to do certain acts on the person's behalf in dealing with a third party.

Agent—One who undertakes to transact some business or to manage some affair for another by authority of the latter.

Agreement of Sale—A written agreement between seller and purchaser in which the purchaser agrees to buy certain real estate and the seller agrees to sell upon terms and conditions set forth therein.

Alienation—A transferring of property to another; the transfer of property and possession of lands, or other things, from one person to another.

Amortization—A gradual paying off of a debt by periodical installments.

Apportionments—Adjustment of the income, expenses, or carrying charges of real estate usually computed to the date of closing of title so that the seller pays all expenses to that date. The buyer assumes all expenses commencing the date the deed is conveyed to the buyer.

Appraisal—An estimate of property's valuation by an appraiser who is usually presumed to be expert in this work.

Appraisal by Capitalization—An estimate of value by capitalization of productivity and income.

Appraisal by Comparison—Comparability with the sale prices of other similar properties.

Appraisal by Summation—Adding together all parts of a property separately appraised to form a whole; e.g., value of the land considered as vacant added to the cost of reproduction of the building, less depreciation.

Appurtenance—Something which is outside the property itself but belongs to the land and adds to its greater enjoyment such as a right of way or a barn or a dwelling.

Assessed Valuation—A valuation placed upon property by a public officer or a board, as a basis for taxation.

Assessment—A charge against real estate made by a unit of government to cover a proportionate cost of an improvement such as a street or sewer.

Assessor—An official who has the responsibility of determining assessed values.

Assignee—The person to whom an agreement or contract is assigned.

Assignment—The method or manner by which a right, a specialty, or contract is transferred from one person to another.

Assignor—A party who assigns or transfers an agreement or contract to another.

Assumption of Mortgage—The taking of title to property by a grantee, wherein the grantee assumes liability for payment of an existing note or bond secured by a mortgage against a property and becomes personally liable for the payment of such mortgage debt.

Attest—To witness to; to witness by observation and signature.

Avulsion—The removal of land from one owner to another, when a stream suddenly changes its channel.

Beneficiary—The person who receives or is to receive the benefits resulting from certain acts.

Bequeath—To give or hand down by will; to leave by will.

Bequest—That which is given by the terms of a will.

Bill of Sale—A written instrument given to pass title of personal property from vendor to vendee.

Binder—An agreement to cover the down payment for the purchase of real estate as evidence of good faith on the part of the purchaser.

Blanket Mortgage—A single mortgage that covers more than one piece of real estate.

Bona Fide—In good faith, without fraud.

Bond—The evidence of a personal debt that is secured by a mortgage or other lien on real estate.

Building Codes—Regulations established by local governments stating fully the structural requirements for building.

Building Line—A line fixed at a certain distance from the front and/or sides of a lot, beyond which no building can project.

Building Loan Agreement—An agreement whereby the lender advances money to an owner with provisional payments at certain stages of construction.

Cancellation Clause—A provision in a lease that confers upon one or more or all of the parties to the lease the right to terminate the party's or parties' obligations thereunder upon the occurrence of the condition or contingency set forth in the clause.

Caveat Emptor—Let the buyer beware. The buyer must examine the goods or property and buy at the buyer's own risk.

Cease and Desist Order—An order executed by the secretary of state directing broker recipients to cease and desist from all solicitation of homeowners whose names and addresses appear on the list(s) forwarded with such order. The order acknowledges petition filings by homeowners listed evidencing their premises are not for sale, thereby revoking the implied invitation to solicit. The issuance of a cease and desist order does not prevent an owner from selling or listing his premises for sale. It prohibits soliciting by licensees served with such order and subjects violators to penalties or suspension or revocation of their licenses.

Cease and Desist Petition—A statement filed by a homeowner showing address of premises owned which notifies the department of state that such premises are not for sale and that he does not wish to be solicited. In so doing, petitioner revokes the implied invitation to be solicited by any means with respect thereto, by licensed real estate brokers and salespersons.

Certiorari—A proceeding to review in a competent court the action of an inferior tribunal board of officer exercising judicial functions.

Chain of Title—A history of conveyances and encumbrances affecting a title from the time the original patent was granted, or as far back as records are available.

Chattel—Personal property, such as household goods or fixtures.

Chattel Mortgage—A mortgage on personal property.

Client—The one by whom a broker is employed and by whom the broker will be compensated on completion of the purpose of the agency.

Closing Date—The date upon which the buyer takes over the property; usually between 30 and 60 days after the signing of the contract.

Cloud on the Title—An outstanding claim or encumbrance that, if valid, would affect or impair the owner's title.

Collateral—Additional security pledged for the payment of an obligation.

Color of Title—That which appears to be good title, but which is not title in fact.

Commission—A sum due a real estate broker for services in that capacity.

Commitment—A pledge or a promise or affirmation agreement.

Condemnation—Taking private property for public use, with fair compensation to the owner; exercising the right of eminent domain.

Conditional Sales Contract—A contract for the sale of property stating that delivery is to be made to the buyer, title to remain vested in the seller until the conditions of the contract have been fulfilled.

Consideration—Anything of value given to induce entering into a contract; it may be money, personal services, or even love and affection.

Constructive Notice—Information or knowledge of a fact imputed by law to a person because the person could have discovered the fact by proper diligence and inquiry (public records).

Contract—An agreement between competent parties to do or not to do certain things for a legal consideration, whereby each party acquires a right to what the other possesses.

Conversion—Change from one character or use to another.

Conveyance—The transfer of the title of land from one to another. The means or medium by which title of real estate is transferred.

County Clerk's Certificate—When an acknowledgment is taken by an officer not authorized in the state or county where the document is to be recorded, the instrument that must be attached to the acknowledgment is called a county clerk's certificate. It is given by the clerk of the county where the officer obtained his/her authority and certifies to the officer's signature and powers.

Covenants—Agreements written into deeds and other instruments promising performance or nonperformance of certain acts, or stipulating certain uses or nonuses of the property.

Cul-de-sac—A blind alley; a street with only one outlet.

Damages—The indemnity recoverable by a person who has sustained an injury, either to his/her person, property, or relative rights, through the act or default of another.

Decedent—One who is dead.

Decree—Order issued by one in authority, an edict or law; a judicial decision.

Dedication—A grant and appropriation of land by its owner for some public use, accepted for such use, by an authorized public official on behalf of the public.

Deed—An instrument in writing duly executed and delivered, that conveys title to real property.

Deed Restriction—An imposed restriction in a deed for the purpose of limiting the use of the land such as:
1. A restriction against the sale of liquor thereon.
2. A restriction as to the size, type, value, or placement of improvements that may be erected thereon.

Default—Failure to fulfill a duty or promise, or to discharge an obligation; omission or failure to perform any acts.

Defendant—The party sued or called to answer in any suit, civil or criminal, at law or in equity.

Deficiency Judgement—A judgment given when the security for a loan does not entirely satisfy the debt upon its default.

Delivery—The transfer of the possession of a thing from one person to another.

Demising Clause—A clause found in a lease whereby the landlord (lessor) leases and the tenant (lessee) takes property.

Depreciation—Loss of value in real property brought about by age, physical deterioration, or functional or economic obsolescence.

Descent—When an owner of real estate dies intestate, the owner's property descents, by operation of law, to the owner's distributees.

Devise—A gift of real estate by will or last testament.

Devisee—One who receives a bequest of real estate made by will.

Devisor—One who bequeaths real estage by will.

Directional Growth—The location or direction toward which the residential sections of a city are destined or determined to grow.

Dispossess Proceedings—Summary process by a landlord to oust a tenant and regain possession of the premises for nonpayment of rent or other breach of conditions of the lease or occupancy.

Distributee—Person receiving or entitled to receive land as representative of the former owner.

Documentary Evidence—Evidence in the form of written or printed papers.

Duress—Unlawful constraint exercised upon a person whereby the person is forced to do some act against the person's will.

Earnest Money—Down payment made by a purchaser of real estate as evidence of good faith.

Easement—A right that may be exercised by the public or individuals on, over, and through the lands of others.

Ejectment—A form of action to regain possession of real property, with damages for the unlawful retention; used when there is no relationship of landlord and tenant.

Eminent Domain—A right of the government to acquire property for necessary public use by condemnation; the owner must be fairly compensated.

Encroachment—A building, part of a building, or obstruction that intrudes upon or invades a highway or sidewalk or trespasses upon the property of another.

Encumbrance—Any right to or interest in land that diminishes its value. (Also Incumbrance)

Endorsement—An act of signing one's name on the back of a check or note, with or without further qualifications.

Equity—The interest or value that the owner has in real estate over and above the liens against it.

Equity of Redemption—A right of the owner to reclaim property before it is sold through foreclosure proceedings, by the payment of the debt, interest, and costs.

Erosion—The wearing away of land through processes of nature, as by streams and winds.

Escheat—The reversion to the state of property in event the owner therof dies, without leaving a will, and has no distributees to whom the property may pass by lawful descent.

Escrow—A written agreement between two or more parties providing that certain instruments or property be placed with a third party to be delivered to a designated person upon the fulfillment or performance of some act or condition.

Estate—The degree, quantity, nature, and extent of interest that a person has in real property.

Estate of Life—An estate or interest held during the terms of some certain person's life.

Estate in Reversion—The residue of an estate left for the grantor, to commence in possession after the termination of some particular estate granted by the grantor.

Estate at Will—The occupation of lands and tenements by a tenant for an indefinite period, terminable by one or both parties at will

Estoppel Certificate—An instrument executed by the mortgagor setting forth the present status and the balance due on the mortgage as of the date of the execution of the certificate.

Eviction—A legal proceeding by a lessor landlord to recover possession of real property.

Eviction, Actual—Where one is either by force or by process of law, actually put out of possession.

Eviction, Constructive—Any disturbance of the tenant's possessions by the landlord whereby the premises are rendered unfit or unsuitable for the purpose for which they were leased.

Eviction, Partial—Where the possessor of the premises is deprived of a portion thereof.

Exclusive Agency—An agreement of employment of a broker to the exclusion of all other brokers; if sale is made by any other broker during term of employment, broker holding exclusive agency is entitled to commissions in addition to the commissions payable to the broker who effected the transaction.

Exclusive Right to Sell—An agreement of employment by a broker under which the exclusive right to sell for a specified period is granted to the broker; if a sale during the term of the agreement is made by the owner or by an other broker, the broker holding such exclusive right to sell is nevertheless entitled to compensation.

Executor—A male person or a corporate entity or any other type of organization named or designated in a will to carry out its provisions as to the disposition of the estate of a deceased person.

Executrix—A woman appointed to perform the duties similar to those of an executor.

Extention Agreement—An agreement which extends the life of a mortgage to a later date.

Fee; Fee Simple; Fee Absolute—Absolute ownership of real property; a person has this type of estate where the person is entitled to the entire property with unconditional power of disposition during the person's life and descending to the person's distributees and legal representatives upon the person's death intestate.

Fiduciary—A person who on behalf of or for the benefit of another transacts business or handles money or property not the person's own; such relationship implies great confidence and trust.

Fixtures—Personal property so attached to the land or improvements as to become part of the real property.

Foreclosure—A procedure whereby property pledged as security for a debt is sold to pay the debt in the event of default in payments or terms.

Forfeiture—Loss of money or anything of value, by way of penalty due to failure to perform.

Front Foot—Property measurement for sale or valuation purposes; the property measures by the "front foot" on its street line, each "front foot" extending the depth of the lot.

Grace Period—Additional time allowed to perform an act or make a payment before a default occurs.

Graduated Leases—A lease that provides for a graduated change at stated intervals in the amount of the rent to be paid; used largely in long-term leases.

Grant—A technical term used in deeds of conveyance of lands to indicate a transfer.

Grantee—The party to whom the title to real property is conveyed.

Grantor—The person who conveys real estate by deed; the seller.

Gross Income—Total income from property before any expenses are deducted.

Gross Lease—A lease of property whereby the lessor is to meet all property changes regularly incurred through ownership.

Ground Rent—Earnings of improved property credited to earning of the ground itself after allowance made for earnings of improvements.

Habendum Clause—The "To Have and To Hold" clause that defines or limits the quantity of the estate granted in the premises of the deed.

Hereditaments—The largest classification of property; including lands, tenements, and incorporeal property, such as rights of way.

Holdover Tenant—A tenant who remains in possession of leased property after the expiration of the lease term.

Hypothecate—To give a thing as security without the necessity of giving up possession of it.

In Rem—A proceeding against the realty directly; as distinguished from a proceeding against a person. (Used in taking land for nonpayment of taxes, etc.)

Incompetent—A person who is unable to manage his/her own affairs by reason of insanity, imbecility, or feeble-mindedness.

Incumbrance—Any right to or interest in land that diminishes its value. (Also Encumbrance)

Injunction—A writ or order issued under the seal of a court to one or more parties to a suit or proceeding from doing an act that is deemed to be inequitable or unjust in regard to the rights of some other party or parties in the suit or proceeding.

Installments—Parts of the same debt, payable at successive periods as agreed; payments made to reduce a mortgage.

Instrument—A written legal document; created to effect the rights of the parties.

Interest Rate—The percentage of a sum of money charged for its use.

Intestate—A person who dies having made no will, or leaves one which is defective in form, in which case the person's estate descends to the person's distributees.

Involuntary Lien—A lien imposed against property without consent of the owner, i.e., taxes, special assessments.

Irrevocable—Incapable of being recalled or revoked; unchangeable; unalterable.

Jeopardy—Peril, danger.

Joint Tenancy—Ownership of realty by two or more persons, each of whom has an undivided interest with the "right of survivorship."

Judgment—Decree of a court declaring that one individual is indebted to another, and fixing the amount of such indebtedness.

Junior Mortgage—A mortgage second in lien to a previous mortgage.

Laches—Delay or negligence in asserting one's legal rights.

Land, Tenements, and Hereditaments—A phrase used in the early English Law, to express all sorts of property of the immovable class.

Landlord—One who rents property to another.

Lease—A contract whereby, for a consideration, usually termed rent, one who is entitled to the possession of real property transfers such rights to another for life, for a term of years, or at will.

Leasehold—The interest or estate which a lessee of real estate has therein by virtue of the lessee's lease.

Lessee—A person to whom property is rented under a lease.

Lessor—One who rents property to another under a lease.

Lien—A legal right or claim upon a specific property that attaches to the property until a debt is satisfied.

Life Estate—The conveyance of title to property for the duration of the life of the grantee.

Life Tenant—The holder of a life estate.

Lis Pendens—A legal document, filed in the office of the county clerk, giving notice that an action or proceeding is pending in the courts affecting the title to the property.

Listing—An employment contract between principal and agent, authorizing the agent to perform services for the principal involving the latter's property.

Litigation—The act of carrying on a lawsuit.

Mandatory—Requiring strict confirmity or obedience.

Market Value—The highest price that a buyer, willing but not compelled to buy, would pay, and the lowest a seller, willing but not compelled to sell, would accept.

Marketable Title—A title that a court of equity considers to be so free from defect that it will enforce its acceptance by a purchaser.

Mechanic's Lien—A lien given by law upon a building or other improvement upon land, and upon the land itself, to secure the price of labor done upon, and materials furnished for, the improvement.

Meeting of the Minds—Whenever all parties to a contract agree to the exact terms thereof.

Metes and Bounds—A term used in describing the boundary lines of land, setting forth all the boundary lines together with their terminal points and angles.

Minor—A person under an age specified by law; under 18 years of age.

Monument—A fixed object and point established by surveyors to establish land locations.

Moratorium—An emergency act by a legislative body to suspend the legal enforcement of contractual obligations.

Mortgage—An instrument in writing, duly executed and delivered, that creates a lien upon real estate as security for the payment of a specified debt, which is usually in the form of a bond.

Mortgage Commitment—A formal indication, by a lending institution that it will grant a mortgage loan on property in a certain specified amount and on certain specified terms.

Mortgage Reduction Certificate—An instrument executed by the mortgagee, setting forth the present status and the balance due on the mortgage as of the date of the execution of the instrument.

Mortgagee—The party who lends money and takes a mortgage to secure the payment thereof.

Mortgagor—A person who borrows money and gives a mortgage on the person's property as security for the payment of the debt.

Multiple Listing—An arrangement among Real Estate Board of Exchange Members, whereby each broker presents the broker's listings to the attention of the other members so that if a sale results, the commission is divided between the broker bringing the listing and the broker making the sale.

Net Listing—A price below which an owner will not sell the property, and at which price a broker will not receive a commission; the broker receives the excess over and above the net listing as the broker's commission.

Notary Public—A public officer who is authorized to take acknowledgments to certain classes of documents, such as deeds, contracts, mortgages, and before whom affidavits may be sworn.

Obligee—The person in whose favor an obligation is entered into.

Obligor—The person who binds himself/herself to another; one who has engaged to perform some obligation; one who makes a bond.

Obsolescence—Loss in value due to reduced desirability and usefulness of a structure because its design and construction become obsolete; loss because of becoming old-fashioned, and not in keeping with modern means, with consequent loss of income.

Open Listing—A listing given to any number of brokers without liability to compensate any except the one who first secures a buyer ready, willing and able to meet the terms of the listing, or secures the acceptance by the seller of a satisfactory offer; the sale of the property automatically terminates the listing.

Open Mortgage—A mortgage that has matured or is overdue and; therefore, is "open" to foreclosure at any time.

Option—A right given for a consideration to purchase or lease a property upon specified terms within a specified time; if the right is not exercised the option holder is not subject to liability for damages; if exercised, the grantor of option must perform.

Partition—The division that is made of real property between those who own it in undivided shares.

Party Wall—A party wall is a wall built along the line separating two properties, partly on each, which wall either owner, the owner's heirs and assigns has the right to use; such right constituting an easement over so much of the adjoining owner's land as is covered by the wall.

Percentage Lease—A lease of property in which the rental is based upon the percentage of the volume of sales made upon the leased premises, usually providing for minimum rental.

Personal Property—Any property that is not real property.

Plat Book—A public record containing maps of land showing the division of such land into streets, blocks, and lots and indicating the measurements of the individual parcels.

Plottage—Increment in unity value of a plot of land created by assembling smaller ownerships into one ownership.

Police Power—The right of any political body to enact laws and enforce them, for the order, safety, health, morals, and general welfare of the public.

Power of Attorney—A written instrument duly signed and executed by an owner of property, that authorizes an agent to act on behalf of the owner to the extent indicated in the instrument.

Premises—Lands and tenements; an estate; the subject matter of a conveyance.

Prepayment Clause—A clause in a mortgage that gives a mortgagor the privilege of paying the mortgage indebtedness before it becomes due.

Principal—The employer of an agent or broker; the broker's or agent's client.

Probate—To establish the will of a deceased person.

Purchase Money Mortgage—A mortgage given by a grantee in part payment of the purchase price of real estate.

Quiet Enjoyment—The right of an owner or a person legally in possession to the use of property without interference of possession.

Quiet Title Suit—A suit in court to remove a defect, cloud, or suspicion regarding legal rights of an owner to retain a parcel of real property.

Quitclaim Deed—A deed that conveys simply the grantor's rights or interest in real estate, without any agreement or covenant as to the nature or extent of that interest, or any other covenants; usually used to remove a cloud from the title.

Real Estate Board—An organization whose members consist primarily of real estate brokers and salespersons.

Real Property—Land, and generally whatever is erected upon or affixed thereto.

Realtor—A coined word which may only be used by an active member of a local real estate board affiliated with the National Association of Real Estate Boards.

Recording—The act of writing or entering in a book of public record instruments affecting the title to real property.

Redemption—The right of a mortgagor to redeem the property by paying a debt after the expiration date and before sale at foreclosure; the right of an owner to reclaim the owner's property after the sale of taxes.

Release—The act or writing by which some claim or interest is surrendered to another.

Release Clause—A clause found in a blanket mortgage that gives the owner of the property the privilege of paying off a portion of the mortgage indebtedness, and thus freeing a portion of the property from the mortgage.

Rem—(See In Rem)

Remainder—An estate that takes effect after the termination of a prior estate, such as a life estate.

Remainderman—The person who is to receive the property after the death of a life tenant.

Rent—The compensation paid for the use of real estate.

Reproduction Cost—Normal cost of exact duplication of a property as of a certain date.

Restriction—A limitation placed upon the use of property contained in the deed or other written instruments in the chain of title.

Reversionary Interest—The interest that a person has in lands or other property upon the termination of the preceding estate.

Revocation—An act of recalling a power of authority conferred, as the revocation of a power of attorney, a license, an agency, etc.

Right of Survivorship—Right of the surviving joint owner to succeed to the interests of the deceased joint owner, distinguishing feature of a joint tenancy or tenancy by the entirety.

Right-of-Way—The right to pass over another's land more or less frequently according to the nature of the easement.

Riparian Owner—One who owns land bounding upon a river or watercourse.

Riparian Rights—The right of a landowner to water on, under, or adjacent to the landowner's land.

Sales Contract—A contract by which the buyer and seller agree to terms of sale.

Satisfaction Piece—An instrument for recording and acknowledging payment of an indebtedness secured by a mortgage.

Seizin—The possession of land by one who claims to own at least an estate for life therein.

Setback—The distance from the curb or other established line, within which no buildings may be erected.

Special Assessment—An assessment made against a property to pay for a public improvement by which the assessed property is supposed to be especially benefited.

Specific Performance—A remedy in a court of equity compelling a defendant to carry out the terms of an agreement or contract.

Statute—A law established by an act of the legislature.

Statute of Frauds—State law that provides that certain contracts must be in writing in order to be enforceable at law.

Stipulation—The terms within a written contract.

Straight Line Depreciation—A definite sum set aside annually from income to pay costs of replacing and improvements, without reference to the interest the sum would earn.

Subdivision—A tract of land divided into lots or plots suitable for home building purposes.

Subletting—A leasing by a tenant to another, who holds a lease under the tenant.

Subordination Clause—A clause that permits the placing of a mortgage at a later date that takes priority over an existing mortgage.

Subscribing Witness—One who writes his/her name as a witness to the execution of an instrument.

Surety—One who guarantees the performance of another; guarantor.

Surrender—The cancellation of a lease by mutual consent of the lessor and the lessee.

Surrogate's Court (Probate Court)—A court having jurisdiction over the proof of wills, the settling of estates, and of citations.

Survey—The process by which a parcel of land is measured and its area ascertained; also, the blueprint showing the measurements, boundaries, and area.

Tax Sale—Sale of property after a period of nonpayment of taxes.

Tenancy in Common—An ownership of realty by two or more persons, each of whom has an undivided interest, without the "right of survivorship."

Tenancy by the Entirety—An estate which exists only between husband and wife with equal right of possession and enjoyment during their joint lives and with the "right of survivorship."

Tenancy at Will—A license to use or occupy lands and tenements at the will of the owner.

Tenant—One who is given possession of real estate for a fixed period or at will.

Tenant at Sufferance—One who comes into possession of lands by lawful title and keeps it afterwards without any title at all.

Testate—Where a person dies leaving a valid will.

Title—Evidence that owner of land is in lawful possession thereof; evidence of ownership.

Title Insurance—A policy of insurance that indemnifies the holder for any loss sustained by reason of defects in the title.

Title Search—An examination of the public records to determine the ownership and encumbrances affecting real property.

Torrens Title—System of title records provided by state law; it is a system for the registration of land titles whereby the state of the title, showing ownership and encumbrances, can be readily ascertained from an inspection of the "register of titles" without the necessity of a search of the public records.

Tort—A wrongful act, wrong, injury; violation of a legal right.

Transfer Tax—A tax charged under certain conditions on the property belonging to an estate.

Unearned Increment—An increase in value of real estate due to no effort on the part of the owner; often due to increase in population.

Urban Property—City property; closely settled property.

Usury—On a loan, claiming a rate of interest greater than that permitted by law.

Valid—Having force, or binding force; legally sufficient and authorized by law.

Valuation—Estimated worth or price. The act of valuing by appraisal.

Vendee's Lien—A lien against property under contract of sale to secure deposit paid by a purchaser.

Verification—Sworn statements before a duly qualified officer to the correctness of the contents of an instrument.

Violations—Acts, deeds, or conditions contrary to law or permissible use of real property.

Void—To have no force or effect; that which is unenforceable.

Voidable—That which is capable of being adjudged void, but is not void unless action is taken to make it so.

Waiver—The renunciation, abandonment, or surrender of some claim, right, or privilege.

Warranty Deed—A conveyance of land in which the grantor warrants the title to the grantee.

Will—The disposition of one's property to take effect after death.

Without Recourse—Words used in endorsing a note or bill to denote that the future holder is not to look to the endorser in case of nonpayment.

Zone—An area set off by the proper authorities for specific use; subject to certain restrictions or restraints.

Zoning Ordinance—Act of city or county or other authorities specifying type and use to which property may be put in specific areas.

READING LIST

The Bank of America publishes the *Small Business Reporter* series covering business operations, business profiles, and professional management. The books are

Business Operations

How to Buy or Sell a Business
Franchising
Management Succession
Crime Prevention for Small Business
Advertising Small Business
Cash Flow Cash Management
Equipment Leasing
Personnel Guidelines
Understanding Financial Statements
Steps to Starting a Business
Financing Small Business
Beating the Cash Crisis

Business Profiles

Home Furnishings Stores
Health Food Stores
Bookstores
Mail Order Enterprises
Bars and Cocktail Lounges
Sewing and Needlecraft Centers
Apparel Stores
Restaurant and Food Services
Hairgrooming/Beauty Salons
Auto Supply Stores
Property Management
Building Contractors
Coin-Operated Laundries
General Job Printing
Gift Stores
The Handcrafts Business

based on California situations, but much of the material applies to businesses anywhere. Titles presently available ($2.00 each) are:

Professional Management

Establishing an Accounting Practice
Establishing a Dental Practice
Establishing a Veterinary Practice

You'd better check with the Bank of America, Department 3120, Box 37000, San Francisco, CA 94137 to see what's currently available. They add subjects—and drop some—periodically.

SBS Publications
These are the publications currently available from the SBA:

Free Publications

The **MANAGEMENT AIDS** (MA's) recommend methods and techniques for handling management problems and business operations.

SMALL BUSINESS BIBLIOGRAPHIES (SBB's) list key reference sources for many business management topics.

STARTING OUT SERIES (SOS's) are one-page fact sheets describing financial and operating requirements for selected manufacturing, retail, and service businesses.

MANAGEMENT AIDS

Financial Management and Analysis

MA	1.001	*The ABC's of Borrowing*
MA	1.002	*What Is the Best Selling Price?*
MA	1.003	*Keep Pointed toward Profit*
MA	1.004	*Basic Budgets for Profit Planning*
MA	1.005	*Pricing for Small Manufacturers*
MA	1.006	*Cash Flow in a Small Plant*
MA	1.007	*Credit and Collections*
MA	1.008	*Attacking Business Decision Problems with Breakeven Analysis*
MA	1.009	*A Venture Capital Primer for Small Business*
MA	1.010	*Accounting Services for Small Service Firms*
MA	1.011	*Analyze Your Records to Reduce Costs*
MA	1.012	*Profit by Your Wholesalers' Services*
MA	1.013	*Steps in Meeting Your Tax Obligations*
MA	1.014	*Getting the Facts for Income Tax Reporting*
MA	1.015	*Budgeting in a Small Business Firm*
MA	1.016	*Sound Cash Management and Borrowing*
MA	1.017	*Keeping Records in Small Business*
MA	1.018	*Check List for Profit Watching*
MA	1.019	*Simple Breakeven Analysis for Small Stores*
MA	1.020	*Profit Pricing and Costing for Services*

Planning

MA	2.002	*Locating or Relocating Your Business*
MA	2.004	*Problems in Managing a Family-Owned Business*
MA	2.005	*The Equipment Replacement Decision*
MA	2.006	*Finding a New Product for Your Company*
MA	2.007	*Business Plan for Small Manufacturers*
MA	2.008	*Business Plan for Small Construction Firms*
MA	2.009	*Business Life Insurance*
MA	2.010	*Planning and Goal Setting for Small Business*
MA	2.011	*Fixing Production Mistakes*
MA	2.012	*Setting up a Quality Control System*
MA	2.013	*Can You Make Money with Your Idea or Invention?*
MA	2.014	*Can You Lease or Buy Equipment?*
MA	2.015	*Can You Use a Minicomputer?*
MA	2.016	*Check List for Going into Business*
MA	2.017	*Factors in Considering a Shopping Center*
MA	2.018	*Insurance Checklist for Small Business*
MA	2.019	*Computers for Small Business—Service Bureau or Time Sharing*
MA	2.020	*Business Plan for Retailers*
MA	2.021	*Using a Traffic Study to Select a Retail Site*
MA	2.022	*Business Plan for Small Service Firms*
MA	2.024	*Store Location: "Little Things" Mean a Lot*
MA	2.025	*Thinking About Going into Business?*

General Management and Administration

MA	3.001	*Delegating Work and Responsibility*
MA	3.002	*Management Checklist for a Family Business*
MA	3.004	*Preventing Retail Theft*
MA	3.005	*Stock Control for Small Stores*
MA	3.006	*Reducing Shoplifting Losses*
MA	3.007	*Preventing Burglary and Robbery Loss*
MA	3.008	*Outwitting Bad-Check Passers*
MA	3.009	*Preventing Embezzlement*

Marketing

MA	4.003	*Measuring Sales Force Performance*
MA	4.005	*Is the Independent Sales Agent for You?*
MA	4.007	*Selling Products on Consignment*
MA	4.008	*Tips on Getting More for Your Marketing Dollar*
MA	4.010	*Developing New Accounts*
MA	4.012	*Marketing Checklist for Small Retailers*
MA	4.013	*A Pricing Checklist for Small Retailers*
MA	4.014	*Improving Personal Selling in Small Retail Stores*
MA	4.015	*Advertising Guidelines for Small Retail Firms*
MA	4.016	*Signs in Your Business*
MA	4.018	*Plan Your Advertising Budget*
MA	4.019	*Learning about Your Market*
MA	4.020	*Do You Know the Results of Your Advertising?*

Organization and Personnel

MA 5.001   *Checklist for Developing a Training Program*
MA 5.004   *Pointers on Using Temporary-Help Services*
MA 5.005   *Preventing Employee Pilferage*
MA 5.006   *Setting up a Pay System*
MA 5.007   *Staffing Your Store*
MA 5.008   *Managing Employee Benefits*

Legal and Governmental Affairs

MA 6.003   *Incorporating a Small Business*
MA 6.004   *Selecting the Legal Structure for Your Business*
MA 6.005   *Introduction to Patents*

Miscellaneous

MA 7.002   *Association Services for Small Business*
MA 237   *Market Overseas with U.S. Government Help*

SMALL BUSINESS BIBLIOGRAPHIES

1. *Handcrafts*
2. *Home Businesses*
3. *Selling by Mail Order*
9. *Marketing Research Procedures*
10. *Retailing*
12. *Statistics and Maps for National Market Analysis*
13. *National Directory for Use in Marketing*
15. *Recordkeeping Systems—Small Store and Service Trade*
18. *Basic Library Reference Sources*
20 *Advertising—Retail Store*
31. *Retail Credit and Collection*
37. *Buying for Retail Stores*
72. *Personnel Management*
75. *Inventory Management*
85. *Purchasing for Owners of Small Plants*
86. *Training for Small Business*
87. *Financial Management*
88. *Manufacturing Management*
89. *Marketing for Small Business*
90. *New Product Development*
91. *Ideas into Dollars*

STARTING OUT SERIES

0101 *Building Service Contracting*
0104 *Radio-Television Repair Shop*
0105 *Retail Florists*
0106 *Franchised Businesses*
0107 *Hardware Store or Home Centers*
0111 *Sporting Goods Store*
0112 *Drycleaning*
0114 *Cosmetology*
0115 *Pest Control*
0116 *Marine Retailers*
0117 *Retail Grocery Stores*
0122 *Apparel Store*
0123 *Pharmacies*
0125 *Office Products*
0129 *Interior Design Services*
0130 *Fish Farming*
0133 *Bicycles*
0134 *Roofing Contractors*
0135 *Printing*
0137 *The Bookstore*
0138 *Home Furnishings*
0142 *Ice Cream*
0145 *Sewing Centers*
0148 *Personnel Referral Service*
0149 *Selling by Mail Order*
0150 *Solar Energy*
0201 *Breakeven Point for Independent Truckers*

Order from:
US Small Business Administration
Box 15434
Ft Worth, TX 76119

Publications For Sale

SMALL BUSINESS MANAGEMENT SERIES

The books in this series discuss specific management techniques or problems.

1. *An Employee Suggestion System for Small Companies*

9. *Cost Accounting for Small Manufacturers*
Assists managers of small manufacturing firms establish accounting procedures that help control production and business costs.

15. *Handbook of Small Business Finance*

20. *Ratio Analysis for Small Business*

25. *Guides for Profit Planning*
Guides for computing and using the breakeven point, the level of gross profit, and the rate of return on investment.

28. *Small Business and Government Research and Development*
Includes a discussion of the procedures necessary to locate and sell to government agencies.

29. *Management Audit for Small Manufacturers*
A questionnaire for manufacturers.

30. *Insurance and Risk Management for Small Business*

31. *Management Audit for Small Retailers*
149 questions to review business operations.

32. *Financial Recordkeeping for Small Stores*

33. *Small Store Planning for Growth*
Covers merchandising, advertising, and display, and provides checklists to increase sales.

35. *Franchise Index/Profile*
Presents an evaluation process that may be used to investigate franchise opportunities.

37. *Financial Control by Time-Absorption Analysis*

38. *Management Audit for Small Service Firms*
A questionnaire for service firms.

39. *Decision Points in Developing New Products*
Provides a path from idea to marketing plan for the small manufacturing or R & D firm.

40. *Management Audit for Small Construction Firms*
A questionnaire for construction firms.

41. *Purchasing Management and Inventory Control for Small Business*

42. *Managing the Small Service Firm for Growth and Profit*

43. *Credit and Collections for Small Stores*

STARTING AND MANAGING SERIES

This series is designed to help the small entrepreneur "to look before leaping" into a business.

10. *Starting and Managing a Small Business of Your Own*

101. *Starting and Managing a Small Service Firm*

NONSERIES PUBLICATIONS

A Basic Guide to Exporting
003-009-00349-1 (Commerce Dept)

U.S. Government Purchasing and Sales Directory
A directory for businesses interested in selling to the U.S. Government. Lists the purchasing needs of various agencies.
045-000-00153-9

Managing for Profits
Discusses the various management functions
045-000-00206-3

Buying and Selling a Small Business
045-000-00164-4

Strengthening Small Business Management
Emphasizes management self-improvement. Available from SBA only.

The Best of the SBI Review—1973-1979
Management ideas for the small business owner-manager.
045-000-00172-5

BUSINESS BASICS

Each of the 23 self-study booklets in this series contains text, questions, and exercises that teach a specific aspect of small business management.

1001 *The Profit Plan*
1002 *Capital Planning*
1003 *Understanding Money Sources*
1004 *Evaluating Money Sources*
1005 *Asset Management*
1006 *Managing Fixed Assets*
1007 *Understanding Costs*
1008 *Cost Control*
1009 *Marketing Strategy*

1010 *Retail Buying Function*
1011 *Inventory Management—Wholesale/Retail*
1012 *Retail Merchandise Management*
1013 *Consumer Credit*
1014 *Credit and Collections: Policy and Procedures*
1015 *Purchasing for Manufacturing Firms*
1016 *Inventory Management—Manufacturing/Service*
1017 *Inventory and Scheduling Techniques*
1018 *Risk Management and Insurance*
1019 *Managing Retail Salespeople*
1020 *Job Analysis, Job Specifications, and Job Descriptions*
1021 *Recruiting and Selecting Employees*
1022 *Training and Developing Employees*
1023 *Employee Relations and Personnel Policies*

ORDER FORM CHECK LIST

Small Business Management Series

No.	Stock No.	Price
1.	045-000-00020-6	$3.50
9.	045-000-00162-8	6.00
15.	045-000-00208-0	4.50
20.	045-000-00150-4	4.50
25.	045-000-00137-7	4.50
28.	045-000-00130-0	4.25
29.	045-000-00151-2	4.25
30.	045-000-00209-8	5.00
31.	045-000-00149-1	4.50
32.	045-000-00142-3	5.50
33.	045-000-00152-1	5.50
35.	045-000-00125-3	4.50
37.	045-000-00134-2	5.50
38.	045-000-00203-9	4.50
39.	045-000-00146-6	4.25
40.	045-000-00161-0	4.25
41.	045-000-00167-9	4.50
42.	045-000-00165-2	4.25
43.	045-000-00169-5	5.00

Starting and Managing Series

No.	Stock No.	Price
10.	045-000-00212-8	$4.75
101.	045-000-00207-1	4.50

Nonseries Publications

Stock No.	Price
003-009-00349-1	$6.50
045-000-00153-9	7.00
045-000-00206-3	5.50
045-000-00164-4	5.00
045-000-00172-5	5.50

Business Basics

No.	Stock No.	Price
1001.	045-000-00192-0	$4.50
1002.	045-000-00193-8	4.50
1003.	045-000-00194-6	4.75
1004.	045-000-00174-1	5.00
1005.	045-000-00175-0	2.75
1006.	045-000-00176-8	4.75
1007.	045-000-00195-4	3.25
1008.	045-000-00187-3	4.75
1009.	045.000-00188-1	4.75
1010.	045-000-00177-6	4.50
1011.	045-000-00190-3	4.50
1012.	045-000-00178-4	4.75
1013.	045-000-00179-2	4.50
1014.	045-000-00180-6	4.75
1015.	045-000-00181-4	4.75
1016.	045-000-00182-2	4.75
1017.	045-000-00183-1	4.75
1018.	045-000-00184-9	4.50
1019.	045-000-00189-0	4.75
1020.	045-000-00185-7	4.50
1021.	045-000-00186-5	4.50
1022.	045-000-00196-1	4.50
1023.	045-000-00196-2	4.50

Order from:
Department 39-CC, Superintendent of Documents
U.S. Government Printing
Office
Washington, DC 20402
Payment by check, Mastercard, or Visa. Include card number and date of expiration.

Other Books I Have Known

Not long ago I spent a day in the Mid-Manhattan Branch of the New York Public Library, going over the books that are available on buying, starting, and running a small business. It's one of the best business libraries around. I spend another day at the New York Public Library doing the same thing. Unfortunately I came up with almost nothing that is helpful to people who are planning to buy a country business. They're all about your typical little business in Toledo, as you might suspect. The basic book among the basic books is still J.K. Lasser's standby:

How To Run a Small Business, J.K. Lasser Tax Institute, Editor: Bernard Greisman. McGraw-Hill Book Company, New York, 1974

Two other interesting items are:

How to Succeed in Your Own Business by William R. Park and Sue Chapin-Park. John Wiley & Sons, New York, 1978. The book has operating and financial data on 80 different types of small businesses and services. Urban-oriented but interesting.

Small Business: Look Before You Leap: A catalog of sources of information to help you start and manage your own small business. Compiled and edited by Louis Mucciolo. Marlu, Dobbs Ferry, NY, 1978.

There are a few other books you might want to skim through:

The Dow Jones-Irwin Guide to Franchises by Peter G. Norback and Craig T. Norback. Dow Jones-Irwin, Homewood, Illinois, 1979.

The Franchise Boom. New Revised Edition by Harry Kursh. Prentice- Hall, Inc., Englewood Cliffs, New Jersey, 1968.

How To Organize and Operate a Small Business, Fifth Edition, by Clifford M. Baumback and Kenneth Lawyer. Prentice-Hall, Inc., Englewood Cliffs, New Jersey, 1979.

How to Pick the Right Small Business Opportunity by Kenneth J. Albert. McGraw-Hill Book Company, New York, 1977.

How to Start, Finance and Manage Your Own Small Business by Joseph R. Mancuso. Prentice-Hall, Inc., Englewood Cliffs, New Jersey, 1978.

J.K. Lasser's Business Management Handbook, Third Edition, edited by Bernard Greisman. McGraw-Hill Book Company, New York, 1968.

Small Business Management by Hal B. Pickle and Royce L. Abrahamson. John Wiley & Sons, Inc., New York, 1976.

Small Business Works! How to Compete and Win in the Free Enterprise System by Eugene L. Gross, Adrian R. Cancel, and Oscar Figueroa. Amacom, a division of American Management Associations, New York, 1977.

Starting a Small Restaurant: A Guide to Excellence in the Purveying of Public Victuals by Daniel Miller. The Harvard Common Press, Harvard, Massachusetts, 1978.

Starting and Succeeding in Your Own Small Business by Louis L. Allen. Grosset & Dunlap, New York, 1968.

Where Have All the Woolly Mammoths Gone? A Small Business Survival Manual by Ted S. Frost. Parker Publishing Company, Inc., West Nyack, New York, 1976.

The Women's Guide to Starting a Business by Claudia Jessup and Genie Chipps. Holt, Rinehart & Winston, New York, 1980.

There is also an interesting group of books you might want to look at entitled *The Small Business Series,* by David M. Brownstone, General Editor, John Wiley & Sons, Inc., New York, 1978. The various titles in the series are:

Credit and Collections by John W. Sedar

Efficient Accounting and Recordkeeping by Dennis M. Doyle

Financing Your Business by Egon W. Loffel

How to Advertise and Promote Your Small Business by Gonnie McClung Siegel

How to Run a Successful Florist and Plant Store by Braum Cavin

How to Run a Successful Specialty Food Store by Douglas L. Brownstone

How to Run a Successful Restaurant by William L. Siegel

People Management for Small Business by William L. Siegel

Protecting Your Business by Egon W. Loffel

Successful Selling Skills for Small Business by David M. Brownstone

Tax-Planning Opportunities by Gerald F. Richards

Index

Notes

Notes

Notes

Notes

Notes

Notes

Notes